God'ed?

DR. LAURENCE B. BROWN

GOD'ED?
THE CASE FOR ISLAM AS THE COMPLETION OF REVELATION

2007

God'ed?

TABLE OF CONTENTS

—Notes on Scriptural Sources and Translations— . . xi

—Introduction— xv

PART I: THE HOLY QUR'AN. 1

   1:   A Brief History of the Holy Qur'an. 3

   2:   Evidence—An Overview 19

   3:   Evidence #1—Innate Appeal. 23

   4:   Evidence #2—The Language of the Qur'an . . . 31

   5:   Evidence #3—Relation of Revelation to
Preceding Events 51

   6:   Evidence #4—Relation of Revelation
to Contemporaneous Events 69

   7:   Evidence #5—Relation of Revelation to
Subsequent Events 75

   8:   Evidence #6—Revelation of the Unknown . . . 91

   9:   Summary of Evidence. 127

PART II: MESSENGERS 133

   1:   Adam to Moses 137

   2:   Moses 141

   3:   Jesus Christ 153

   4:   Muhammad. 161

PART III: PROOF OF PROPHETHOOD. 171

   1:   Miraculous Signs .173

   2:   Miracles Performed 179

   3:   Character. 185

   4:   Persistence and Steadfastness. 201

   5:   Lack of Disqualifiers. 213

6:    Maintenance of the Message 225

PART IV: THE UNSEEN. 233

   1:    Angels. 235

   2:    Day of Judgment 239

   3:    Divine Decree 243

PART V: CONCLUSIONS 249

   1:    The "Deviant" Religion 251

   2:    Surrender. 255

   3:    The Consequences of Logic 261

Appendix 1—Idolatry. 267

Appendix 2—Recommended Reading. 287

Bibliography. 291

Glossary of Terms 301

ENDNOTES. 303

Lines lead from the very first Jewish Christianity to the seventh century, indeed to Islam ... The analogies between the Qur'anic picture of Jesus and a Christology with a Jewish-Christian stamp are perplexing. These parallels are irrefutable and call for more intensive historical and systematic reflection.

—Hans Küng, *Islam, Past, Present and Future* (2007, One World Publications. pp. 37, 44)

NOTES ON SCRIPTURAL SOURCES AND TRANSLATIONS

Biblical quotes in the following work, unless otherwise noted, are taken from the New King James Version. The reason for selecting this version of the Bible does not relate to the degree of scriptural fidelity, which is debatable, but rather to the popularity of the text. In English-speaking countries, the 1611 edition of the King James Version is the most widely read translation of the Bible. The *New* King James Version (NKJV) grew from an effort to render the 1611 translation more accessible to modern readers, tossing the *thees* and *thous* out the window. Unfortunately, little effort has been made to reconcile differences between the 1611 King James Version and the Sinaiticus and Vaticanus codices, which were discovered two centuries afterward and contain the oldest and most authoritative New Testament manuscripts found to date. Now that they are available, one can reasonably expect to see their influence upon more modern translations, but this is not the case in the New King James Version, which retains verses and passages in conflict with the most ancient and respected New Testament manuscripts. Therefore, while this book predominantly cites the New King James Version in the interest of satisfying the Protestant majority of Western Christianity, a complementary version is employed where greater scholastic accuracy is required.

The New Revised Standard Version (NRSV) fills this gap. Like its predecessor, the Revised Standard Version (RSV), the

NRSV is an ecumenical collaboration, reflected in its three separate Protestant, Roman Catholic, and Eastern Orthodox editions. More importantly, the NRSV reflects modern biblical scholarship hitherto unavailable. Indeed, the dust had barely been blown off the Dead Sea Scrolls when the RSV translation of the Old Testament was first published in 1946. For these reasons, the NRSV has effectively replaced the Revised Standard Version and enjoys the broadest acceptance of all Bible translations.

Quotations from the *World Bibliography of Translations of the Meanings of the Holy Qur'an* (hereafter TMQ), unless otherwise noted, are taken from Abdullah Yusuf Ali's *The Holy Qur'an: Translation and Commentary.* Where more exacting translation is required, those of Saheeh International or of Muhammad Al-Hilali and Muhammad Khan (i.e., *The Noble Qur'an*) are employed.

Those who question the use of multiple translations need to understand that no language, and most especially one as complex as Arabic, can be translated with complete accuracy. As Professor A. Guillaume stated, "The Qur'an is one of the world's classics which cannot be translated without grave loss."[1]

Hence the need for multiple translations, for no single translation can adequately convey the meaning of the original.

INTRODUCTION

Life is rather like a tin of sardines—we're all of us looking for the key.

—Alan Bennett, *Beyond the Fringe*[2]

This is the second of two books devoted to an analysis of the three Abrahamic faiths of Judaism, Christianity, and Islam. As stated in the first book, *MisGod'ed*, the goals of this analysis are to define the valid links in the chain of revelation, trace this chain to its conclusion, and in the process expose the faithful and unfaithful (i.e., the "God'ed" and "mis-God'ed") from among those who claim divine guidance. I assume readers have already finished the first book in the series, but for those who haven't, *MisGod'ed* defined the differences between the Judaic, Christian, and Islamic understandings of God, analyzed the doctrinal differences that separate Christianity from Islam, and exposed the weaknesses of Judeo-Christian scripture and dogma. With regard to the latter, many of these weaknesses have become compounded, such as when false tenets of Christian faith were derived from scribal errors or scriptural forgeries. In other cases, illegitimate tenets of Christian faith were derived from non-biblical sources, which, of course, means scripture had little or nothing to do with them. Where elements of Christian canon *were* derived from biblical sources, it is shocking to find Paul's teachings given priority over those of Jesus Christ, especially when the two teachings openly conflict.

This unreliability of Judeo-Christian sources forces many sincere seekers to look elsewhere for guidance. Hence this second volume in the series. Many who question institutionalized Jewish or Christian dogma find their logical objections opposed by the fiery emotion that accompanies blind indoctrination.

Not so with Islam.

In the words of Margaret Nydell, "They [i.e., Arab Muslims] are secure in their belief about the completeness of Islam, since it is accepted as the third and final refinement of the two previously revealed religions, Judaism and Christianity."[3]

Many find the Islamic approach to religion refreshing, for Islam condemns blind indoctrination and demands derivation of religious truths from foundational evidence. Islam teaches accepted beliefs, to be sure, but it also claims not to overstep the boundaries of reason. Objective study is expected to reveal the chain of revelation and expose the unacceptable, ungodly elements of all scriptures and philosophies superseded by the revelation of the Holy Qur'an. Those who agree with this opinion recognize "submission to the will of God" as the only code of life acceptable to the Creator, and discover the teachings of Islam not only in the Holy Qur'an, but also in the scriptures that preceded it.

The Islamic claim is that sincere seekers should not feel intimidated, for Islam is nothing more than a revival and confirmation of the teachings of all the prophets. As stated in the Holy Qur'an, "This Qur'an is not such as can be produced by other than Allah; on the contrary, it is a confirmation of (revelations) that went before it, and a fuller explanation of the Book—wherein there is no doubt—from the Lord of the Worlds" (TMQ 10:37). On the other hand, Jewish and Christian institutions might feel very much threatened, for Islam exposes the false foundations upon which these institutions were constructed—foundations that, more often than not, were fabricated from followers' teachings in preference to those of the prophets themselves.

How did this happen? According to Islam, in the days of oral tradition, Allah (i.e., God) sent a prophet to every nation. But when Allah gifted mankind with written language, the books of scripture supplanted the need for such a plethora of prophets. Revelation reached subsequent generations through the combination of oral tradition, written scripture, and religious men and women who served as pious examples to their communities.

God reportedly gifted mankind with a series of scriptures, having revealed the *suhuf* ("sheets") to Abraham, the *zaboor* (psalms) to David, the *tawraat* (Torah) to Moses, the *injeel* (gospel) to Jesus, and the Qur'an to Muhammad. Each book replaced the preceding record once the pristine message of God's revelation became sufficiently adulterated to warrant correction.

This scenario might sound familiar, for history is no stranger to the numerous individuals who altered or selectively interpreted revelation in accordance with deviant desires. With regard to these individuals, Allah teaches, "There is among them a section who distort the Book with their tongues, (as they read) you would think it is a part of the Book, but it is no part of the Book; and they say, 'That is from Allah,' but it is not from Allah: it is they who tell a lie against Allah, and (well) they know it!" (TMQ 3:78), and "Then woe to those who write the Book with their own hands, and then say: 'This is from Allah,' to traffic with it for a miserable price!—woe to them for what their hands do write, and for the gain they make thereby" (TMQ 2:79).

The historical result is that a common theme runs throughout the scriptural threads of the Abrahamic religions.

As discussed in *MisGod'ed*, both Old and New Testaments bear undeniable earmarks of corruption. And yet a common creed courses through the revelation chain of the Old Testament, New Testament, and the Holy Qur'an. All three books teach divine unity and command adherence to God's commandments. The deviations crept in when the job of recording, translating, or canonizing fell into the hands of those who sought to design religion closer to their hearts' desire.

Consider, for example, the Psalms of David. If anyone believes that what remains in the hands of man is a complete and unadulterated book of guidance, capable of standing on its own merit, they had better have another read. Consider next the Old Testament, which is sufficiently riddled with errors to render the entire work suspect. Then consider the New Testament, which excluded anywhere between an estimated 250 and 2,000 non-canonical acts, epistles and gospels (which were discarded and burned with only a handful of "apocryphal" survivors).[4(EN)] One wonders about the character of the men who made *that* editing choice, their intention and religious orientation, and their willingness to compromise scriptural truth in support of group ideology.

And then we have the renowned expert of textual criticism, Professor Bart D. Ehrman, telling us that scholars estimate the number of New Testament manuscript variants in the hundreds of thousands, some estimating as high as 400,000.[5] In Ehrman's now famous words, "There are more variations among our manuscripts than there are words in the New Testament."[6]

So where does this leave the seeker of religious truth, if not searching for the final, unadulterated book of God's revelation? And could that final revelation be the Holy Qur'an? I leave all readers to answer that question themselves, based upon the evidence that follows.

Lastly, the problem with heavily referenced works such as this is that the reader doesn't always know whether it's worth flipping pages to read the endnotes. To solve this problem, endnotes containing explanatory text are denoted by the endnote number followed by (EN), like this,[36(EN)] which means, "Endnote number 36: Explanatory Note." Endnote numbers lacking the (EN) denotation contain purely bibliographical information.

PART I
THE HOLY QUR'AN

When Satan makes impure verses,
Allah sends a divine tune to cleanse them.
——George Bernard Shaw, *The Adventures of the Black Girl*
in Her Search for God

1
A Brief History of the Holy Qur'an

One reason that history repeats itself is that so many people were not listening the first time.

—Margaret Hussey

The Holy Qur'an was revealed at the beginning of the seventh century, approximately six hundred years following the ministry of Jesus Christ. Muslims contend that, word for word, the revelation was placed in the mind and mouth of the prophet Muhammad during the last twenty-three years of his life. Conversely, nonbelievers charge Muhammad with a full rapsheet of false prophecy. Claims of scriptural plagiarism, deception, lying, and delusional thinking have all been advanced, as has the patronizing view of Muhammad having been a man of extraordinary intelligence and insight, but nothing more. Some have even gone so far as to suggest that Muhammad was epileptic, and the Holy Qur'an is a compilation of his mutterings while in the throes of seizure.

Perhaps this is due to recorded descriptions of Muhammad's altered appearance while receiving revelation. His beloved wife, A'ishah, noted that he broke out in a sweat when receiving revelation, even on a cold day. Those who seek to summarily execute Muhammad's character can fashion whatever garment of conclusions suits their taste from such scraps of evidence. However, those more circumspect might consider an altered appearance not just excused, but expected. What, after all, should we expect to read from the face of any mortal confronted with the spiritual assault of direct revelation?

Those who have experienced the pounding pulse, crawling skin, rising hair, spinal chill, and quickening of senses that accompany a spiritual anomaly can easily imagine the angel of revelation to elicit greater shock. Certainly a focused attention, a sweat on the brow, a blank stare would in no way exceed expectations. Far more unreasonable would be to assume that any mortal could converse with the angel of revelation in casual and comfortable terms—say, over a cappuccino and biscotti at one's local café. Many people break out in a sweat simply facing their boss. Just how much tighter their nerves might be stretched should they face the Creator of *all* bosses is hard to predict. Furthermore, anybody who has witnessed *grand mal* seizures knows epileptics do not produce intelligible speech, and cannot communicate during a seizure or even during the recovery of senses that follows. As W. Montgomery Watt comments,

> Opponents of Islam have often asserted that Muhammad had epilepsy, and that therefore his religious experiences had no validity. As a matter of fact, the symptoms described are not identical with those of epilepsy, since that disease leads to physical and mental degeneration, whereas Muhammad was in the fullest possession of his faculties to the very end. But, even if the allegation were true, the argument would be completely unsound and based on mere ignorance and prejudice; such physical concomitants neither validate nor invalidate religious experience.[7]

Hartwig Hirschfeld, a man never short of slanders against the Qur'an, a man who exposed his prejudice in the preface to his *New Researches into the Composition and Exegesis of the*

Qoran with the words, "The *Qoran*, the text-book of Islam, is in reality nothing but a counterfeit of the Bible,"[8] nonetheless concluded,

> What remains now of epileptic or hysterical influence on the origin of Islam? Absolutely nothing. Never has a man pronounced a sentence with more circumspection and consciousness than Muhammad did in the *iqra'* [the 96th *surah*, or chapter, of the Qur'an]. Should he have proclaimed it with nothing but prophetic enthusiasm, he must have been the greatest genius that ever lived.[9]

Of course, Muslims claim Muhammad pronounced the entire Qur'an, Surah (i.e., chapter) Al-'Alaq (commonly known as the *Iqra' Surah*) included, completely devoid of circumspection, for he only repeated what was revealed to him. Hirschfeld, though in clear disagreement with the Muslim viewpoint, nonetheless dismissed the charge of epilepsy as a blatant slander.

Delusional thinking should also be dismissed, for Muhammad did not appear to fully comprehend his first experience of revelation. So traumatic was his initial encounter with the angel Gabriel that Muhammad required convincing. As per the *New Catholic Encyclopedia*, "Mohammed himself was frightened, incredulous, and unsure of the meaning of the experience. It required persuasion from his wife and friends before he was convinced and believed that he had actually received a revelation from God."[10]

Deluded people readily believe their delusions. That is what the word implies: a readiness to accept the implausible due to some warpage in the thought process. Furthermore, a significant period of time passed (some say as little as forty days, others as much as two years) between Muhammad's first and second revelation. Now, a deluded person's mind summons up bizarre ideas on a frequent basis. That is the nature of those who are psychologically disturbed—their bent reasoning does not spontaneously straighten out for a couple of days, much less a week, much less forty days or more. Such is also the case with charlatans and pathologic liars, who seem incapable of turning off their deceptions, which eventually become recognized in any case.

History having cleared Muhammad of the charges of delusion, lying and deception, no true scholar entertains such slanders. For example, Thomas Carlyle commented,

> How he (Muhammad) was placed with Kadijah, a rich widow, as her steward, and traveled in her business, again to the fairs of Syria; how he managed all, as one can well understand, with fidelity, adroitness; how her gratitude, her regard for him grew: the story of their marriage is altogether a graceful intelligible one, as told us by the Arab authors. He was twenty-five; she forty, though still beautiful. He seems to have lived in a most affectionate, peaceable, wholesome way with this wedded benefactress; loving her truly, and her alone. It goes greatly against the impostor-theory, the fact that he lived in this entirely unexceptionable, entirely quiet and commonplace way, till the heat of his years was done. He was forty before he talked of any mission from Heaven. All his irregularities, real and supposed, date from after his fiftieth year, when the good Kadijah died. All his "ambition," seemingly, had been, hitherto, to live an honest life; his "fame," the mere good-opinion of neighbours that knew him, had been sufficient hitherto. Not till he was already getting old, the prurient heat of his life all burnt out, and *peace* growing to be the chief thing this world could give him, did he start on the "career of ambition;" and, belying all

his past character and existence, set up as a wretched empty charlatan to acquire what he could now no longer enjoy! For my share, I have no faith whatever in that.
Ah no: this deep-hearted Son of the Wilderness, with his beaming black eyes, and open social deep soul, had other thoughts in him than ambition. A silent great soul; he was one of those who cannot but be in earnest; whom Nature herself has appointed to be sincere ... We will leave it altogether, this impostor-hypothesis, as not credible; not very tolerable even, worthy chiefly of dismissal by us.[11]

With regard to other attempts to disqualify the revelation Muhammad claimed, we must turn to an analysis of the Qur'an itself.

To begin with, the word *Qur'an* does not refer to a book, but to a revelation. Islamic tradition holds that this revelation was transmitted verbally to the prophet Muhammad by the angel of revelation, Gabriel. And so it has been maintained—as an oral tradition preserved to this day in the hearts and minds of devout *hafith* (memorizers, or "protectors" of the Qur'an), whose number in the present day is conservatively estimated to be no less than thirty million.

The Qur'an was also recorded by scribes, who faithfully transcribed each element of revelation at the time it was revealed. Unlike the New Testament, whose earliest books were written decades following Jesus' ministry, the Holy Qur'an is the only book of scripture recorded at the time of revelation and preserved unchanged to the present day. Writing material was scarce, so the Holy Qur'an was originally recorded on palm leaves, sheets of leather, shoulder blades of large animals, and whatever else was immediately available. This bulky and inconvenient record was commissioned by Abu Bakr (the first Caliph)[12(EN—Explanatory Note, as opposed to a bibliographical reference)] to be copied and compiled into an official *mushaf* (book) roughly two years after Muhammad's death.

This project was overseen by Zaid ibn Thabit, one of Muhammad's faithful scribes. Between four and eight copies were completed during the caliphate of Uthman, and each copy was dedicated to one of the territories of the Islamic world. Two of these books still exist—one in Tashkent, Uzbekistan, the other in Istanbul, Turkey—and continue to serve as templates. Any Qur'an, anywhere in the world, can be authenticated against these "originals" to demonstrate the integrity and preservation of the sacred book of Islam. It is this very preservation that many consider a miraculous proof of the sanctity of the Holy Qur'an. Dr. Laura Vaglieri adds this element of authenticity to her list of evidence: "We have still another proof of the divine origin of the Quran in the fact that its text has remained pure and unaltered through the centuries from the day of its delivery until today …"[13]

Professor Arthur J. Arberry, Professor of Arabic at Cambridge University from 1947 to 1969, contributes: "Apart from certain orthographical modifications of the originally somewhat primitive method of writing, intended to render unambiguous and easy the task of reading the recitation, the Koran as printed in the twentieth century is identical with the Koran as authorized by Uthman more than 1300 years ago."[14]

This opinion is not new. Sir William Muir, the nineteenth-century Orientalist and biographer of Muhammad, penned the following: "The recension of Othman has been handed down to us unaltered … There is probably in the world no other work which has remained twelve centuries with so pure a text."[15]

Whereas a more contemporary opinion can be summed up in the words of Adrian Brockett,

> The transmission of the Qur'an after the death of Muhammad was essentially static, rather than organic. There was a single text, and nothing significant, not even allegedly abrogated material, could be taken out nor could anything be put in. This applied even to the early caliphs … The transmission of the Qur'an has always been oral, just as it has always been written.[16]

Tens of thousands of *sahaba* (Muslims who lived and interacted with the prophet Muhammad) unanimously approved the written record of the Holy Qur'an. All of these *sahaba* had memorized portions of the Qur'an and many were *hafith*, having memorized the Qur'an in its entirety. When the Qur'an was first compiled into a book, many *sahaba* possessed personal copies of their own recording. Many of these copies were incomplete and others (such as those of Abdullah ibn Masud, Ubay ibn Kab and Ibn Abbas), while correct in one reading, did not leave room for the multiple readings that constitute one of the miracles of the Qur'an.[17(EN)] Consequently, these partial records were not acknowledged, *even by their possessors*, as having been either complete or authoritative.

The only written record of the Qur'an to be accepted by unanimous approval was the officially adopted *mushaf* compiled by Zaid ibn Thabit and commissioned by Abu Bakr. To prevent confusion and the possibility of division in future generations, all other personal copies were voluntarily turned in and, along with the remnants of the bones, animal skins, and papyrus etched with the scripture, destroyed. Had this not been done, future generations may have fallen prey to ignorance or pride, preferring one of the incomplete works passed down in a family or tribe to the true and complete revelation. Tribal solidarity and religious schism almost certainly would have resulted. The pious *sahaba* appear to have recognized and eliminated this risk by preserving only the complete revelation, discarding the bits and pieces which, at the very least, could have become sources of contention.

Muslims are fond of pointing out that not a single one of Muhammad's contemporaries disagreed with the text of the official *mushaf*. Not a single *sahaba* claimed a passage was left out or a non-Qur'anic passage inserted. Most importantly, the texts that were gathered and destroyed were *incomplete* records and not *differing* records. The possessors voluntarily relinquished their copies, because the *mushaf* compiled by Zaid ibn Thabit was comprehensive: there simply were no accurate records unrepresented therein. Furthermore, as stated above, the Qur'an has primarily been preserved not in writing, but in the memories of the faithful. Memorizers cross-checked and confirmed the official *mushaf*, and validated its completeness and accuracy. Not a single *hafith* dissented. And they numbered in the thousands.

The existence of even a few memorizers of the Qur'an after 1,400 years is extraordinary, but the existence of tens of millions? That ... well, that seems miraculous.

According to contemporary census statistics, there are a billion Christians and many millions of Jews in the world, but not one of them holds the original scripture of their religion in memory. A rare rabbi might have memorized the Torah—not as it was revealed, but as it was reconstructed roughly two centuries following the destruction of the original, during the sacking of the Temple of Solomon by the conquering Babylonian empire in 586 BC. The only known version of the Old Testament, whether in memory or in print, contains the ungodly errors discussed in depth in my previous book, *MisGod'ed*.

Moreover, it is an *extremely* rare Christian who has memorized the entire New Testament, in the translation of just one of the thousands of versions known to exist. Even rarer, if not completely nonexistent, is the Christian who has memorized one of the 5,700 extant Greek manuscripts. But nowhere in the world and nowhere in history has anyone ever been known to have memorized the original Gospel of Jesus—simply because, as far as we know, it no longer exists. If it *did* exist, the Christian world would cease struggling to rectify the hundreds of thousands of variations in their extant Greek manuscripts, and would face the world with the uncorrupted original.

The Qur'an, then, is unique. It's the only book of scripture recorded at the time of revelation and maintained in the purity of the original to the present day. There may be different translations into non-Arabic languages, but there is only one original. Hence, there is no confusion such as exists with the many versions of the Bible. There is no frustration, such as results from lacking a definitive original scripture. There is no uncertainty, such as wondering what truths are sequestered from the public eye in the private library of the Vatican or in the fiercely guarded Qumran (Dead Sea) scrolls. No one need wonder how much the predominantly *Koiné* Greek differs from the spoken Aramaic of the prophet Jesus. Should the errors of translation from Aramaic and ancient Hebrew to *Koiné* Greek have been as numerous and grave as the errors that occurred translating *Koiné* Greek to English, all hope of biblical accuracy should have been dismissed long ago.

One huge difference between the Bible and the Qur'an is that the Qur'an was always in the hands of the people, whereas the Bible most definitely was not. Anybody who ever wanted a Qur'an could have one. First of all, the Bible did not exist in its present form—meaning with the present table of contents—until it was canonized at the council of Trent in the year 367 CE. Even then, it was strictly maintained in the Latin Vulgate for more than a millennium. And when John Wycliffe's English translation of the New Testament in 1382 was followed by that of William Tyndale (completed by Miles Coverdale and edited by John Rogers) and Martin Luther's translation of the Bible into German (both of which were translated only as recently as the sixteenth century), what was Tyndale's reward? Death—burned at the stake in 1536. Rogers'? Same fate, different stake, in 1555. Their predecessor, Wycliffe, escaped execution but not the fire, for the ecumenical Council of Constance condemned him *posthumously* in 1415, and his bones were exhumed and publicly burned. Had it not been for the intercession of Denmark, Miles Coverdale would have been similarly condemned. And like their authors, Wycliffe's and Tyndale's translations were publicly burned.

So for over 1500 years the Christian scriptures were available only in Greek or Latin: languages only the educated class and the more learned clergy could read, for many Catholic clergy were illiterate with regard to their own scripture. It is a sobering thought to realize that were Jesus Christ to return, even he would not be able to read either the Greek of our New Testament manuscripts or the Latin of the Catholic Vulgate, for his native tongue was Aramaic.[18] Indeed, the educated class were a miniscule percentage of the population compared to today; only they could read the Bible, and then only if they had one. The combination of the great expense and scant availability of Bibles (all copied by hand), along with harsh laws prohibiting Bible possession by laity, severely curtailed their acquisition. Many of these laws prescribed death, especially for possession of translations in the vernacular or of unauthorized translations considered to be aligned with heresies, of which Protestant Bibles were considered the most offensive examples.

Not until Gutenberg's invention of moveable type in the 1450s was mass production of Bibles feasible, and not until the Protestant Reformation of the sixteenth century was the Bible not only translated into languages of the literate laity (i.e., German and English), but mass-produced and permitted to the public.

For the first time in history, the sixteenth century witnessed the production of Bibles translated into the vernacular, together with the growth of new, non-Catholic churches endorsed by a sympathetic monarchy. Responding to the pressures of the Protestant Reformation, the Catholic Church produced the Douay-Rheims Bible, which presented the translation of the Latin Vulgate into English for the first time. The New Testament portion was completed in Rheims, France in 1582, and the Old Testament was completed in Douay in 1609–10. All the same, even with mass production then feasible, availability was severely constrained, for, "...it was calculated that there must have been about 25,000 printed Bibles in circulation in western Europe around 1515, one third of them in German, for about fifty million inhabitants; i.e. one Bible for every 2,000 souls."[19]

What this means is that for over 1,500 years the common citizen could not verify the teachings of the Christian scriptures, both for lack of literacy and lack of Bibles. For an even greater period, laity could not question the canonized doctrines forced upon them for fear of a "bloodless death"—the pleasant-sounding euphemism by which burning at the stake came to be known.

Catholics argue that restriction of scriptural interpretation and religious education to the offices of the church was (and remains to this day) necessary to maintain orthodox understanding. Others argue that the church was less concerned with sheltering scripture from misinterpretation than it was with sheltering their power base and privileged position in society. Well do we know that the church believed the intricacies of the Christian mysteries were unlikely to be understood through deductive reasoning and the conclusions of laity. What is less well known is that the church did not even trust their own scholars with biblical interpretation. As Pope Innocent III stated in 1199,

> The mysteries of the faith are not to be explained rashly to anyone. Usually in fact, they cannot be understood by everyone, but only by those who are qualified to understand them with informed intelligence ... The depth of the divine Scriptures is such that not only the illiterate and uninitiated have difficulty understanding them, but also the educated and the gifted.[20]

The Protestant stand, however, was that all humans were created with brains and the ability to interpret scripture for themselves. Protestants argue now, as they did in the past, that once people could freely read and study the Bible in their own language, they were able to discern biblical fact from canonized fiction. Once the errors of Catholicism were laid bare and the foundation of Catholic theology exposed as predominantly (and in many cases, entirely) non-biblical, gravitation toward Protestantism was inevitable.

Muslims take this argument one step further and assert that the shaky foundation of Christian scriptures should not drive people from one Christian sect to another, still basing beliefs upon a scriptural canon peppered with demonstrable errors and inconsistencies. Rather, they believe those seeking the truth of God should recognize the need for the Creator to have renewed His revelation.

Claiming this final revelation to be The Holy Qur'an, Muslims point out that the Qur'an was always in the hands and minds of the people. The Qur'an has been recited aloud in the daily prayers of the Muslims ever since revelation. Every year, in the month of Ramadan, the Qur'an is recited in its entirety aloud, in virtually every mosque in the world. Any Muslim listening could voice correction, but for 1,400 years there has never been so much as a single letter in dispute among orthodox (Sunni) Muslims. At the present day, that adds up to a billion unanimous votes. Amazingly enough, over time there have been many factions among the Sunni Muslims, some of them at war with one another. Uthman, the third Caliph, was assassinated while reading the Qur'an, and his dried blood is still to be seen on the pages. However, among all of these differing Muslim groups, and throughout all of these centuries, the authenticity of the Qur'an has never been questioned. Certainly the same cannot be said of the Bible. As F.F. Arbuthnot commented a century ago,

> From a literary point of view, the Korân is regarded as a specimen of the purest Arabic, written in half poetry and half prose. It has been said that in some cases grammarians have adapted their rules to agree with certain phrases and expressions used in it, and that, though several attempts have been made to produce a work equal to it as far as elegant writing is concerned, none have as yet succeeded. It will thus be seen, from the above, that a final and complete text of the Korân was prepared within twenty years after the death (A.D. 632) of Muhammad, and that this has remained the same, without any change or alteration by enthusiasts, translators, or interpolators, up to the present time. It is to be regretted that the same cannot be said of all the books of the Old and New Testaments.[21]

The Qur'an, furthermore, exists in a living language, understood by hundreds of millions of devout followers even to the present day. The Bible exists primarily in the dead language of *Koiné* Greek, with snippets of equally necrotic ancient Hebrew (not the Modern Hebrew spoken today) and Aramaic. In the entire world there are only a few scholars with partial understanding of these dead languages, and even they don't agree on translation. Evidence of the difficulty is found in the Preface to the Revised Standard Version of the Bible, which was authorized by vote of the National Council of the Churches of Christ in the USA in 1951. The RSV appears to have subsequently enjoyed the widest popular acceptance throughout the Christian world, but despite its ecumenical scholarship and global acceptance, the RSV admits,

> Many difficulties and obscurities, of course, remain. Where the choice between two meanings is particularly difficult or doubtful, we have given an alternative rendering in a footnote. If in the judgement of the Committee the meaning of a passage is quite uncertain or obscure, either because of corruption in the text or because of the inadequacy of our present knowledge of the language, that fact is indicated by a note. It should not be assumed, however, that the Committee was entirely sure or unanimous concerning every rendering not so indicated.[22]

Understanding of biblical manuscripts increases with each new discovery, as evidenced by the motivation of church authorities to revise the King James Version of 1611 to the American Standard Version of 1901, and subsequently to the Revised Standard Version fifty years later. The motivation for such revisions lay, as stated in the Preface of the RSV, in that the KJV suffers from "grave defects." More specifically, it contends, "The King James Version of the New Testament was based upon a Greek text that was marred by mistakes, containing the accumulated errors of fourteen centuries of manuscript copying."[23]

And while understanding of the Greek New Testament continues to be refined, it is far from comprehensive at the present time, and is unlikely ever to be. In such a climate of uncertainty, mistranslation—whether deliberate, accidental, or well-intentioned—is easily passed off as accurate to those who lack the linguistic background to know better. The same is not true if the language is understood by the faithful, which is precisely the case with the Arabic language and the Holy Qur'an.

We might wonder, then, how Muslims support the assertion that the Qur'an is unique and unchanged. Unsubstantiated claims are not acceptable. Most of humanity have been asked— correction, *forced* to blind belief for too long. The sophisticated laity are tired of the appealing but unsubstantiated lines, sprinkled with the spittle of the proselytizers, and spiritually cold to the bone. Sincere seekers need a blanket of evidence to warm their convictions. Not just a cover that looks nice and cozy at a distance, but one that does the job.

What follows, then, are the myriad Qur'anic facets that stitch much of the quilt of evidence with which Muslims comfort their convictions.

2
Evidence—An Overview

When speculation has done its worst, two and two still make four.

—Samuel Johnson

T he lack of references in the following discussion of Islamic history and Qur'anic constitution might seem surprising to those unfamiliar with Islamic history, but in fact are considered common knowledge among educated Muslims. Consequently, just as such well-known statements as, "The Bible is the foundational book of Christianity and contains the gospels attributed to Matthew, Mark, Luke, and John" needs no reference, neither does most of that which follows.

Nonetheless, details can be confirmed through a number of respected source books, among them *Manaahil al-'Irfaan fee 'Uloom al-Qur'an* by Shaykh Muhammad 'Abd al Adheem az-Zarqaanee, *al-Madkhal li Dirasaat al-Qur'an al-Kareem* by Muhammad Abu Shahbah, and two books, both by the title of *Mabaahith fee 'Uloom al-Qur'an*, one by Dr. Subhee al-Saalih, the other by Dr. Mannaa' al-Qattaan. These books have yet to be translated from Arabic, but there are two excellent books in English. *'Ulum Al-Qur'an: An Introduction to the Sciences of the Qur'an*, by Ahmad Von Denffer, is a basic though superficial introduction to the subject. A more scholarly and comprehensive work is *An Introduction to the Sciences of the Qur'aan*, by Abu Ammaar Yasir Qadhi.[24]

On the other hand, the conclusions of many, if not most, non-Muslim authors are often tainted by religious prejudice. Most of these critical works rate so low in objective scholastic value as to have been cast out not only by Muslims, but by educated clergy, orientalists, and religious scholars as well, leading one author to lament,

> The totally erroneous statements made about Islam in the West are sometimes the result of ignorance, and sometimes of systematic denigration. The most serious of all the untruths told about it are, however, those dealing with facts; for while mistaken opinions are excusable, the presentation of facts running contrary to the reality is not. It is disturbing to read blatant untruths in eminently respectable works written by authors who *a priori* are highly qualified.[25]

Furthermore, many so-called "scholastic works" are discredited by the author's own educated co-religionists. For the most part, however, the following details are simply omitted from such books, presumably because discussion of the subject is uncomfortable for those who deny the signs that seem to validate the Islamic revelation.

On the other hand, there is virtually zero disagreement throughout the Muslim world on the following subjects, and verification thereof is relatively easy considering the accuracy of historical record-keeping typical of the Islamic sciences and traditions.

Admittedly, some modern books of Muslim authorship also suffer inaccuracies, frequently from overzealous attempts to either modernize or glorify the religion. Nonetheless, the same commonly accepted elements of Qur'anic history are found to course through most such works with remarkable consistency. It is just these commonly accepted elements that will be discussed in this present work. Items of personal, sectarian, deviant (such as Ahmadi'ite, Shi'ite and Nation of Islam), or minority opinion are avoided herein, being left for those who wish to explore the less mainstream sects of Islam on their own.

3
Evidence #1—Innate Appeal

All truth, in the long run, is only common sense clarified.
—Thomas Henry Huxley, *On the Study of Biology*

On the most superficial level, Muslims hold the truth of the Qur'an to be self-evident by the simple fact that it makes sense, precisely conforming to our inborn understanding of God and His methodology. But what religion lacks this claim? No proof satisfies all mankind, as evidenced by the fact that the world is not Muslim. However, on an individual level the proof is in the exposure. Many who read the foundational books of various religions find themselves inexplicably drawn to one specific book and the ideologies expressed therein. The Qur'an is no different. People simply have to sit down and read it.

Those who do will encounter a book of strikingly different character than those of the other Abrahamic faiths. Whereas the Old Testament is largely a book of laws, lengthy "begat" lists and dry history, the New Testament exudes spirituality while denying the reader concrete guidance on the significant issues of life. The Holy Qur'an, on the other hand, provides the foundation not only for the Islamic religion, but also for Islamic law, government, social conduct, family structure, and every facet of worldly and spiritual existence. H. G. Wells commented on the teachings of Islam as follows:

They established in the world a great tradition of dignified fair dealing, they breathe a spirit of generosity, and they are human and workable. They created a society more free from widespread cruelty and social oppression than any society had ever been in the world before ... It [i.e., Islam] was full of the spirit of kindliness, generosity, and brotherhood; it was a simple and understandable religion; it was instinct with the chivalrous sentiment of the desert; and it made its appeal straight to the commonest instincts in the composition of ordinary men. Against it were pitted Judaism, which had made a racial hoard of God; Christianity talking and preaching endlessly now of trinities, doctrines, and heresies no ordinary man could make head or tail of; and Mazdaism, the cult of the Zoroastrian Magi, who had inspired the crucifixion of Mani. The bulk of the people to whom the challenge of Islam came did not trouble very much whether Muhammad was lustful or not, or whether he had done some shifty and questionable things; what appealed to them was that this God, Allah, he preached, was by the test of the conscience in their hearts, a God of righteousness, and that the honest acceptance of his doctrine and method opened the door wide in a world of uncertainty, treachery, and intolerable divisions to a great and increasing brotherhood of trustworthy men on earth, and to a paradise not of perpetual exercises in praise and worship, in which saints, priests, and anointed kings were still to have the upper places, but of equal fellowship and simple and understandable delights such as their soul craved for. Without any ambiguous symbolism, without any darkening of altars or chanting of priests, Muhammad had brought home those attractive doctrines to the hearts of mankind.[26]

The keystone of Islamic faith, as emphasized over and over again in the Holy Qur'an, is the simple message of monotheism.

Muslims propose this message to have the greatest innate appeal of *all* knowledge, since the Creator instilled knowledge of His oneness and unique attributes into the mind, heart, and soul of every human being. Thus, no person (unless conditioned in life to do so) is likely to object when taught the oneness of the Creator, His many and unique names, and His perfect attributes.

With regard to the oneness of Allah, Islamic ideology is explicit on this point. Allah is One, eternal and absolute, not begotten and not begetting, without partner or co-sharer in divinity:

> Say: He is Allah, The One and Only;
> Allah, The Eternal, Absolute;
> He begets not, nor is He begotten;
> And there is none like unto Him.
> (TMQ 112:1–4)

It is this clarification of Allah's uncompromised Unity to which Trinitarian Christians object, for Trinitarian ideology teaches that God is indeed One, but also three in One. Trinitarian arguments were discussed at length in my previous book, *MisGod'ed*, so here we can propose a test of innate understanding. Should we assume that convictions are comforted by embracing inherent understandings, the opposite most certainly should be true. Embracing teachings in conflict with inborn knowledge should bring stress and discomfort. Hence the test. Those living a religion that conforms to innate, God-given understanding (such as the oneness of the Creator) will be at ease explaining their convictions, for their explanation will match their audience's inherent understanding as well. On the other hand, those who attempt to explain notions that conflict with inborn knowledge will manifest frustration, both in the weakness of their arguments and in their inability to force their notions upon an audience that knows better. Resorts to emotional appeals, plays at self-righteousness and histrionics are the hallmark of those who fail in rational debate.

Secondary to creed, the Holy Qur'an presents many teachings applicable to everyday life. Manners are corrected, with an emphasis on modesty. The use of money, time, and energy is addressed, with focus on a balanced application to person, family, religion, and society. Miserliness is condemned, as is unwarranted extravagance. Even war is regulated, with laws laid down to foster honorable conflict, beginning with war being allowed only in circumstances where all other options are exhausted. Even then, Muslims are instructed not to abuse an advantage won, and to be merciful as much as the situation permits.

Fairness and equality, mercy and love are underlying Qur'anic themes that at times give way to a system of justice that is fair but harsh against those whose transgressions threaten the peace of Islamic society. No laws in the history of man have been more successful in restricting the evils of murder, rape, theft, adultery, fornication, homosexuality, alcohol, and drugs. Cheating, lying, bribery, usury, prejudice, and all forms of injustice are condemned, giving way to a social reform that, if implemented, would likely unite all mankind under the One God.

Polygamy, while practiced by only a minority of Muslims, permits a lawful avenue for those whose lusts might otherwise drive them to adultery. Women, on the other hand, are protected. Fourteen hundred years ago, Islam gave women rights to property, inheritance, religion and education— rights that were denied in Western society and Old and New Testament religions up until the twentieth century.

As the Holy Qur'an emphasizes the merits of freeing

slaves, so too it frees the mind—correcting wrong beliefs and encouraging free thought. Objective truth is given priority over personal opinion, societal customs, family tradition, canonized institutional teachings, and all prejudicing outside influences. Compulsion of religion is forbidden in all circumstances. In addition, the Qur'an challenges and stimulates the intellect while soothing the spirit. In short, the Qur'an may be viewed as a "final testament," giving mankind balanced guidance in all facets of life.

Muslims conceive the revelation to be undeniable. Non-Muslims disagree; they consider the revelation very much deniable, and profess the Muslims' claim to innate appeal false. After all, it doesn't appeal to them.

How do Muslims resolve this difficulty? Muslims believe *unprejudiced* minds will be receptive to teachings of the Holy Qur'an. Like a fertile field, open minds will best cultivate that which they were created to receive. However, most minds are very much prejudiced. By the time most Westerners learn about Islam, they have been subjected to a lifetime of anti-Islamic propaganda in social, religious and media circles. As a result, their hearts and minds are closed.

By analogy, the photon theory of light and prismatic effects on the visible spectrum will mean little or nothing to a blind person. Likewise, those whose hearts and minds are closed to Islam are not expected to appreciate Islamic evidence. But like light to a blind person, failure to perceive does not negate reality; it just won't convince those who fail to appreciate it. Those who study the message and find it a source of strength will understand the Islamic viewpoint; those who don't, won't.

Allah tells us He could have ordered mankind to all be of one mind: "If your Lord had so willed, He could have made mankind one People: but they will not cease to dispute" (TMQ 11:118), but for reasons best known to Him, He didn't. The obvious implication is that God guides some and leaves others to stray, and this is exactly what the Qur'an teaches: "Truly Allah leaves to stray, whom He will; but He guides to Himself those who turn to Him in penitence" (TMQ 13:27). The fact that God guides some and not others is far from arbitrary. In fact, it's the result of each individual's actions and receptiveness, for "We send the Messengers only to give good news and to warn: so those who believe and mend (their lives), upon them shall be no fear, nor shall they grieve. But those who reject Our Signs, punishment shall touch them, for that they did not cease from transgressing" (TMQ 6:48–49), and "Whatever of good reaches you, is from Allah, but whatever of evil befalls you, it is from yourself" (TMQ 4:79).

In other words, God guides those who acknowledge Him, seek His guidance, and prove worthy. All others slam their own doors in the face of His guidance. That God guides only those who acknowledge Him and seek His guidance is no less understandable than the fact that teachers only instruct those who attend class, and gas station attendants only give directions to those who ask. As the Bible reports Jesus having stated, "Ask, and it will be given to you; seek, and you will find; knock, and it will be opened to you. For everyone who asks receives, and he who seeks finds, and to him who knocks it will be opened" (Matthew 7:7–8). Don't ask, don't seek and, well, what do people expect, if not to be left in the state of ignorance they themselves choose?

All this is one more link in the chain of continuity from the Old and New Testaments to the Holy Qur'an. The Old Testament teaches, "They do not know nor understand; For He has shut their eyes, so that they cannot see, *And* their hearts, so that they cannot understand" (Isaiah 44:18). The New Testament effectively repeats this lesson in Mark 4:11–12 and Matthew 13:11–15.

The burden of choice, then, is upon the individual. Those who seek guidance will answer the call to righteousness. Those who deny Allah will earn His wrath, but will have nobody to blame but themselves. That Allah guides those who turn to Him with sincerity is a manifestation of His mercy; that He leaves astray those who deny Him is a manifestation of His justice.

This viewpoint may seem elitist, but then so are all religions. The world is a heterogeneous mix of our-sect-is-saved-by-the-grace-of-God-and-all-others-will-burn-in-hell religious factions. Many religions paint themselves the elect of God and argue why they, and only they, will achieve salvation. Such arguments usually fall short not in reasoning why any one particular group is "saved," the explanation of which always sounds good to those who belong, but in the inability to explain why the rest of mankind are condemned. The difference between the Islamic religion and others in this regard is that Islam provides a concrete explanation that satisfies both ends of the equation. Other religions largely fail to address this subject, and leave the outsider questioning why God would guide some and not others. The concept of an arbitrary God is simply not acceptable in the minds of most.

Muslims claim that, for those exposed to all the evidence Islam offers, one or more will appeal. Consistent with the purpose of revelation, Allah provides something from among all the evidence to convince each and every individual of the divine origin of His revelation. Recognition is easy; refusal requires obstinacy.

Hence, reward versus punishment.

4

Evidence #2—The Language of the Qur'an

Language, as well as the faculty of speech, was the immediate gift of God.

—Noah Webster

The Holy Qur'an exists in one written form but ten different (though complementary) readings or recitations, and in seven different dialects. A person may wonder how this is possible. The answer lies in the intricacies of the Arabic language that, unlike non-Semitic languages, maintains an extraordinary flexibility owing to the fact that the alphabet does not contain short vowel letters. Short vowels, the most common vowels in Arabic, are designated by diacritical marks (distinguishing signs, like a slash or a whorl) placed above or below consonants. For example, the Arabic letter equivalent to B in English would be pronounced *ba* if a slash is above the letter, but *bi* if the slash is below the letter. Other formulations may render the letter *bu, baan, been, buun, baa, bii, buu, bai, bau,* etc.

When words are written with their diacritical marks, we readily understand their correct pronunciation and meaning. However, when Arabic is written without diacritical marks, we must rely upon context to determine each word's correct meaning, for identically spelled words can have different meanings depending upon how they are vowelled. For example, in the sentence, "A speck of dust flew into my eye," the Arabic word for "eye" can be vowelled to mean a spy, an important person or a high-ranking official, or even nobody. In fact, this one word can have over thirty meanings, including such diverse possibilities as a fountainhead of water and a capital asset. But only one meaning typically makes sense in any given context. Rarely, multiple meanings can apply, but only *extremely* rarely can all possible meanings apply in the context in which a word is written. Imagine a sentence that contains one or more words that have multiple possible meanings, with all of these meanings making sense. Now *that* is a rich language. Moreover, that is one of the miracles Muslims cite regarding the Holy Qur'an, for that is how the Qur'an is written, from beginning to end.

To begin even to grasp the complexity of this issue, we can leaf through any respected Arabic-English dictionary, such as Hans Wehr's *A Dictionary of Modern Written Arabic*. What we will find is that the overwhelming majority of Arabic words bear multiple translations. If we look up the same words in the most respected reference book, Lane's *Arabic-English Lexicon*, we find the English explanation of a single Arabic word frequently runs into not just paragraphs, but *pages*.

In light of this complexity, there is little wonder that the Qur'an can exist in ten officially recognized recitations in seven different dialects. To accommodate this diversity, the original *mushaf* (book) of the Qur'an lacks diacritical marks, allowing for differences in pronunciation and meaning according to the rules of how vowel points can be assigned to the unvowelled text. What *is* astonishing, however, is that despite the many linguistic possibilities, all recitations not only make sense, but also complement one another. Nowhere does a single sentence, much less a word, of one recitation contradict another. For example, the Arabic words for *owner* and *king* differ by only one vowel point, and yet both are appropriate descriptions of Allah. The result is that Qur'anic recitation, to a person endowed with comprehensive knowledge of Arabic, does not convey one specific lesson, but rather evokes a kaleidoscope of imagery and understanding.

Jews and Christians who find difficulty with the concept of an unvowelled scripture should recognize the common ground between the Bible and the Qur'an in this respect, for the foundational manuscripts of the Old Testament are similarly unvowelled. As per the *Encyclopaedia Britannica*:

> Since texts traditionally omitted vowels in writing, the Masoretes[27(EN)] introduced vowel signs to guarantee correct pronunciation. Among the various systems of vocalization that were invented, the one fashioned in the city of Tiberias, Galilee, eventually gained ascendancy. In addition, signs for stress and pause were added to the text to facilitate public reading of the Scriptures in the synagogue.[28]

Similarly, modern books of the Qur'an are predominantly recorded in the *Hafs 'an 'Aasim* recitation, which has become the most popular of the many accepted recitations among Muslims. One important difference between these two examples is that the Masoretic text of the Old Testament "gained ascendancy" from "among the various systems of vocalization that were invented" (and let's pause over that word, *invented*), whereas the *Hafs 'an 'Aasim* recitation of the Holy Qur'an is one of the recognized recitations of the original.

As discussed in the previous volume, *MisGod'ed*, neither of the original revelations sent down to Moses or Jesus are known to exist, but like the Arabic of the Qur'an, both were written in Semitic languages (ancient Hebrew for the Torah of Moses;

Aramaic—Jesus' native language—for the Gospel of Jesus). Hence, were the original Gospel of Jesus available, we would expect the text to be unvowelled. But because the original Torah and Gospel of Jesus are *not* available, Old and New Testament translators have attempted to compensate for this deficiency. The Preface of the Revised Standard Version of the Bible notes the following, with regard to the Old Testament: "The vowel signs, which were added by the Masoretes, are accepted also in the main, but where a more probable and convincing reading can be obtained by assuming different vowels, this has been done."[29]

Oh. Well, doesn't *that* give us a warm and comfortable feeling, considering our salvation hangs in the balance.

The room for textual manipulation is obvious, and the thought teases the imagination: prior to standardization by the Masoretes, the Jewish Bible lacked punctuation marks, vowels, capital letters, and even word spaces. Just for fun, we can run the words of any sentence in any language together, reduce capital letters to small case, remove punctuation, vowel letters and diacritical marks, and then see how easily this model of the original message can be corrupted.

For example, the teaching, "God is One" would be written *gdsn,* which could be re-expanded to "God is One." However, *gdsn* could just as easily be misinterpreted to mean "Good son," "Good sin," "Go do sin," "God's son" (following the rules of Semitic languages a single consonant, such as the S in this case, can be doubled), or even "Sun-God" (in Semitic languages, a modifier follows its noun. Hence, *gdsn* could be expanded to "God-Sun," the Semitic equivalent of "Sun-God" in English).

In this manner, we could easily misinterpret or manipulate the condensed *gdsn* from orthodoxy to heresy, and those reading the translation would be clueless to our corruption. How much more easily could we (or, more to the point, the

Bible translators) misinterpret entire pages of Old and New Testament manuscripts closer to our desires than to the actual meaning? And yet, the same can not be done with the Holy Qur'an, for at no time was the scripture of Islam ever lost; the original was always available as a primary source by which to identify errors.

Punctuation is critical as well, as pointed out by F. F. Arbuthnot, who relates the amusing story of a British Member of Parliament forced to issue a retraction after calling another member a liar. The member worded his retraction as, "I said the gentleman lied, it is true; and I am sorry for it." However, the following morning the retraction appeared in the local paper as, "I said the gentleman lied. It is true; and I am sorry for it."[30] A reversal in meaning can result from a mistake in a single punctuation point in such circumstances.

We can fairly question, then, who determined what constituted a "more probable and convincing reading" of the relatively featureless, unvowelled, unpunctuated, uncapitalized Jewish scriptures? Was that decision based upon doctrinal prejudice or objective research? And if the vowel system of the Masoretes was trustworthy enough to be accepted as the scriptural authority for an entire religion, why the need to assume "different vowels" in certain places in order to obtain "a more probable and convincing reading"? Lastly, why restrict audience awareness of these controversies to the rarely read preface rather than note them where they occur in the text?

The answer to this last question is easy—the controversies are too numerous. Entire books have been written regarding these disputes, and to include these discussions in the text of the Jewish Bible would more than double its size. It would also discourage the readership. Even blind faith has trouble overlooking too many controversies.

The conditions rightfully provoke no small degree of suspicion on the part of those who recognize the potential for adjusting translation to match doctrinal preference. The Preface to the RSV continues as follows: "Sometimes it is evident that the text has suffered in transmission, but none of the versions provides a satisfactory restoration. Here we can only follow the best judgment of competent scholars as to the most probable reconstruction of the original text."[31]

The fact that the most universally accepted Bible in history admits to the text having "suffered in transmission" does not necessarily imply any fault of modern scholarship, but it does imply an uncertain foundation.

So while both the Bible and the Qur'an were recorded in consonantal texts, the two vary greatly in reliability. The Qur'an was revealed and maintained as an oral tradition until the present day, so pronunciation and meaning have never been in question. The various readings of the Qur'an are all complementary, unlike the Bible where the "more probable and convincing reading" seeks definition, since the various verbal possibilities differ significantly in meaning. The Qur'an has been maintained unchanged to the present day, whereas (to quote again from the RSV Preface) "for the New Testament we have a large number of Greek manuscripts, preserving many variant forms of the text."[32] No single one of which is authoritative.

The context in which the literary miracle of the Qur'an was revealed is important in this regard, for each prophet appears to have been endowed with a sign that was uniquely impressive to those to whom he was sent. The skill most revered by ancient Egyptians was magic, and that most respected by Jews, doctoring. No surprise, then, that Moses was given miracles that stunned Pharaoh's court sorcerers into submission. Equally, there should be no surprise that Jesus was given the miracle of healing.

So what was the highest skill and most respected art of the Arabs? Poetry, and eloquence of the spoken word. The complexity of the Arabic language stems from a profusion of dialects that, "could diversify the fourscore names of honey, the two hundred of a serpent, the five hundred of a lion, the thousand of a sword, at a time when this copious dictionary was entrusted to the memory of an illiterate people."[33]

So devoted were the Arabs to the impact of the spoken word that they held annual festivals, described as follows:

> Thirty days were employed in the exchange, not only of corn and wine, but of eloquence and poetry. The prize was disputed by the generous emulation of the bards; the victorious performance was deposited in the archives of princes and emirs, and we may read, in our own language, the seven original poems which were inscribed in letters of gold, and suspended in the temple of Mecca.[34]

R. Bosworth Smith comments,

> What the Olympic Games did for Greece in keeping up the national feeling, as distinct from tribal independence, in giving a brief cessation from hostilities, and acting as a literary center, that the annual fairs at Okaz and Mujanna were to Arabia. Here tribes made up their dissensions, exchanged prisoners of war, and, most important of all, competed with one another in extempore poetic contests. Even in the "times of ignorance," each tribe produced its own poet-laureate; and the most ready and the best saw his poem transcribed in letters of gold, or suspended on the wall of the entrance of the Kaaba, where it would be seen by every pilgrim who might visit the most sacred place in the country.[35]

In short, the Arabs liked their poetry.

The consistency plays out, for as the miracles of Moses overwhelmed the magic of Pharaoh's sorcerers, and as Jesus' ministrations humiliated the physicians of his time, Muhammad transmitted a revelation composed in the most beautiful Arabic ever known to man. One passage of the Holy Qur'an can reduce hardened desert dwellers to tears, while another can elevate the spirits of the faithful to heights of ecstasy. The novelist James A. Michener, in his essay, "Islam: The Misunderstood Religion," writes:

> The Koran is probably the most often read book in the world, surely the most often memorized, and possibly the most influential in the daily life of the people who believe in it. Not quite so long as the New Testament, written in an exalted style, it is neither poetry nor ordinary prose, yet it possesses the ability to arouse its hearers to ecstasies of faith.[36]

The miraculous beauty of the Qur'an is so affecting as to have spawned a plethora of testimonies. Most convincing is the historical record of the *enemies* of Muhammad, many of whom were so drawn by the beauty of the Qur'an that they would sneak at night through the inky desert darkness to eavesdrop on nighttime recitations. On one such occasion, a number of these men bumped into one another on the way home from the reading. Identifying one another as the *leaders* of Muhammad's enemies (Abu Sufyan and Abu Jahl being two of the three), they vowed never to return. The next night they ran into one another under the same circumstances again. This time they *really* swore not to return, pledging an oath by their idols in testimony to their sincerity. The next night they collided in the darkness once again.[37] Muslims regard this story as evidence of the irresistible beauty of the Holy Qur'an—a beauty so affecting that it drew the ears and imaginations of even the most hardened of detractors, the staunchest of enemies.

The conversion of Umar, one of the greatest warriors of his time and, up to the moment of his conversion, a greatly feared opponent of Islam, is frequently cited. Setting out to kill Muhammad, he was diverted to his sister's home where, upon hearing the recitation of just one *surah*, he converted on the spot.

Other exemplary cases are to be found in the examples of Unays al-Ghifaaree and Al-Kindii, two of the greatest Muslim poets of Muhammad's time. Unays al-Ghifaaree had this to say after his first encounter with Muhammad: "I have met a man of your religion in Makkah who claims to be sent by Allah. The people claim that he is a poet, or a sorcerer, or a magician. Yet, I have heard the words of sorcerers, and these words in no way resemble those uttered by a sorcerer. And I also compared his words to the verses of a poet, but such words cannot be uttered by a poet. By Allah, he is the truthful, and they are the liars!"[38] Al-Kindii, when asked to compose a passage like that found in the Qur'an, stated that it simply wasn't possible. Al-Kindii indicated that he would need to write books in order to convey the meaning of just a few lines of the Qur'an. His inability to match the beauty and content of the Qur'an is held by Muslims as testimony to the divine nature of Allah's challenge to mankind: "And if you [Arab pagans, Jews and Christians] are in doubt concerning that which We have sent down (i.e. the Qur'an) to Our slave (the prophet Muhammad), then produce a *surah* [chapter] of the like thereof and call your witnesses (supporters and helpers) besides Allah, if you are truthful" (TMQ 2:23). The reader is reminded that the "We" and "Our" in the above quote are English translations of the "royal plural" (as discussed in *MisGod'ed*) and not the plural of numbers. Having said that, the quote benefits from closer examination.

Allah is recorded as having challenged mankind no less than five times to attempt to match the Qur'an. The first challenge (in order of revelation, not in the order presented in the chapters) was to write an entire book equal to that of the Qur'an (*surahs* 17:88 and 52:33–34). When the greatest poets of the Arabic language could not produce even a single contestant, Allah issued a second challenge to write ten chapters the like of the Qur'an (*surah* 11:13). When the Arabian nation hung its head in abject literary humiliation, Allah reduced the challenge to producing one lone *surah* the like of that found in the Qur'an (*surah* 10:38, followed by *surah* 2:23). For 1,400 years native Arabic-speaking Jews, Christians, pagans, and atheists have struggled to disprove the Qur'an for religious, political, and personal reasons. And Arabic is their native tongue.

Something seems almost surreal about this scenario, for the shortest *surah* in the Qur'an is Al-Kauthar, number 108, weighing in at a power-packed, meaning-filled three lines. *Three.* Three lines totaling a scant ten words. So why has mankind been unable to write three lines equal or better for the past 1,400 years? Why has mankind been unable to "produce a *surah* of the like thereof"?

Muslims point out that human standards are easily broken. Seemingly impossible barriers are routinely transgressed, unbeatable records beaten, and previously unimagined successes achieved. The four-minute mile has been broken, the speed of sound shattered, the moon trod upon, the atom split, and electrons frozen. But why has all of mankind been unable to write the like of the Qur'an? After 1,400 years? It's not for lack of time to think about it, that's for sure.

Al-Waleed ibn al-Mughera, a lifelong antagonist of Islam and a poet in his own right, admitted, "By Allah, I heard a speech (the Qur'an) from Muhammad now; it is not from men or jinn (spirits)—it is like sweetness. It is like the highest fruit in a tree growing in rich soil, and nothing can be above it."[39] When the best poets and the most avowed enemies admit the supremacy of the revelation, such opinions should be respected.

While some assert that Muhammad was just a very great poet, Muslims point out that one character trait of great artists is that when they finish cutting their ears off, they fret over their dissatisfaction with their work. Would a person expect Beethoven, who struggled mightily over his masterpieces, as his heavily marked-over scores attest, to challenge the world to write better music? Or would Michelangelo, who shattered his statues to shards because he felt they weren't good enough, challenge the world to sculpt a better statue? Such a bold challenge could only be made, with confidence, by the One Who orders creation and knows He will never allow the challenge to be met. And so, 1,400 years later, as noted by numerous authors, the challenge still stands. Professor A. J. Arberry states: "The Koran undeniably abounds in fine writing; it has its own extremely individual qualities; the language is highly idiomatic, yet for the most part delusively simple; the rhythms and rhymes are inseparable features of its impressive eloquence, and these are indeed inimitable."[40]

Dr. Laura Vaglieri contributes,

The Miracle of Islam *par excellence* is the Quran, through which a constant and unbroken tradition transmits to us news of an absolute certainty. This is a book which cannot be imitated. Each of its expressions is a comprehensive one, and yet it is of proper size, neither too long nor too short. Its style is original. There is no model for this style in Arab literature of the times preceding it. The effect which it produces on the human soul is obtained without any adventitious aid through its own inherent excellences. The verses are equally eloquent all through the text, even when they deal with topics, such as commandments and prohibitions, which must necessarily affect its tone. Stories of Prophets, descriptions of the beginning and the end of the world, enumerations and expositions of the divine attributes are repeated but repeated in a way which is so impressive that they do not weaken the effect. The text proceeds from one topic to another without losing its power. Depth and sweetness, qualities which generally do not go together, are found together here, where each rhetoric figure finds a perfect application ... We find there vast stores of knowledge which are beyond the capacity of the most intelligent of men, the greatest of philosophers and the ablest of politicians.[41]

And A. Guillaume sums up as follows:

The Qurān is one of the world's classics which cannot be translated without grave loss. It (The Holy Qurān) has a rhythm of peculiar beauty and a cadence that charms the ear. Many Christian Arabs speak of its style with warm admiration, and most Arabists acknowledge its excellence ... indeed it may be affirmed that within the literature of the Arabs, wide and fecund as it is both in poetry and in elevated prose, there is nothing to compare with it.[42]

One notable point about the language of the Qur'an is that Muhammad first received revelation when he was forty years old. People knew his character, his walk, his talk, his ethics, his morals. They *knew* his speech. The observation is frequently made that habits and personality traits do not markedly change past the age of thirty. An ancient Chinese proverb correctly states, "With men as with silk, it is most difficult to change colors once the dye has set."

By the age of forty, most people have settled into a solid framework of character traits. Not only had Muhammad proved himself no author (a point referred to in the verse, "And you were not [able] to recite a Book before this [Book came], nor are you [able] to transcribe it with your right hand; in that case, indeed, would the talkers of vanities have doubted" [TMQ 29:48]), but the language of Muhammad was identifiably on a much lower plane than that of the Qur'an. Furthermore, Muhammad was very specific about which words were recorded as revelation. He initially forbade his companions to record his own words in any form whatsoever, and commanded, "Do not write anything from me except the Qur'an. Whoever writes anything besides the Qur'an should burn it."[43]

Even later, when Muhammad permitted the recording of *hadith*, his words and those of the revelation were never mixed, and there is no confusion over the fact that the words of Muhammad never approached the divine eloquence of the Qur'an. To this day, we can verify this language difference by comparing any book of *hadith* with the Holy Qur'an. The traditions of Muhammad were recorded in scores of volumes of *hadith*, preserving his speech in a multitude of sources that give the reader extraordinary insight into his character and literary abilities. Yet the rhyme and rhythm, the emotionally evocative essence of the message and the unique beauty of the Qur'an are nowhere found in Muhammad's own speech. As Dr. Laura Vaglieri questioned, "How could this marvelous book be the work of Muhammad, an illiterate Arab who in all his life composed only two or three verses, none of which reveals the least poetic quality; e.g. 'I am the Prophet and do not lie. I am the son of Abd el-Muttalib.'?"[44]

Professor A. J. Arberry elaborates as follows:

> We know quite well how Mohammed spoke in his normal, everyday moods; for his *obiter dicta* have been preserved in great abundance. It is simply untrue therefore to say, as Margoliouth said, that "it would be difficult to find another case in which there is such a complete identity between the literary work and the mind of the man who produced it." Accepting, as we have good reason to accept, the sayings of Mohammed recorded in the books of Traditions as substantially authentic, and supposing, as Margoliouth supposed, that the Koran was Mohammed's conscious production, it would be more reasonable to say that it would be difficult to find another case in which the literary expression of a man differed so fundamentally from his ordinary speech.[45]

The point is that the difference between the language of Muhammad and that of the Qur'an is so readily identifiable that detractors of Islam have driven their imaginations great distances in order to deny the Qur'an as revelation. Many non-Muslims, such as the above-referenced Oxford orientalist, David Margoliouth, have gone so far as to allow religious prejudice to override scholastic standards. These orientalists disingenuously deny what, to less biased scholars, is a clear reality. Non-Muslim Arabic scholars (such as the aforementioned A. J. Arberry[46(EN)]) readily appreciate the difference between Muhammad's speech and the literary miracle of the Qur'an. Consequently, this difference demands explanation. For if not from the mind of Muhammad, what was the source of the Holy Qur'an?

In trying to provide an explanation without crediting revelation, some scholars have gone so far as to suggest that Muhammad must have had a teacher who tutored the composition of the Qur'an. This, they propose, would explain the difference. And indeed it might. However, Muhammad's contemporaries recognized that the structure of the Qur'an was completely foreign to all lexical forms of Arabic poetry.[47] It remains so to this day. Furthermore, if ever there had been such an accomplished tutor, who was he (or she) and what happened to his other works? Where are his other equally glorious and distinctive compositions? Common sense tells us a people who valued their literature as much as the Arabs would have preserved such treasures from this alleged tutor. And yet none are known to exist.

To expand the argument, the Holy Qur'an broke many, if not most, of the pre-existing literary rules. For one thing, poetry most frequently concerns matters of common interest—wine, women and song, for example—with excursions into the esoteric at the pens of the masters. In Muhammad's time Arabic poetry, like its Western parallel, reveled in romantic and hedonistic delights. However, issues of tribal superiority, the virtues of people and animals of noble breeding or notable qualities, contests of strength and wit, local heroes and history were also the subject of poetic glorification. As can be imagined, much of Arabic poetry extolled the virtues of one's own person, tribe, kith and kin, while denigrating all others.[48(EN)]

The Qur'an broke this mold. Exaggeration was avoided, descriptions were confined to the limits of reality, and chosen topics strayed into the fields of law and legislation, manners and morals, social and civil responsibilities, and religious beliefs and practices. The combination of such seemingly dry topics with unembellished accounting fails to constitute what most people would consider ingredients for a literary masterpiece. And yet, fourteen hundred years of Arab poets identify the Holy Qur'an as the most eloquent and provocative expression of their language the world has ever seen.

Hard to believe.

But isn't that what a miracle is? An extraordinary reality that defies reasonable expectations?

Though repetitive, the Qur'an is not monotonous; though conveyed through a human conduit (i.e., Muhammad), it does not betray the fluctuations of mood and tone that is unavoidable among poets; though revealed over a period of twenty-three years, there is no evolution of style, no development of technique typical of a work written over such a long period of time. In defiance of normal human variability, the Qur'an remained consistent in its expression and superlative in its eloquence, from topic to topic, from beginning to end.

One of the most intriguing aspects of the superlative beauty of the Holy Qur'an is that it was not revealed in chronological order. As verses were revealed, Muhammad was commanded to place each new verse in a specific spot in the framework of what had been revealed up to that point. Frequently new verses were sandwiched between two previously revealed verses, inserted at a divinely ordained position in the scripture. In the Preface to his translation of the Holy Qur'an, Professor A. J. Arberry commented on this process as follows:

> I have followed the traditional arrangement for all its admitted perplexities. The Suras themselves are in many instances—and this has been recognized by Muslim students from the earliest times—of a composite

character, holding embedded in them fragments received
by Muhammad at widely differing dates ...[49]

Again, Muslims point out the inconsistency between
this process and human methodology. People tell stories and
relate historical accounts, and attempt to link them together.
Whether we examine a history book or the Bible, the pattern is
the same—stories are strung together end-to-end, in an effort
to achieve continuity. Constructing the Qur'an piecemeal, as
was done, violates both human capacity and methodology.
Furthermore, if Muhammad had faked revelation, literary
contortionism just was not necessary, for throughout history
false messiahs have mislead the masses with far, far less, and
for good reason—false messiahs are lazy. No false messiah can
be imagined to ever have worked this hard!

Consequently, to be fair, those who believe they can come
up with three verses that rival those of the Qur'an now have
to do it backwards! Now they have to write the last line first
(without having previously conceived the first two lines), the
first line next and the second line last. Or something like that.
Now they have to do it in such a way that each stage of the
composition stands by itself, bears an intelligent message, and
achieves an unrivaled literary eloquence. Additionally, the
teachings have to foretell a future event, address a current
concern, or teach a scientific fact that will not be known for
the next 1,400 years. Ten different readings in seven different
dialects at each stage of passage construction are required—
each one complementary in meaning, each one embodying the
above qualities. If it sounds impossible, the Muslim claim is
that, from a human perspective, it is!

Yet the Qur'an was recorded in just this fashion over a period
of twenty-three years, with the revelation transmitted through

the lips of an illiterate man, Muhammad. If construction of just three lines seems impossible, how could Muhammad have composed a complete book in this manner, when he could neither read nor write in the first place? And lacking the luxury of a written work-in-progress to which he could refer, how could he have filled in the missing pieces over a period of two decades? Each stage of the work bears a comprehensible message of such practicality and beauty that no human has been able to match as little as three lines. There are no demonstrable errors, inconsistencies, or disruptions in flow. Can we imagine all of the above, at *each* of the hundreds (if not thousands) of stages of revelation, having been accomplished by a human being? Most people can't assemble a do-it-yourself project without putting the long bolt in the short hole, misplacing shelves and partitions, or similar errors—and all that despite having a manual in hand. In the end, human efforts approach perfection through a series of corrected errors.

So could a book of such complexity have been written by one man, or even a team of men? Muslims assert that the revelation and content of the Holy Qur'an defy both human ability *and* methodology. After just a few years, if not a couple months, events would have conspired to negate planned verses, the plan to put such-and-such a verse here or there would have been forgotten, and the whole thing would have degenerated into an incoherent mess.

If nothing else, no human could predict they would live long enough to complete the task; an early demise would have left the work with gaping holes where future passages were planned.

Fourteen centuries ago, a forty year-old man living in the desert could have reasonably expected to be at the end of his life, and to have had a good run of it. To have expected to live another twenty-three years in that time and under conditions of persecution and warfare against overwhelming odds would have seemed grossly unrealistic at best. An even greater breach from reality would have been to imagine that anyone could foresee the events around which future passages of the Qur'an would be revealed.

One of the first lessons a con artist learns is that good liars have to have better memories. But the Islamic view is that no human has ever lived with the memory necessary to compose such a complex work. And yet, this is how the Qur'an was revealed. Verse by verse, over a period of twenty-three years, the Qur'an was pieced together and filled out in such a manner that it was, at all stages of development, an incomparable, eloquent revelation of such sublime force and beauty as to change the hearts of man and the direction of mankind.

The question as to Who the author was, in the mind of the Muslim, does not entertain a human candidate.

There are those who agree that no human could write such a book, but who assert it must be the work of Satan. Such assertions are disappointing, at best, for the New Testament relates that many disbelieving Jews made the same claim about Jesus—that his works were not of God, but of Satan, the prince of devils (Matthew 12:24, Mark 3:22, Luke 11:15).

On one hand, Christian hearts melt at the stories of the miracles of Jesus, wondering how the disbelieving Jews could possibly have denied these miracles as evidence of Jesus' prophethood. The Christians who read these biblical stories think that, had they been there, they wouldn't have been so blind—they would have believed. But would they have? After all, these are frequently the same Christians who slander the miracle of the Qur'an as the work of the devil. Such Christians begin to look very much like the disbelieving Jews in Jesus' day, for despite the weight of evidence (miracles included), they not only adopt elaborate excuses to dismiss the Muslim scripture, but they frequently advance the same reflexive claim—that it is the work of the "prince of devils."

Even that challenge has an answer, though, for Muslims point out that the Holy Qur'an's teachings preclude such a possibility. *Surah* 16, *ayah* 98 (i.e., chapter and verse) directs the Muslim, "When you do read the Qur'an, seek Allah's protection from Shaytan the Rejected One" (Yusuf Ali translation). The Muhammad Al-Hilali and Muhammad Khan translation is even more explicit: "So when you want to recite the Qur'an, seek refuge with Allah from Shaitan (Satan), the outcast (the cursed one)." Common sense tells us that Satan would not write a book that directs a person to take refuge from himself with Almighty God. Some might stretch their imaginations far enough to assert that Satan is just that tricky, but only the hypocritical Christian can make such a claim, for the Bible reads,

> But Jesus knew their thoughts, and said to them: "Every kingdom divided against itself is brought to desolation, and every city or house divided against itself will not stand. If Satan casts out Satan, he is divided against himself. How then will his kingdom stand?" (Matthew 12:25–26)

This teaching is echoed in Mark 3:23–27 and Luke 11:17. To deny the argument is to deny not only Jesus, but also three of the New Testament gospels. And for those who consider the Bible the word of God, it is denial of God Himself. The point? That *surah* 16, *ayah* 98 is not just a Muslim argument. It is, in fact, a biblical argument!

The Islamic world thus presents this challenge: If man and Satan are excluded as authors, exactly Whom does that leave?

5

Evidence #3—Relation of Revelation to Preceding Events

The past is a foreign country; they do things differently there.
—L.P. Hartley, *The Go-Between,* Prologue

M any biblical stories are retold in the Qur'an, but with significant differences. A frequent challenge is the assertion that the Qur'an was copied from the Old and New Testaments. There are many difficulties with this proposal, the first being that Muhammad was illiterate, and could not have read the Jewish and Christian scriptures had he tried. For that matter, Arab Jews and Christians could not have read their Bibles, even had they tried. Why? Because they didn't exist. Evidence suggests there was no such thing as an Arabic Bible during the lifetime of Muhammad, and for centuries to follow.

This lack of an Arabic Bible is disturbing to those who propose that Muhammad copied biblical stories into the Qur'an. Although discovery of an Arabic Bible predating the seventh century would bring considerable joy to such claimants, this search has proved disappointing. *The Encyclopedia of Religion and Ethics*, a series of voluminous tomes filled with poison and slanders aimed at Islam, nonetheless admits, "There is no evidence of any parts of the Bible having been translated into Arabic before Islam."[50] Hasting's *Dictionary of the Bible* attributes the first Arabic translation of the Bible to the tenth century,[51] while *Encyclopedia Judaica* attributes the first Arabic translation of the Old Testament either to Hunayn ibn Ishaq (800–873 CE) or to Saadiah (born Joseph Gaon, 882–942 CE).[52]

Thus, we have to wonder what Jewish and Christian sources existed in Muhammad's day. If there was no Arabic Bible, what was there? Copying something that didn't exist would be, well, tough—even tougher for the illiterate.

The presence of Jews and Christians in the Arabian Peninsula during Muhammad's time is well known. Khadijah (Muhammad's first wife) had an aged cousin, Waraqah ibn Nawfal, who was Christian. Furthermore, Muhammad came into contact with Bahira-Sergius, a Nestorian monk of Syria, at a young age. Contact with the Jews of his community, and the opportunity for instruction in their religion, was no less likely. Thus a case can be made for Muhammad having learned the basics of the Jewish and Christian religions through their oral traditions. As the Jews and Christians passed the teachings of their religions to one another, they also could have conveyed them to Muhammad. Such a case can be made. And such a case can be destroyed.

The problem with this proposal is not that Jewish and Christian oral traditions were unavailable, for no doubt they were readily available. No, the problem relates to exactly *what* Jewish and Christian teachings circulated in the Arabian Peninsula during Muhammad's time. For in fact, the Arabs do not appear to have embraced the mainstream views of the Jewish and Christian religions during this period. Regarding the period of Muhammad's prophethood, the *New Catholic Encyclopedia* comments,

Neither Arabian Jews nor Arabian Christians, unfortunately, were to be classed among the better representatives of their faiths at the time. The former had lived in comparative isolation possibly since the middle of the 1st millennium B.C., although they had been mildly successful in proselytism, and the latter were mainly heretical Monophysites, remote in every sense from the centers of Christian learning.[53]

Paul D. Wegner, author of *The Journey from Texts to Translations,* contributes this:

The Scriptures do not seem to have been extant in an Arabic version before the time of Muhammad (570–632), who knew the gospel story only in oral form, and mainly from Syriac sources. These Syriac sources were marked by Docetism (believed that Jesus had only a divine nature and only appeared to be incarnate—they thought the material world and thus one's body was inherently evil) ...[54]

Hence the problem. The proposal is that Muhammad copied from Jewish and Christian sources, even though he was illiterate, hard copies of the Bible didn't exist, and the only sources of Jewish and Christian oral traditions were those of the poorer "representatives of their faiths." In other words, these were the traditions of the heretical Monophysites, Docetists, and Nestorians. Why, then, doesn't the Qur'an just copy the dogma peculiar to these heretical sects? Why does the Qur'an condemn associating Jesus Christ with divinity, rather than endorse the Monophysite belief in a union of godhead and manhood in the one nature of Jesus Christ? Why does the Qur'an validate Jesus Christ as a man, and not advocate the Docetist concept of Jesus having been a phantasm? And why does the Qur'an reject the Nestorian claim to union of God (the son) with Jesus (the man)? If the Qur'an was copied from oral traditions, and the Jewish and Christian Arabs were poor representatives of their faiths, why are their heresies not argued in the Holy Qur'an? Why does the Qur'an address the valid beliefs of the Jewish orthodoxy, the commonly accepted historical accounts of both Old and New Testaments, and the mainstream issues of the Trinitarian Christianity of Constantinople? Why doesn't it present the unorthodox concepts of the Arab Jews and Christians of Muhammad's time?

Similarly, we have to wonder why the Qur'an records history differently from how the Arabs understood it. The Qur'an repeatedly claims to reveal historical details previously unknown to the Arabs—Jews and Christians included. Following the story of Noah, the Qur'an teaches, "Such are some of the stories of the Unseen, which We have revealed to you: before this, neither you nor your people knew them" (TMQ 11:49).

And yet no one, whether well-traveled pagan, scholarly Jew or Christian, or even Muslim, ever ran to the front of the congregation yelling, "Wait a minute, I knew that!" Once again, copying Jewish or Christian traditions that didn't exist, either on paper or in oral tradition, would be, well, troublesome. What could possibly have been the source of such information if the other religious *authorities* were themselves clueless?

The most significant point, however, is that the Qur'an corrects, rather than repeats, biblical errors. What should we think of a book that corrected the as-yet unrecognized errors considered "gospel truth" during Muhammad's lifetime? A man-made book designed to appeal to the masses would be expected to confirm, rather than deny, popular opinion. True revelation, however, would be expected to correct falsehoods, no matter how distasteful the truth may seem. And such is the case with the Holy Qur'an—correct beliefs were reinforced and unrecognized errors were rectified.

The most important corrections relate to elements of belief, as discussed in the first volume of this series, *MisGod'ed*. The Holy Qur'an challenges Christians by telling them to look in their own book, for they will find that Jesus never called himself "Son of God" (see *MisGod'ed*). Now, how could Muhammad have known that? As discussed above, he couldn't read their book. For that matter, *they* couldn't read their book; it would be two centuries before a translation would be available to them. So what were Muhammad's sources? Again, the most he could have heard were snippets of Christian oral traditions. But how could he have known he had heard them all? Or correctly? Without a Bible for reference, how could he have known that throughout the New Testament, Jesus never identified himself as the "Son of God"? The safer bet, given what he must have been told, would have been to state the exact opposite. To this day, it is the rare Christian who knows Jesus never called himself "Son of God" in the Bible. So how did Muhammad know this?

Examples of more objective, verifiable corrections include scientific evidence. But we can also consider such simple elements as Jesus' age at the beginning of his ministry.

According to the Bible, "Now Jesus himself began his ministry at about thirty years of age ..." (Luke 3:23)

So says the Bible.

And so say most Christians.

However, history suggests Jesus was considerably older—perhaps as old as forty-six, but not less than thirty-eight.[55] Where do we get these numbers? Jesus was born during the reign of King Herod the Great of Judaea (who died shortly after a lunar

DR. LAURENCE B. BROWN

eclipse dated by astronomers to March 12–13, 4 BC) and began his ministry after John the Baptist's imprisonment. Why was John the Baptist imprisoned? For rebuking Antipas—King Herod the Great's son, also known as Herod the Tetrarch (i.e., governor) of Galilee and Perea—for marrying his own niece and sister-in-law. Now, we can fairly assume that Antipas could not have married his sister-in-law unless his brother was, by one means or another, out of the picture. Some small degree of sibling rivalry might otherwise have ensued. Sure enough, in his *Jewish Antiquities,* the first-century historian Josephus documents that Herod's dear brother Philip died "in the twentieth year of the reign of Tiberius," which corresponds with 33–34 CE.[56] A soap opera here, a battle there, a journey to fetch the questionably grieving widow, a marriage, a public rebuke, and John the Baptist found himself in jail waiting for the manipulative step-daughter to dance. The timing works out to Jesus having started his ministry on or after 34 CE, as per the gospels of Mark and Luke: "Now after John was put in prison, Jesus came to Galilee, preaching the gospel of the kingdom of God" (Mark 1:14).

The time span from 4 BC to 34 CE being thirty-eight years, Jesus could not have started his ministry before the age of thirty-eight.

Assuming that Jesus was not born on the day King Herod the Great died, and allowing a more reasonable period of time for his son, Herod Antipas, to have acquired his sister-in-law, Jesus was more likely well into his forties. Such an assumption is not unreasonable. To understand why, let us consider the sequence of events:

1.   Jesus Christ was born during the reign of King Herod the Great. (Matthew 2:1)

2. Following Jesus' birth, the Magi (wise men), having seen the star signaling his miraculous birth, came to Jerusalem from the east. (Matthew 2:1)

——That's one major trip. In a period of history when first-class transportation meant a camel that didn't spit, such things took time.

3. Herod sent the Magi on a reconnaissance trip to Bethlehem. (Matthew 2:8)

——That's a second trip.

4. The Magi returned to their countries, unbeknownst to Herod. (Matthew 2:12)

——That's a third trip.

5. An angel of God directed Joseph to "arise," and flee. (Matthew 2:13)

6. Joseph arose…(Matthew 2:14)

——That may only have taken a minute or so.

7. And took the family to Egypt for an indefinite leave of absence. (Matthew 2:14)

——That probably took slightly longer. A fourth trip.

8. Herod found out about the deception. (Matthew 2:16)

——That probably took some time, too. A fifth trip (by the messenger).

9. Herod, being a man of such paranoia as to have executed his beloved wife Mariamne and, on separate occasions, three sons thought to threaten his throne, sent his flunkies in tyranny to kill all the male children two years old and less in Bethlehem and the vicinity. (Matthew 2:16)

——Why two years old and younger? "…according to the time which he had determined from the wise men" (Matthew 2:16). In other words, Jesus Christ was getting on in infancy.

10. After an unspecified period of time, Herod died. (Matthew 2:19)

Given the above scenario, we can reasonably expect Jesus to have been born at least two years prior to King Herod the Great's demise. In other words, he was born in or before 6 BC. Similarly, we can reasonably expect that events surrounding Herod Antipas' shady marriage unfolded somewhat slower than a snap of the fingers.

Suddenly the question posed to Jesus in John 8:57, "You are not yet fifty years old, and have you seen Abraham?" makes sense. We can logically expect that, had Jesus been in his thirties, this challenge would have been worded, "You are not yet *forty* years old ..." But it isn't. And now we understand why.

Illustrating yet another biblical difficulty is not the point. The take-home message is that to this day Christians read Luke 3:23 ("Now Jesus himself began his ministry at about thirty years of age ...") and assert that Jesus started his ministry around the age of thirty. Had Muhammad asked, this is almost certainly what he would have been told. Now, what does the Qur'an say? That Jesus spoke to the people in childhood, and when he was *kahlan* (*surah* 5:110). *Kahlan* describes a man aged between thirty and fifty.[57] Had the Bible been copied, we would expect to find "Luke's" claim that Jesus was "about thirty." However, just as historical evidence defies the biblical record, the Qur'anic description corrects, rather than repeats, this biblical error.

How about another example? The title *pharaoh* was applied to Egyptian rulers only during the years 1539–1292 BC and *circa* 945–730 BC.[58] To quote, "The Egyptian term became a title of respect for the king during the 18th dynasty … Any use of 'Pharaoh' for kings preceding Thutmose III is an anachronism."[59] And Thutmose III lived—drum roll, please—from approximately 1490 to 1436 BC.[60] So any use of the term *pharaoh* prior to the 1490s BC would be an anachronism: "an attribution of a custom, event, etc., to the wrong period."[61]

What does this have to do with the Bible and the Holy Qur'an?

During the prophet Joseph's time (around 1700 BC), Egypt was ruled by a different line of monarchy. And had been for some time. The Hyksos Dynasty were ethnic Arabs who usurped the Egyptian throne *circa* 2000 BC, and ruled Egypt to the end of the fifteenth century BC. They never called their kings "Pharaoh." And here Joseph was, in the minus-seventeen hundreds, smack-dab in the middle of the Hyksos Dynasty. Yet the Bible labels both the kings of Joseph (Genesis, chapters 39–50) and of Moses (Exodus 2–18) as "Pharaoh." What we know of history, however, conflicts with the use of this term during the time of Joseph. But oh, well, one out of two isn't bad, if that is the standard of accuracy we seek in a book of revelation.

Now, what about the Qur'an?

The Qur'an correctly acknowledges the king of Moses' time as "Pharaoh," but identifies the king of Egypt in the time of Joseph as just that—the "King" (See *Surah* Yusuf—i.e., *surah* 12). Here again, the Qur'an corrects, rather than repeats, a biblical error, despite the fact that the Qur'an mentions the title "Pharaoh" over seventy times. However, each of these mentions refers to a historical period when the monarch of Egypt was actually identified as "Pharaoh." Considering this context, the conspicuous avoidance of this term in reference to the ruler during Joseph's time appears significant.

Speaking of Egypt, the Qur'an records Pharaoh having ordered a man called Haman to bake bricks for construction (TMQ 28:38). The word *haman* comes to us from hieroglyphics and is believed to mean "the chief of the workers in the stone-quarries."[62] In other words, in a time and place where construction was largely tantamount to stacking blocks, "Haman" was in charge of supplies.

Now, hieroglyphics died out centuries before Muhammad's time, and was only relearned with the discovery of the Rosetta Stone in 1799 CE. Here is what happened: After the deaths of Marcus Antonius (i.e., Marc Antony) and Cleopatra in 30 BC, Roman governorship superseded the Egyptian dynastic system, and Latin became the language of the realm. Consequently, the writing system of hieroglyphics died out within the next century. Discovery of the Rosetta Stone resuscitated the hieroglyphics, but this was by no means easy. Even with the Rosetta Stone in hand, the effort demanded time (more than twenty years), inspiration, and some of the most brilliant minds of Europe. All of which leads us to question how the author of the Qur'an knew to title the man in charge of construction supplies "Haman." With hieroglyphics dead and buried for over five hundred years, and such titles presumably extinct as well, what was the source of such knowledge in Muhammad's day?

Now let's consider a less obscure example.

Jesus never identified his followers as "Christians." In fact, his followers did not adopt this label until years following his ministry. Nonetheless, once adopted, the label stuck. So if Muhammad had asked the Christians of his time what they called themselves, they would have said, "Christian" (or *Masihiyyun*, in Arabic). *Masihiyyun* describes the followers (-*iyyun*) of Christ (*Messiah* in Hebrew, *Masih* in Arabic).

Makes sense? Sure. To this day, Western Christians identify themselves as just that—Christians. Likewise, their Arab counterparts identify themselves as *Masihiyyun* (followers of Christ). By what name, then, would Muhammad have known Jesus' followers? As *Masihiyyun*. Why, then, is this word not mentioned once in the Qur'an? Not one, single, solitary time?

The Qur'an mentions Christians repeatedly, not as "Christians" or *Masihiyyun*, but as *Nasara* (Nazarenes). Now, wait a minute. How many Christians, anywhere in the world, have ever called themselves "Nazarenes"? Very few, I suspect. Why then does the Qur'an employ the faithful biblical term of "Nazarene," rather than the popular Arabic label of *Masihiyyun?* Who told Muhammad that although virtually all Christians identify themselves as "Christian," Jesus never did? We find in Acts 11:26 that "the disciples were called Christians first in Antioch." In other words, non-believers first applied this term to Christ's followers around 43 CE, roughly ten years following his ministry.

Furthermore, it doesn't appear to have been a polite term.

Contrary to popular belief, the term *Christian* appears to have been conceived as a name of contempt. It's what disbelievers called the followers of Christ—a distasteful name to believers who knew themselves as Jews, following the latest in the line of Jewish prophets. And yet that very label is now worn with pride, despite the fact that, "it appears to have been more widely used by pagans, and according to Tacitus it was in common use by the time of the Neronian persecution (Annals, 15.44)."[63]

In other words, "Christian" was a derogatory label imposed upon believers by their enemies. And yet the term stuck and, with typical Christian humility, was eventually adopted.

Fine. Now we know. But how many readers knew this fact before reading it here? More to the point, who told

Muhammad? Who told Muhammad the term "Christian" (*Masihiyyun* in Arabic) began its life as a derogatory term, and was never uttered by Jesus Christ? Who told Muhammad a more respectful biblical term is *Nasara?* And why would Muhammad bother to swim against such an overwhelmingly strong current of public opinion? Unless, that is, he only conveyed words given to him—words that corrected his own opinion as well as that of most of the rest of mankind?

The above issues, while addressing relatively small details of historical accuracy, are highly significant. It is these minute details that function as tripwires upon which false prophethood snags a toe. Nobody trips over a building; it is always the small, seemingly insignificant bumps people stumble over. However, rather than painting a new gloss over old errors, it is just these minute points of detail the Qur'an corrects with exquisite accuracy.

The Bible teaches, "He who is faithful in what is least is faithful also in much; and he who is unjust in what is least is unjust also in much" (Luke 16:10). If this teaching is applied to the Bible, the significance of even the smallest error (i.e., unfaithfulness to detail) becomes apparent. Even as little as a copying error should sound the alarm to the fact that "he who is unjust in what is least is unjust also in much." Details are important, for it is on the basis of detail that we differentiate between human fallibility and divine inerrancy.

And then there is Iram.

The Holy Qur'an makes passing mention of a city named Iram (TMQ 89:7). As it turns out, Iram was lost to history for over 3,500 years, and only recently discovered. Who, then, knew to mention Iram in the Holy Qur'an? For two thousand years prior to the revelation, there was no evidence it had ever existed.

The archeological roadmap to Iram passes through the ancient city of Ebla, as discussed in the December 1978 issue of *National Geographic*. The article, "Ebla, Splendor of an Unknown Empire" outlines one of the greatest archeological finds of the present epoch—the discovery of the city of Ebla in Northwest Syria.[64] The magnitude of the Ebla find is related as follows:

> In 1975, Matthiae {Paolo Matthiae, one of the two archaeologists in charge of the dig} hit an archeological jackpot. In the ruins of a palace apparently destroyed in the 23rd century B.C., he came upon the greatest third-millennium archive ever unearthed. More than 15,000 cuneiform tablets and fragments—the commercial records, treaties, chronicles—whispered, through the mists of ancient and ambiguous syntax, of an unknown Semitic empire, with Ebla as its seat, that once dominated much of the Middle East ... this find struck the scholarly world like a thunderbolt.[65]

How big is this find? To quote Dr. Ignace J. Gelb, "Ebla was a mighty kingdom, treated on an equal footing with the most powerful states of the time."[66] How important are the cuneiform tablets? To quote Dr. Giovanni Pettinato, "*All* the other texts of this period recovered to date do not total a fourth of those from Ebla."[67]

This massive collection of cuneiform plates (clay tablets inscribed with wedge-shaped writing) lifts the veil of obscurity from the face of history to reveal an image contrary to many classical preconceptions. These tablets reveal a rich culture in a thriving community—so much so that archeological experts conclude: "Ebla rivaled Egypt and Mesopotamia as a major power of the ancient world."[68]

Wow.

So what happened to so great a culture? Where did it go? Into the ground.

Around 2300 BC, Sargon defeated Ebla and razed the city. The burning of the palace turned the library into a kiln, and the fire baked the clay tablets into ceramic preservation. Excavated layers of the ruins reveal that Ebla was rebuilt only to be destroyed again around three centuries later, most likely by the Amorites. Rebuilt upon the ruins once more, "Ebla flourished briefly once again, but around 1800 B.C. the city began to decline, and within two hundred years finally disappeared from history."[69]

What does this have to do with Iram? Ebla, like all major world powers, kept records of all cities with which they transacted business or from which they exacted tribute. These records were stored in the palace library. And what do we find there? Mention of Beirut, Damascus, Gaza, Sodom, Gomorrah, among others. What else? "Also included is Iram, an obscure city referred to in *surah* 89 of the Koran."[70] So in 1975 Iram, as mentioned in the Holy Qur'an 1,400 years ago, became historically verified.

What else was verified? Ebla's library records also mention the cities of Ad and Shamutu (believed to be the city of the early Arabian people known as the Thamud): two other lost civilizations mentioned in the Qur'an.[71] As a matter of fact, five short Qur'anic verses (89:6–10) mention four lost civilizations, all of which are now historically identified: Iram, Ad, Shamutu, and the people of Pharaoh.

Could Muhammad have known of Iram? Ad? No doubt he knew of the people of Pharaoh, and almost certainly he knew of Shamutu, in structure if not in name, for the ruins of Shamutu exist to this day in the Arabian city of *Mada'in Salih*. But Iram and Ad? Could Muhammad have known of cultures that disappeared thousands of years before the sun rose on his first day in his mother's arms? Could he have known the names of lost cities in a time and place where the closest thing to an information superhighway was a level trail and a fast camel?

Not likely.

The average American can't name the first three settlements in the United States, and might miss the correct answer even if offered in the form of a multiple-choice question. And those settlements are not only well known, but are only a few centuries old. So by what means did Muhammad come up with the names Iram, Ad, and Thamud? To reference lost names is risky—unless, that is, you're God.

And that, Muslims assert, is the point.

When we conjure up an image of a false prophet, we tend to imagine someone who struggles to gain confidence from his followers. A false prophet would be foolish to deal in any facts, prophecies, or beliefs other than the commonly accepted ones, whether valid or not. So why would Muhammad have gone out on a limb by naming lost civilizations when he could have limited his comments to famous cities, like Nazareth? The Christians around Muhammad must have filled his ears with tales of Nazareth, so we have to wonder why Nazareth isn't mentioned in the Qur'an. Giving Nazareth a plug would have fostered considerable goodwill among his Christian compatriots, and we are hard-pressed to imagine the harm. Unless, that is, Nazareth didn't exist. And, as a matter of fact, it may not have.

Nazareth is mentioned twenty-nine times in the New Testament, but no town by that name appears to have existed in the time of Jesus. Now, whether or not Nazareth did in fact exist isn't terribly important. But it is interesting to note that the Romans had comprehensive mercantile and tax records of all the towns in Palestine. They were methodical about these records, for they didn't like having to scour the countryside seeking pockets of peasants to beat the taxes out of. Nazareth, however, is not mentioned. In addition, Nazareth "is not among the places mentioned in Joshua 19:10f., nor is it referred to by Josephus, who gives the names of forty-five Galilean towns, nor by the Talmud, which names sixty-three."[72]

In fact, *Encyclopedia Judaica* informs us that outside of the Bible, Nazareth isn't mentioned in the historical record until the third century CE.[73] We have to wonder if this reflects a deficiency in the historical record or an error in the Bible. Was there, or was there not, a Nazareth in Jesus' day?

Some scholars speculate that Nazareth and modern day *en Nasira* are one and the same. But no one knows for sure.

Why, then, was Jesus Christ called the Nazarene? Hard to say. However, *Nazarene* is the English translation of the Greek *Nazoraios*, which appears to derive from the Hebrew *Nozrim*, which itself stems from *Nozrei ha-Brit*—the ancient Hebrew name by which the Qumran community identified themselves as "Keepers of the Covenant."[74] If the extraction seems strained, we might consider that the modern-day *Tsar* (or *Czar*) derives from *Kaiser,* itself derived from *Caesar,* and bearing no relation to either seeded hamburger rolls or gourmet salads. As all etymologists know, words separated by two thousand years wrinkle with age.

But to get back to *Nazarene,*

> Contrary to the assumptions of later tradition, it has nothing whatever to do with Jesus' alleged upbringing in Nazareth, which, the evidence (or lack of it) suggests, did not even exist at the time. Indeed, it seems to have been the very perplexity of early commentators encountering the unfamiliar term "Nazorean" that led them to conclude

Jesus' family came from Nazareth, which by then had appeared on the map.[75]

Search Palestine now, and we find Nazareth in lower Galilee (i.e., Northern Palestine). The problem is, the city by this name does not appear to have existed in biblical times. So, does the naming of a Palestinian city as "Nazareth" represent a Christian effort to backfill a scriptural deficiency? Maybe. But more likely, as is the case with the American city of Bethlehem, Pennsylvania, the founding fathers of the Palestinian city of Nazareth adopted its biblical name simply because they liked it.

One thing we can say for sure is that Jesus Christ wasn't born in Bethlehem, Pennsylvania. Similarly, there is no good reason to presume he had any association with the Palestinian city that now claims the title of Nazareth.

However this juggling of biblical names occurred, the point is that this constitutes one more point of Qur'anic accuracy. The Bible mentions a place that appears not to have existed in Jesus' lifetime, whereas the Qur'an doesn't. Avoiding repetition of this little-known biblical error tells us something important about the Qur'an and its author. "Nazareth" is just the kind of popular scriptural currency that would have appealed to the Christians of Muhammad's time, yet it bears no mention in the Holy Qur'an.

Weird.

That is, if we assume the Qur'an to have been authored by a man.

But back to Iram. To propose the existence of a city for which there was no record during Muhammad's lifetime (not to mention for the next fourteen centuries) is pretty bold for a man. Even bolder would be the mention of not just one but *three* such cities, *in succession*. That's … that's … well, that's beyond unlikely. Muhammad would had to have been both foolish and historically fortunate. And what, we might ask, was the motivation? For there was nothing to be won and a great deal to be lost from such a mention.

On the other hand, Muslims propose that our all-knowing God would have known that 1,400 years later evidence of Iram, Ad, and the Thamud people would be identified, providing signs for this present age.

Hmm.

Muslims hold that one of the miracles of the Qur'an is just this—it is timeless. Although the revelation was completed roughly 1,400 years ago, the miracles continue to surface even in the present day.

6

Evidence #4—Relation of Revelation to Contemporaneous Events

Truth would become more popular if it were not always stating ugly facts.

—Henry H. Haskins

The fact that specific passages of the Holy Qur'an were revealed at the same time as the events they describe is not particularly surprising. What *is* surprising, however, is not what the revelation contains, but what is conspicuously absent.

For example, Muhammad outlived his first love and first wife, the woman with whom he spent twenty-five years of his youth, Khadijah. She died after two long, painful years during which the Makkan pagans ostracized, persecuted, and starved Muhammad and his followers. Twenty-five years of love, support, caring, and kindness—gone. His first wife, so beloved that he remained faithful to her throughout their marriage and throughout his youth—gone. The first person to believe in his prophethood, the wife who bore all but one of his eight children—gone. So devoted was she that she exhausted her wealth and sacrificed her tribal relationships in support of him. After which, she was gone.

Musicians croon over their lost loves; artists immortalize their infatuations in marble and on canvas, photographers fill

albums with glossy memorials and poets pour their hearts
onto paper with the ink of liquid lamentation. Yet despite
what a person might expect, nowhere does the Qur'an mention
the name Khadijah. Not once. The wives of Pharaoh, Noah,
and Lot are alluded to, but Khadijah is not mentioned a
single solitary time. Why? Because she wasn't loved? When
Muhammad later had several wives, his then favorite wife,
A'ishah, commented that she was never as jealous of any
woman as she was of Khadijah, for Muhammad remembered
her frequently, with love and respect. A'ishah once related that
Muhammad commented,

> She believed in me when no one else did. She embraced
> Islam when people disbelieved in me. And she helped and
> comforted me in her person and wealth when there was
> none else to lend me a helping hand. I had children only
> from her.[76]

And yet the woman who so filled the life and mind of
Muhammad was never mentioned in the Qur'an. For that
matter, neither his father (who died before his birth), his
mother (who died while he was a child), nor his wife Khadijah,
nor any of his sons or daughters is mentioned. They are not
even hinted at.

Many orientalists claim that the Qur'an is not true
revelation, but came from Muhammad's mind. Compounding
the peculiarity of this claim is the startling fact that the *only*
woman the Qur'an mentions by name is Mary, an Israelite and
the mother of Jesus. And she is mentioned in glowing terms.
As a matter of fact, a whole *surah* bears her name. The Muslim
questions if this could be the product of the mind of a man.
To declare Muhammad a false prophet, when he excluded the
women who filled his life and memory from the revelation he

claimed, in favor of an Israelite woman and the mother of an Israelite prophet, drives recklessly against the flow of reasonable expectation.

During Muhammad's life, he saw every one of his four sons die. All but one of his four daughters predeceased him. His favored uncle, Hamzah, was killed in battle and mutilated in a horrific manner. Muhammad and his followers were regularly insulted, humiliated, beaten, and on occasion murdered. On one occasion the offal of a slaughtered camel was dumped on Mohammad's back while he was prostrate in prayer. The sheer weight of this offal reportedly pinned him to the ground until his daughter uncovered him. Now, camels smell bad enough while they're living. Try to imagine the smell of their decomposing guts in the tropical sun. Then try to imagine being buried in the tangled mass of their slimy offense, rivulets of rotting camel juice running down exposed arms, cheeks and, oh yes, behind the ears. A refreshing massage-head shower is a couple thousand calendar pages away, with soap not yet registered in the patent office.

Such events must have tortured Muhammad's memory. Yet they are described nowhere in the Qur'an.

On a more positive note, Muhammad was obsessed about oral hygiene. He brushed his teeth before every prayer, which equates to no less than five times a day. Furthermore, he taught his companions to brush the tongue as well, over 1,300 years before the tongue was recognized as the primary source of halitosis. Cleanliness was a passion of the Prophet's, and a practice associated with Muslim prayer. Mentioned in the Qur'an? Not once.

Muhammad taught that every illness has a cure. Whether true or not, reliable traditions relate that he firmly believed this. Why, then, don't we find the Qur'an filled with home remedies? The only mention of any product of medicinal value is a reference to honey, in which "there is healing for men" (TMQ 16:69). Certainly the throat lozenge and cold-and-flu pharmaceutical companies do not dispute this point.

So the Qur'an is remarkable in that its content does not reflect the mind of the messenger. In fact, in some cases the Qur'an does the exact opposite, and corrects Muhammad's errors in judgment.

For example, many passages defined issues with which Muhammad and his companions were immediately concerned, or delivered lessons regarding contemporaneous events. Such passages are legion. However, instead of affirming Muhammad's judgment, the Qur'an not only admonishes certain of the believers, but even corrects Muhammad on occasion. *Surah* 80 admonishes Muhammad for having frowned and turned his back on a blind Muslim who, in seeking guidance, interrupted a conversation to which Muhammad mistakenly assigned priority. The error in judgment was understandable, but it was an error nonetheless. And according to the Holy Qur'an, it was an error deserving of correction.

On other occasions, revelation admonished Muhammad for forbidding himself the use of honey (after being deceived into believing it gave his breath a bad odor—TMQ 66:1), for directing his adopted son to keep his marriage when divorce was preferable (TMQ 33:37), and for praying for forgiveness of the Hypocrites (Muslims-in-name-only who were denied the mercy of Allah due to their obstinate rebellion—TMQ 9:80). The admonishment for his error of judgment with regard to his adopted son, Zaid, and his unhappy marriage to Zainab, was of such extreme embarrassment that Muhammad's wife, A'ishah, later commented to the effect that, "Were Muhammad to have concealed anything from the revelation, he would have concealed this verse [i.e., TMQ 33:37]"[77]

In one case Muhammad was corrected for being vengeful,[78(EN)] in another for being lenient.[79(EN)] Although such errors of judgment were rare, they highlight his humanity.[80(EN)] Equally important, they reveal his sincerity, for Muhammad's errors required correction by the One Whom Muhammad represented, lest they be misperceived as bearing God's approval. However, unlike a false prophet, who would have concealed his shortcomings, Muhammad conveyed revelation that immortalized his mistakes, and Allah's admonition thereof.

So here is a man who claimed every letter of revelation was from God, including the passages that corrected his own errors and instructed him to repent. Weird. If, that is, we imagine the Qur'an to have been authored by a false prophet. False prophets are either liars or deluded, and both types attempt to build confidence in their followers by portraying themselves as perfect. The author of the Qur'an fails to fit this profile. So if not a man, Who, then, authored the Qur'an?

7

Evidence #5—Relation of Revelation to Subsequent Events

I don't know what the future may hold, but I know who holds the future.

—Ralph Abernathy

A s Albert Einstein wisely commented, "I never think of the future. It comes soon enough." The problem is that when the future *does* come, it is frequently contrary to expectations. Hence the difficulty with predictions. The only One who can know the future with certainty is the One who determines it. All others expose their human fallibility when they play with predictions, for future events typically prove them wrong, at least part of the time.

The validity of biblical predictions is no surprise to those who presume much of the Bible to be from God. So, too, with the Holy Qur'an. What *is* problematic, however, is to consider the Qur'an to have been of human authorship in the face of the remarkable accuracy of its predictions.

Unlike other books, the Bible included, Muslims assert there is not a single prediction made in the Qur'an that is assailable from a historic or scientific point of view. And, in fact, those who desire to discredit the holy book of Islam have desperately sought a weak link in Qur'anic prophesies for nearly 1,400 years. To date, they have discredited nothing, for no such error has ever been found. For this reason, we must note that detractors of the Islamic religion typically focus their criticisms upon emotional issues, such as Islamic practices considered distasteful in Western society. In other words, they tell us what they don't like about Islam, rather than discredit the Islamic evidence. This is, at best, a capricious approach.

We should bear this phenomenon in mind, for the fact is that there is no book in history, other than the Qur'an, which succeeds so completely with its predictions. Choose any book of a philosopher, soothsayer or false prophet, and you may find a few predictions that came true, but you'll also find a great many that didn't. Not so with the Holy Qur'an, the accuracy of which repels any reasonable criticism.

For example, early in the history of the Qur'an, while the Muslims were still an oppressed minority in Makkah, a verse was revealed in the "Moon" *surah* that promised victory (in battle) to the Muslims over the pagan Quraysh (i.e., the dominant tribe in Makkah):

> Are you Unbelievers (O Quraysh) better than they?
> Or do you have an immunity in the Sacred Books?
> Or do they say: "We, acting together, can defend ourselves?"
> Soon will their multitude be put to flight, and they will show their backs.
>
> (TMQ 54:43–45)

Now, at the time of this revelation, the Muslims were few, weak, and regularly beaten and killed by the pagan majority. Five years later, when emigrating to Medina, the Muslims were still so weak that the main tribe of Makkah, the Quraysh, confiscated their land, property and wealth, detained their wives, and tortured and killed those unfortunate few who lacked tribal protection. Not only were the Muslims no force to contend with, but they lacked sufficient numbers to expect anything but a life of persecution. The syrup on the *kanafa*[81(EN)] was that the verses of the Qur'an that command the Muslims to fight oppression and tyranny had not yet been revealed. Furthermore, among a people whose family ties were tight enough to chafe, the concept of waging war on one's own tribe was foreign to all but the most sociopathic of imaginations.

So seemingly out of place was this prediction that the future second caliph of Islam, Umar ibn al-Khattab, questioned, "Which group will we defeat?"[82] Even he did not immediately grasp that the revelation spoke of the Muslims defeating the pagans of his own tribe of Quraysh. And only later, when the Muslims were actually commanded to fight tyranny and oppression, did they have sufficient numbers to do so. The following verse from the "Light" *surah* was subsequently revealed in Makkah, prior to the Muslim emigration to Medina:

> Allah has promised, to those among you who believe and work righteous deeds, that He will, of a surety, grant them in the land, inheritance (of power), as He granted it to those before them; that He will establish in authority their religion—the one which He has chosen for them; and that He will change (their state), after the fear in which they (lived), to one of security and peace: "They will worship Me (alone) and not associate anything with Me." If any do reject Faith after this, they are rebellious and wicked. (TMQ 24:55).

As predicted in the "Moon" *surah*, the "multitude" of unbelieving Quraysh were "put to flight" and "showed their backs" at the Battle of Badr. The Quraysh army outnumbered the Muslims by more than four to one, but it was the Quraysh who suffered the greatest losses. Rather than massacring the Muslims, as their overwhelming superiority in men and arms might have led us to expect, the Quraysh dead outnumbered the Muslim dead five to one. Both sides reported seeing angels fighting among the Muslim ranks, and the Quraysh fled in terror.[83,84]

Subsequently, in fulfillment of the "Light" *surah*, the Muslims were decisively victorious when they peacefully retook Makkah in 8 AH.[85(EN)] True to the prediction, their fear and insecurity was replaced by security and peace, due to their established authority both in power and religion.

The peace and security encountered in Makkah is itself a fulfillment of revelation, as follows:

> Have We not established for them a secure sanctuary (Makkah), to which are brought fruits of all kinds, a provision from Ourselves ...
>
> (TMQ 28:57[86])

And this as well:

> Have they not seen that We have made (Makkah) a secure sanctuary, while men are being snatched away from all around them?
>
> (TMQ 29:67[87])

As foretold, Makkah has not only remained a "secure sanctuary" to this day, but despite the barren land and harsh desert climate, the plethora of food and fruit stores stands testimony to the promise of "fruits of all kinds, a provision from Ourselves ..."

This mention of fruits and provision in revelation may at first seem peculiar, for to what purpose would such a mention be made? Speculation aside, the fact is that such a mention *was* made, and despite the barren volcanic terrain, harsh desert climate, and geographic isolation, the holy city of Makkah has since enjoyed a most ample and unlikely food supply.

With regard to the above conquest, this verse was revealed:

> When comes the Help of Allah, and Victory, and you see the people enter Allah's Religion in crowds ... (TMQ 110:1–3)

Following the conquest and conversion of Makkah, delegates from all over the Arabian Peninsula bore the pledge of allegiance of entire tribes and communities. Such history of *en-masse* voluntary conversions defies religious norms. And yet it was foretold.

What else was foretold?

Prior to their conquest of Makkah, the Muslims faced tremendous hardship, for they were sandwiched between the opposition of the disbelievers and the treachery of the Hypocrites within their ranks. While in Medina, the Jewish tribe of Bani Nadir reneged on their treaty with the Muslims, and were ordered to leave the city within ten days. Abdullah ibn Ubayy, the head of the Hypocrites in Medina, pledged support to the Bani Nadir in the form of an army of two thousand men, and promised to follow the Jews if they left or were expelled. The following days were a tense period for the Muslims, who took solace in the revelation,

> Have you not observed the Hypocrites say to their misbelieving brethren among the People of the Book (i.e. the Christians and/or Jews)? "If you are expelled, we too will go out with you, and we will never hearken to anyone

in your affair; and if you are attacked we will help you."
But Allah is Witness that they are indeed liars. If they are
expelled, never will they go out with them; and if they
are attacked, they will never help them ...

(TMQ 59:11–12)

Any fears vanished with the expulsion of the Bani Nadir
within the ten-day ultimatum. True to the Qur'anic prediction,
the Hypocrites neither accompanied nor defended them. At
a time when the Muslims were still weak and vulnerable,
predictions such as the one above would be considered supremely
optimistic, if not frankly foolish, had they come from a man.

A prediction that must have seemed similarly rash, given
the circumstances, was the following:

Say to the desert Arabs who lagged behind: "You shall be
summoned (to fight) against a people given to vehement
war; then you shall fight, or they shall submit" (TMQ
48:16).

Putting ourselves in a similar circumstance, we can't help
but wonder how we would have felt as new converts to Islam,
were we told that we would be called upon to fight "a people
given to vehement war." Surely this disheartening revelation
would have been considered a peculiar way of encouraging
a following, were it to come from a man. However, the
prediction *was* made, and years following Muhammad's death
the Muslims not only battled, but defeated, the Roman and
Persian empires, great world powers "given to vehement war."
Can we accuse Muhammad of having manipulated events to
fulfill the revelation he transmitted? Of having attacked the
Roman and Persian empires for the purpose of *making* the
revelation come true?

Uh, *no.* He passed away before the prophesy was fulfilled. And in any case, who could possibly foresee that *any* group would ever conquer either the Roman or Persian empires, much less both?

One of the most interesting predictions in the Holy Qur'an is *surah* 111's condemnation of Abu Lahab (one of Muhammad's uncles) and his wife to hell. Now, quite obviously, nobody can witness to the final disposition of this couple. However, Islam teaches that all Muslims will eventually achieve salvation. Why? Because Islam teaches that Allah may punish unrepentant believers for their sins, but that Allah will eventually rescue all Muslims from the tortures of hell and place them in paradise in reward for their faith. That is what Muslims believe, and it is a cornerstone of their convictions.

How does this pertain to the prediction of Abu Lahab and his wife being condemned to hell? Simple. Abu Lahab was one of Muhammad's most notorious antagonists. His animosity drove him to contradict virtually everything Muhammad said, and he used to follow Muhammad around town for just this purpose. So why, when a *surah* was revealed that implied that Abu Lahab would never repent, didn't he just stand up and say, "I repent"? After all, that was his nature—whatever Muhammad said, he would contradict. Even in hypocrisy, all he or his wife had to do was say the *shahada* (testimony of faith), and *pretend* to become Muslim. Had either of them done so, they could have created a conflict sufficient to damage or even destroy the religion. Either the Qur'an's prediction of their condemnation would have been proven to be wrong, or the teaching that all Muslims would eventually be blessed with paradise would have been contradicted by their conversion. Either way, to the satisfaction of observers, the revelation would have been invalidated.

So why didn't either or them do it? Why didn't either of them pretend to convert?

It's not for lack of time to think about it, that's for sure.

Surah 111, which contained the prediction under discussion, was revealed in 3–4 BH ("before Hijra"), and Abu Lahab died in 2 AH.[88] His wife died roughly six years later.[89] So Abu Lahab and his wife had over five and ten years respectively to speak out. No doubt there were Muslims who pressed them to do so, and anti-Islamic friends who tried to goad them into claiming conversion. Now remember, this couple's code of ethics included lying, torture and murder of the believers. So why did they draw the line at hypocrisy?

Muslims maintain that only one thing held them back— they didn't have permission. The One who makes the rules of this life, the One who has lent mankind minds and bodies (and will demand their return), the One who can open or close the minds, mouths, and hearts of His creation, this One can make the boldest of claims, the most assured of predictions. Why? Because He not only knows the future; He *determines* the future. And if He decrees that certain words will not pass the lips of specific people, well, that's all there is to it.

Muslims claim that no human can make promises such as this. That promise can only be made by the One who knows He will not allow His book to be contradicted.

The prophesy is doubly impressive, not just because of the boldness of the claim, but because the example is repeated. *Surah* 74:11–26 condemns another of Muhammad's antagonists—this time Al-Walid ibn Al-Mughirah.[90] Al-Walid organized a convention of antagonists in an attempt to consolidate their criticism of the Holy Qur'an. The story of the conflict between his private realization and public profession beautifully exemplifies how rational thought can be overridden by pride.

The story is as follows: Al-Walid heard Muhammad reciting the Qur'an and seemed moved by it. He stated that the recitation was not poetry, magic, or madness, but could only be the speech of Allah. When news of this got to Abu Jahl (another notorious antagonist), he accused Al-Walid of trying to curry favor with the prophet: a rumor circulating among the Quraysh. Al-Walid succumbed to pride and replied, "Quraysh knows that I am the richest of them and do not need anything from Muhammad." Abu Jahl said, "Then you should let your position be known. Tell them what you think of Muhammad." Al-Walid responded, "What should I say of him? By Allah there is none among you more knowledgeable of Arabic poetry and its scales than me, nor of the poetry of the Jinn [spirits]. What he [Muhammad] says does not resemble any of that. By Allah, it is a beautiful speech and it crushes that which is below it and it surpasses that which is above it." Abu Jahl stated, "People will not be pleased with this. You must think of something to say." Al-Walid said, "Leave me to think." When he returned to commune with the leaders of Quraysh over what they should say about Muhammad, some said Muhammad was a magician, and others said he was crazy. Al-Walid stated, "All of these things that you are saying I know are untrue, but the closest of these sayings is that he is a magician, because magic breaks apart a son from his father, a person from his brother, a husband from his wife, or a person from his tribe."[91]

Such also is the effect of revelation, incidentally, for Jesus Christ is recorded as having taught, "Do you suppose that I came to give peace on earth? I tell you, not at all, but rather division. For from now on five in one house will be divided: three against two, and two against three. Father will be divided against son and son against father, mother against daughter and daughter against mother, mother-in-law against her daughter-in-law and daughter-in-law against her mother-in-law" (Luke 12:51–53).

But I digress. The point is that Al-Walid succumbed to pride, and shortly afterward the verses were revealed:

> Leave Me (i.e., Allah) alone, (to deal) with the (creature)
> whom I created (bare and) alone!
> To whom I granted resources in abundance,
> And sons to be by his side!
> To whom I made (life) smooth and comfortable!
> Yet is he greedy—that I should add (yet more)
> By no means! For to Our Signs he has been refractory!
> Soon will I visit him with a mount of calamities!
> For he thought and he plotted;
> And woe to him! How he plotted!
> Yes, woe to him: how he plotted!
> Then he looked round;
> Then he frowned and he scowled;
> Then he turned back and was haughty;
> Then he said: "This is nothing but magic, derived from
> of old;
> This is nothing but the word of a mortal!"
> Soon will I cast him into Hell-Fire!
>
> (TMQ 74:11–26)

This verse was revealed ten years before the subject of these verses, Al-Walid ibn Al-Mughirah, died.[92] So once again, the boldness of the Qur'anic prediction demands explanation. How could the author of these verses have known that Al-Walid would never return to his initial impression and convert—or just fake it in order to throw the revelation into question? And would a false prophet have risked his claim to prophethood on such a risky and unnecessary prediction?

For another of these unlikely predictions, we have to return to the Romans and the Persians, and ask if a false prophet would have risked his reputation on long shots such as these:

Surah Ar-Rum (i.e., the Romans), *surah* 30, *ayah* 2–4, was revealed at the time of a Persian victory over Rome, *prior* to news of the battle reaching Makkah. These verses acknowledged Persia's victory and predicted a reversal of fortunes within three to nine years. As history records, Persia celebrated victory over Rome at Antioch in 613 CE, and the Byzantines were subsequently defeated in Damascus, driven out of Armenia, and overrun in their cherished city of Jerusalem.[93] The Persians took Chalcedon in 617 CE and conquered Egypt in 619.[94,95] The Persians were on a roll and the situation looked bleak for the Roman Empire, right up until Heraclius launched his historic campaign of 622–627 CE. The Romans decisively pounded the Persian forces on Armenian soil in 622 CE, three years after losing Egypt, nine years after the defeat at Antioch, and bracketing the other above-mentioned defeats within a period of three to nine years.[96,97] *Surah* 30:2–4 reads:

> The Romans have been defeated.
> In the nearest land (Syria, Iraq, Jordan, and Palestine), and they, after their defeat, will be victorious.
> Within three to nine years. The decision of the matter, before and after (these events) is only with Allah.
> And on that Day, the believers (i.e. Muslims) will rejoice.
> (TMQ 30:2–4[98])

The history is remarkable, for by this time the Roman Empire was in decay (historians date the Fall of the Roman Empire to 395–476 CE). The Visigoths sacked Rome in 410 CE, the Vandals and the Alani plundered it in 455 CE, Attila the Hun overran the area a short time later, and the last emperor of the undivided Roman Empire was deposed in the late fifth century. So a prophecy that the already disintegrating Roman Empire would gain a victory over the seemingly superior Persian army in the early seventh century would have seemed rash, if made by a man. And so it was judged by those who denied the revelation. Men like Ubay ibn Khalaf.

The story is narrated in many accounts of Arabian history. The Arabs perceived the conflict between Persia and Rome as a contest between paganism and revealed religion. The pagan Arabs considered the fire-worshiping Persians to be brothers in paganism whereas the Muslims deemed the Romans, who were Christian by this time, to be followers of the prophets and the chain of revelation, worshippers of the same God. Many Arabs believed victory on the battlefield reflected superiority of the god of the winner. Hence, when the Persians were victorious over Rome, the pagan Arabs celebrated. Following this, the above *ayat* (verses) were revealed, strengthening the hearts of the believers. When the future first caliph, Abu Bakr As-Siddiq, learned the revelation, he bet one of the pagan Arabs, Ubay ibn Khalf, a hundred camels that the Persian victory would be overturned in three to nine years, as foretold. Nine years later Abu Bakr gained a herd of camels and the encyclopedia of Islamic evidence gained one more entry.[99]

The icing on the cake of this prediction is the final line, "And on that Day, the believers (i.e. Muslims) will rejoice." In Muhammad's time, news took weeks to months to find its way across the Arabian sands. How, then, could the Qur'an predict the Muslims would be rejoicing on the same day the Persians were defeated? Yet such was precisely the case, for the Persians were defeated on the exact same day that the Muslims celebrated their own victory over the disbelievers at the Battle of Badr. An unlikely human coincidence—or divine plan?

But enough about Rome.

Let's turn to *surah* 15, *ayah* 9, which promises that "we (i.e., Allah) have, without doubt, sent down the Message; and We will assuredly guard it (from corruption)" (TMQ 15:9). This promise is remarkable on several levels, the first being that, to date, it has been fulfilled—the present-day Qur'an is unchanged from the original revelation.

The extent of this miracle is apparent when we compare the Qur'an with the scriptures of other world religions, for, as discussed in *MisGod'ed*, no other book of revelation exists in the purity of the original, the Old and New Testaments included. And while the revelation transmitted through Moses seems to be partially preserved, the gospel of Jesus is lost in entirety.

Another point is that the above prediction (that Allah will guard the Qur'an from corruption) would have been both foolish and unnecessary had Muhammad been an imposter. He stood to gain nothing from such a sweeping prophesy, and would have lost everything had a single letter of revelation been misplaced or forgotten. And there were over 300,000 letters at stake.

Another strikingly bizarre prophesy is encountered in *surah* 5, *ayah* 82:

> Strongest among men in enmity to the Believers will you find the Jews and Pagans; and nearest among them in love to the Believers will you find those who say, "We are *Nasara* [i.e., Nazarenes, or Christians]": because among these are men devoted to learning and men who have renounced the world, and they are not arrogant.

Taken in context, the uniqueness of this prophesy is not only the fact that 1,400 years of history have proven it true, but also that Muhammad forged several cooperative treaties with different Jewish tribes. Consequently, this *ayah* (verse) is just one of many at risk of having been disproved within Muhammad's lifetime. But such was not the case. Despite reasonable expectation for the Jews to have sided with the increasingly powerful Muslims, the various Jewish tribes violated virtually every treaty they made—a trend maintained to the present day in Zionist Israel's lengthy track record of UN and peace accord violations in Palestine.

A wonder, then, that Muhammad discharged his bodyguards. Living among hatred and treachery, the Prophet survived multiple attempts upon his life. On separate occasions he was severely beaten, choked with his own mantle, and stoned until blood filled his shoes. One tribe attempted to crush him with a boulder; another poisoned his food. Different enemies took up swords to kill him, and not just in battle. Twice Bedouins pulled Muhammad's own sword (once while he was sleeping in the desert and once while sitting at a well), intending to kill him in a defenseless state. Both Bedouins dropped the sword, for they found themselves physically unable to hold it. On the evening of his emigration to Medina, every tribe in Makkah sent a representative to kill Muhammad according to a pact to share the deed, so as to escape the blame. The list goes on. And so, not unreasonably, Muhammad kept bodyguards while he slept. Yet when the following verse was revealed, he discharged them:

> O Messenger! Proclaim the (Message) which has been sent to you from your Lord. If you did not, you would not have fulfilled and proclaimed His Mission. And Allah will defend you from men (who mean mischief). For Allah guides not those who reject faith (TMQ 5:67).

Muhammad heard Allah's promise of divine protection, and immediately announced to his guards, "Oh people, leave me for Allah the most High has protected me."[100]

And so it happened.

Following the discharge of his guards, attempts upon the Prophet's life continued but were somehow always frustrated. In the end, Muhammad's soul departed within the walls of his own home, his head cradled in the arms of his favorite wife, A'ishah, after suffering a brief but fatal illness. Point of the story? In a time and place and under circumstances where a person might reasonably feel the whole world was out to get him, Muhammad discharged his bodyguards on the promise of revelation, and that promise was fulfilled.

The bizarreness of the scenario has an undeniable ring of truth. False prophets are rightfully paranoid. As attempts upon their lives increase in number, they raise their guard and become reclusive. To release their bodyguards in a time of war—and with a history of serial assassination attempts—defies worldly reason. If the Qur'an came from the mind of a charlatan, we would expect the exact opposite. We would expect the "prophet" to convey false revelation that exhorts his believers to protect him from his enemies. But it didn't happen that way with Muhammad, once again challenging mankind to consider the divine source of the Qur'an. Furthermore, who has the power to fulfill such bold promises of lifelong protection? Beyond a doubt, it is not a man.

The final entry of this chapter involves a familiar Old Testament story. Pharaoh was a tyrant who oppressed a nation, killed upon whim, and slaughtered the children of the Jews, fearing the multitude of their race. While Pharaoh's soldiers doled out infanticide in the village, Moses washed up in a gift-basket on the riverbank of Pharaoh's palatial estate. So while big stones were being hoisted off the squashed slaves and stacked according to royal decree, Moses grew up to stun the world with his fear of God and piety.

A couple of heated court conversations, a few ignored divine signs, and several periods of plague and pestilence later, Moses took his people on a divinely ordained nature walk. The point is that no matter how the story is told, everybody knows how it ended: Pharaoh's pathetic dog-paddle didn't stand up to the raging torrent of two walls of water clapping its unforgiving hands over his mis-commanding mouth.

This story is so well known, in fact, it is unimaginable that Muhammad didn't know it. However, the common impression is that Pharaoh was buried beneath a couple million tons of seawater, where he and his men slept with the fishes—until the fish woke up and ate them, that is. It is not commonly accepted that Pharaoh's body was preserved. And yet, the Qur'an records just this: Allah's promise to preserve Pharaoh's body after his death:

> This day shall we save you in your body, that you may be a sign to those who come after you! But verily, many among mankind are heedless of Our signs! (TMQ 10:92)

Only in 1898 CE was the mummified body of Merneptah, successor to Rameses II—and the most likely candidate to the title of "Pharaoh of the Exodus," according to biblical history and archaeological evidence—discovered at Thebes in the King's Valley.[101] The body is on display, along with various other royal mummies, in the Cairo Museum. Hence, over 1,200 years after the revelation, the Qur'anic promise of preserving Pharaoh's body as a sign to future generations appears to be satisfied. But how could Muhammad have foretold such a find, and why would he have gone out on such a thin limb of speculation over such a seemingly insignificant detail?

Unless, that is, the words were not his own.

8

Evidence #6—Revelation of the Unknown
(That Which Was Beyond the Experience of the Prophet)

No one ever approaches perfection except by stealth, and unknown to themselves.
—William Hazlitt, *Sketches and Essays*, "On Taste"

P erhaps a better title of this chapter would be "Scientific Evidence." However, such a title might strike the audience as overly bizarre, for most Westerners consider science and religion to be mutually exclusive. The examples of Giordano Bruno (convicted of heresy and burned at the stake in the year 1600 CE) and Galileo (who escaped punishment in 1633 only by issuing a retraction) are well known. Both were persecuted for having supported the "heretical," but correct, Copernican theory of heliocentrism (the theory of the sun being the center of the solar system), contrary to the officially sanctioned, though incorrect, Ptolemaic theory of geocentrism (the planet Earth being the center). This conflict gave rise to the Western perception that science and religion are incompatible housemates.

In fact, considering the many church teachings that ran contrary to what are now known to be evident truths, an odder couple than science and religion is difficult to imagine. The voices of those who dared to oppose such church teachings, stilled by the fires that consumed their mortal bodies, would be expected to have agreed.

The horrors perpetuated by an intolerant, oppressive and, most importantly, *wrong* church won sufficient condemnation to eventually force a separation of church, science and state. The process was bloody, as seems to have been typical of any circumstance where church doctrine and beliefs bumped up against a contrary reality, and incalculable suffering was the result. This left the present generation with a tradition in which religion and science remain shy to dabble in one another's affairs. For many, no other system can be imagined.

On the other hand, separation of church and science has no place in Islam. The Islamic revelation is comprehensive, and influences most areas of human life. Islam defines not only tenets of faith and articles of worship, but also the will of the Creator with regard to politics, personal conduct, family and social structure, economic principles, civil and criminal law, and many other practicalities of human existence. Science and nature are nurtured by a revelation that encourages investigation while condemning closed-mindedness. Multiple passages of the Holy Qur'an direct people to think for themselves, and condemn those who violate God-given logic. Among the things Allah has forbidden are "sins and trespasses against truth or reason …" (TMQ 7:33)

The Muslim world witnessed an explosion of knowledge following Muhammad's time, in no small part because the needs of the religion stimulated certain lines of investigation. A religion that enjoins prayer within set times of the day and fasting in a particular month naturally stimulated advances in timekeeping and calendar computation. Similarly, a religion that requires payment of varying percentages of wealth according to category (e.g., agricultural products versus gold) as a poor-due can be expected to have led to advancements in methods of estimation and calculation (i.e. weights and measures, and mathematics).

The origins of Arabic numerals (along with the mathematically revolutionary zero), were absorbed into European mathematics in the twelfth century. The Arabic system replaced the troublesome and zero-less Roman numerals and the laborious system of writing numbers longhand. This, as well as the development of algorithms and algebra, can all be traced to Muslims.

The Islamic religion forbade representational art, so Muslim artists channeled their skills to the geometrically based, arabesque arts of masonry, inlay, weaving, and carpentry. Whether it was cause or effect, the fields of geometry and trigonometry gained significant contributions from Muslims. Sine and cosine tables were constructed, cubic equations defined, the roots of quadratic equations determined, spherical, analytical and plane trigonometry expanded, and geometry advanced.

Muslims were commanded to spread the word of revelation, and so a new breed of travelers and merchants was born. Furthermore, the mandate to direct prayer toward the *Kaba* (the house built by Abraham) in Makkah gave rise to the need for accurate directional determination; consequently, a need for improvements in navigation and map-making arose. The magnetic compass, latitude and longitude tables, construction of star maps and the astrolabe (a medieval navigational instrument) came into play. Observatories were built as astronomy developed as a science, and geographic maps were produced that remained unrivaled for centuries.

With an emphasis upon learning and teaching, paper became a critical commodity. The Kufic letters, the foundation of the modern Arabic alphabet, were invented on the banks of the Euphrates. Although paper was first invented by the Chinese, who used the cocoon of the silkworm, Muslims adopted and further refined the manufacture by using cotton, wood, and rags in addition to silk.

Similar advancements were made in the fields of metallurgy, mechanical, optical, and theoretical physics, organic and inorganic chemistry, medicine, geography, agriculture, and other disciplines. Technological improvements included such instruments as the scale, axle, lever, pulley, windmill, waterwheel, and toothed wheel, and such processes as calcination (a method of extracting metals from ore), reduction, distillation, and crystallization. Theories of gravity and the elasticity of air were advanced. Hospitals were built, and great advancements were made in the field of medicine, including the development of new medicines and surgical techniques. The caesarean operation for childbirth was originally developed by a Muslim.

According to Jared Diamond, "In the Middle Ages the flow of technology was overwhelmingly from Islam to Europe, rather than from Europe to Islam as it is today. Only after around A.D. 1500 did the net direction of flow begin to reverse."[102]

The magnitude and significance of such advancements are best known to scholars in the respective fields, but a short and easily readable treatise titled *Islam and Science*[103] is a good starting point for those who wish to research further.

Lest the reader misunderstand, no attempt is made in this book to validate the Holy Qur'an based upon such fruits of revelation. Rather, the simple observation is offered that a separation between church and science never was an element of the Islamic religion. In fact, during the pre-Renaissance period, Muslims were at the technological forefront of civilization. As Victor Robinson noted in his book *The Story of Medicine*,

> Europe was darkened at sunset, Cordova [the capital of Moorish Spain] shone with public lamps; Europe was dirty, Cordova built a thousand baths; Europe was covered with vermin, Cordova changed its undergarments

daily; Europe lay in mud, Cordova's streets were paved; Europe's palaces had smoke-holes in the ceiling, Cordova's arabesques were exquisite; Europe's nobility could not sign its name, Cordova's children went to school; Europe's monks could not read the baptismal service, Cordova's teachers created a library of Alexandrian dimensions.[104]

Although H.G. Wells is best remembered primarily as the author of *The Time Machine* and other works of science fiction, his works on history are perennial best-sellers. From his crowning work, *The Outline of History,* Wells had this to say about the intellectual life of Islam:

From a new angle and with a fresh vigour it [the Arab mind] took up that systematic development of positive knowledge which the Greeks had begun and relinquished. If the Greek was the father, then the Arab was the foster-father of the scientific method of dealing with reality, that is to say, by absolute frankness, the utmost simplicity of statement and explanation, exact record and exhaustive criticism. Through the Arabs it was and not by the Latin route that the modern world received that gift of light and power ... And a century or so in advance of the west, there grew up in the Moslem world at a number of centers, at Basra, at Kufa, at Bagdad and Cairo, and at Cordoba, out of what were at first religious schools dependent upon mosques, a series of great universities. The light of these universities shone far beyond the Moslem world, and drew students to them from east and west. At Cordoba in particular there were great numbers of Christian students, and the influence of Arab philosophy coming by way of Spain upon the universities of Paris, Oxford, and North Italy and upon Western European thought generally, was very considerable indeed.[105]

It is worth another look at James A. Michener's 1954 essay, "Islam: The Misunderstood Religion," to reflect on this quote:

> Many Westerners, accustomed by their history books to believe that Muslims were barbarous infidels, find it difficult to comprehend how profoundly our intellectual life has been influenced by Muslim scholars in the field of science, medicine, mathematics, geography and philosophy. Crusaders who invaded the Holy Land to fight Muslims returned to Europe with new ideas of love, poetry, chivalry, warfare and government. Our concept of what a university should be was deeply modified by Muslim scholars, who perfected the writing of history and who brought to Europe much Greek learning.[106]

And from the pen of German scholar Hartwig Hirschfeld, renowned expert on Arabic and Jewish cultures:

> We must not be surprised to find the Qoran regarded as the fountain-head of the sciences. Every subject connected with heaven or earth, human life, commerce and various trades are occasionally touched upon, and this gave rise to the production of numerous monographs forming commentaries on parts of the holy book. In this way the Qoran was responsible for great discussions, and to it was indirectly due the marvelous development of all branches of science in the Muslim world.[107]

The list of endorsements is long, but one last quote by Thatcher and Schill is worth including. It was so highly valued by H. G. Wells that he quoted it in his best-selling *A General History of Europe*:

The origin of the so-called Arabic numerals is obscure. Under Theodoric the Great, Boethius made use of certain signs which were in part very like the nine digits which we now use. One of the pupils of Gerbert also used signs which were still more like ours, but the zero was unknown till the twelfth century, when it was invented by an Arab mathematician named Muhammad-ibn-Musa, who also was the first to use the decimal notation, and who gave the digits the value of position. In geometry the Arabs did not add much to Euclid, but algebra is practically their creation; also they developed spherical trigonometry, inventing the sine, tangent, and cotangent. In physics they invented the pendulum, and produced work on optics. They made progress in the science of astronomy. They built several observatories, and constructed many astronomical instruments which are still in use. They calculated the angle of the ecliptic and the precession of the equinoxes. Their knowledge of astronomy was undoubtedly considerable.

In medicine they made great advances over the work of the Greeks. They studied physiology and hygiene, and their *materia medica* was practically the same as ours to-day. Many of their methods of treatment are still in use among us. Their surgeons understood the use of anaesthetics, and performed some of the most difficult operations known. At the time when in Europe the practice of medicine was forbidden by the church, which expected cures to be effected by religious rites performed by the clergy, the Arabs had a real science of medicine. In chemistry they made a good beginning. They discovered many new substances, such as alcohol, potash, nitrate of silver, corrosive sublimate, and nitric and sulphuric acid … In manufactures they out-did the world in variety and beauty of design and perfection of workmanship. They worked in all the metals—gold, silver, copper, bronze, iron, and steel. In textile fabrics they have never been surpassed. They made glass and pottery of the finest quality. They knew the secrets of dyeing, and they manufactured paper. They had many processes of dressing leather, and their work was famous throughout Europe. They made tinctures, essences, and syrups. They made sugar from cane, and grew many fine kinds of wine.[108(EN)] They practiced farming in a scientific way, and had good systems of irrigation. They knew the value of fertilizers, and adapted their crops to the quality of the ground. They excelled in horticulture, knowing how to graft and how to produce new varieties of fruit and flowers. They introduced into the west many trees and plants from the east, and wrote scientific treatises on farming.

One item in this account must be underlined here because of its importance in the intellectual life of mankind, the manufacture of paper. This the Arabs seem to have learnt from the Chinese by way of Central Asia. The Europeans acquired it from the Arabs. Until that time books had to be written upon parchment or papyrus, and after the Arab conquest of Egypt Europe was cut off from the papyrus supply. Until paper became abundant, the art of printing was of little use, and newspapers and popular education by means of books was impossible. This was probably a much more important factor in the relative backwardness of Europe during the dark ages than historians seem disposed to admit …[109]

The evidence Muslims consider supportive of the divine origin of the Holy Qur'an involves the many passages that comment on the nature of mankind and the universe in which we live. Many of these verses survived as unsubstantiated mysteries for nearly 1,400 years, only to be verified in light of modern knowledge.

How does this differ from biblical predictions?

Well, to begin with, we have to question why the Bible describes God as having bestowed light upon His creation three days before he created the stars (compare Genesis 1:3–5 with Genesis 1:14–19). Possibilities within the realm of Divine decree are beyond human imagination, but a basic scientific premise with regard to the nature of light is that before light can exist, a source of photon emission must assume some degree of responsibility. Similarly, we can fairly ask how an evening and a morning occurred (Genesis 1:3–5) two days before the creation of the Earth (Genesis 1:9–13) and three days before the creation of the sun (Genesis 1:14–19), for without a horizon upon which the sun could rise and set, and without a sun in the first place, exactly how could there even *be* an evening and a morning?

There is more. The Bible describes birds as having been created on the fifth day (Genesis 1:20–23), one day prior to the creation of the beasts of the Earth (Genesis 1:24–25), whereas the fossil record indicates the reverse order. Biblical genealogies are the basis of the Jewish calendar, which proposes the world to be 5,768 years old (as of the year 2007 CE). With a solar system estimated at 4½ billion years old and the origin of hominoids measured in millions of years, this estimate falls somewhat short of the scientific evidence.

The global flood, as dated in the Bible to approximately three hundred years before the time of Abraham, would have corresponded with the twenty-first to twenty-second centuries BC. As such, this flood failed to wash away both the Third Dynasty at Ur in Babylonia and the First Intermediate Period before the Eleventh Dynasty in Egypt—two civilizations that history testifies were uninterrupted. So the period to which the biblical narratives attribute the global flood could stand revision.

However, putting all that aside and assuming, for the sake of discussion, that the Bible reads like the synthesis of a science library and a Farmer's Almanac, the "So what?" challenge remains. Islam acknowledges both Judaism and Christianity originated from revelation, and points out that both religions are awaiting the final prophet, as predicted by their scriptures. The question, then, is not which of the Abrahamic religions of Judaism, Christianity, and Islam take origin from divine revelation, for they all do. Rather, the question is which is the *last* religion to have been divinely revealed. For if that is not the religion our Creator intends for us to follow, why did He reveal it?

The challenge, then, is for Christians and Jews to disqualify the Qur'an from the competition. As we have seen, the challenge to write just one *surah* to equal that of the Qur'an has yet to achieve success. According to Muslims, no attempt ever will. And given 1,400 years of failed attempts, it is hard to argue the point.

A word of caution is necessary at this point, for religious zeal leads many people to overstep the bounds of reason in defense of their position. Certain passages from the Holy Qur'an speak of things we do not yet understand. As such, the significance of these passages is speculative. To attempt to assign more meaning than actually exists, whether to support or refute the Qur'an, would be unreasonable. The best that can be said of such passages is that they speak of mysteries, and as such can be regarded as neither scientific evidences nor examples of inconsistency. Perhaps with time and advancement in scientific knowledge such passages will become understood. Until then, speculation is probably inappropriate. An example, by way of illustration, is this: the fourth *ayah* of the seventieth *surah* (TMQ 70:4) is translated, "The angels and the spirit ascend unto Him in a day the measure whereof is (as) fifty thousand years."

Some Muslims have suggested that this verse, from the *surah*, "The Ways of Ascent," can be related to Einstein's Special Theory of Relativity, and in fact it might. Then again, it might not. But, to pursue the hypothesis, according to Einstein's theory, the perception of time, size, and mass vary between two differing inertial frames of reference in motion relative to one another. What that means is that two observers moving at different speeds will perceive time, size, and mass to be different. At speeds such as those traveled by humans in the present age, such differences are negligible. However, should future generations shift their Ford 2800 year-model intergalactic positron-harvesting star-skippers into one-millionth gear and shimmy up to the speed of light, such differences will become increasingly great. The space traveler and the stationary observer will then see two very different views of the same world.

According to the Special Theory of Relativity, as speed approaches that of light (5.88×10^{12} miles/year) perception of time slows, size becomes reduced, and mass increases. Should Max Planck, the "father of quantum physics," have hijacked a bunch of his theoretical quanta, pulled in the reins a tad, and screamed past Martha's Vineyard at near the speed of light, his bedside alarm clock would have run imperceptibly slow, appeared infinitesimally small, and possessed an infinitely heavy mass.

The concept is a little tough on most intellects, so the world has Albert Einstein to thank for the Lorentz transformations—mathematical equations by which the differential perception of space and time by two observers can be related to one another. With regard to time, the equation is as follows:

$t' = (1-v^2/c^2)^{-1/2} (t-vx/c^2)$

where v = speed traveled

c = the *speed* of light (5.88 x 10^{12} miles/year)

x = *position* in space (defined by the equation $x^2 = c^2t^2$)

t' and t are the *two* differing time perspectives

Plug the numbers from the above *ayah* into the equation, with t equaling 50,000 years and t being a single day (2.7397 x 10^{-3} years) and v calculates out to be, in gross scientific terms, a billionth of a hair of a balding smidgen less than the speed of light. The difference is small. Indeed, so close is the value of v to the speed of light, that the last decimal point in the chain of 9's resulting from the fraction of v/c cannot be reached with a common calculator.

How does this relate to the Holy Qur'an? Well, according to the Qur'an and *hadith,* man was made from clay, *jinn* (spirits) from fire, and angels from light. So here is a passage of the Holy Qur'an that not only presents the differing perceptions of time later defined as "time dilation" by the theory of relativity, but the values presented describe the angels as traveling at the speed of that from which they were reported as having been created: light.

Now, this analysis is nice and neat, and may even be correct. But to assert that this is what the above *ayah* actually means is to make some bold assumptions. Far better, perhaps, would be to note the amazing correlation, but not go past discussion of the theory of "time dilation." The simple fact that differing perceptions of time were mentioned 1,400 year ago, when the fastest movement witnessed by the eye of man might have been the swoop of a hawk or the flight of an arrow, is enough. To analyze any further seems speculative to an unacceptable extreme.

But that is precisely what detractors of Islam do—chase their prejudices so far out on the limb of speculation that their unbalanced conclusions snap the branch from the trunk of logic. For example, some detractors have claimed that the "Ways of Ascent" verse conflicts with *surah* 32, *ayah* 5, which reads: "He rules (all) affairs from the heavens to the earth: in the end (all affairs) will go up to Him, on a day, the space whereof will be (as) a thousand years of your reckoning" (TMQ 32:5).

To claim that these two verses conflict with one another is to invite a Lithium prescription, for the two verses speak of completely different entities and circumstances. The common understanding among Muslims is that the "Ways of Ascent" verse speaks of the ascent of the angels and spirit, whereas the second refers to the Day of Judgment, when all affairs will return to Allah for determination.[110]

To analyze scientific evidences, then, requires us to remain objective, and to that end, Muslim analysts should not trespass into the realm of speculation, and non-Muslim detractors should abandon superfluous arguments. Furthermore, detractors of Islam should recognize that showing a particular passage to lack scientific proof does not invalidate that passage; many passages of the Holy Qur'an endured 1,300 years without substantiating evidence, only to achieve validation by the growth of scientific knowledge in the nineteenth and twentieth centuries. Lack of substantiating evidence equates to lack of proof, not lack of truth. In order to disprove a claim, we must prove a contradictory truth; all else is speculation and prejudice. And this is what is conspicuously absent from the Holy Qur'an: one or more passages, such as the Old Testament Creation verses cited above, which are provably, hopelessly inconsistent with the world as we know it, or which are self-contradictory. Either scenario would suggest a less-than-divine author, but lack of such inconsistencies—as is the case of the Qur'an—would suggest the exact opposite. And, in fact, the Qur'an offers this challenge: "Do they not consider the Qur'an (with care)? Had it been from any other than Allah they would have found therein many a discrepancy" (TMQ 4:82).

Indeed, given the wealth of information presented in the Qur'an, the lack of one such discrepancy should be considered significant.

The Qur'an does not imitate the Bible by assigning dates or disorder to the sequence of Creation. Considering the number and primacy of such biblical narratives, the assertion that the Qur'an was in part copied from previous scriptures looks sadly suspect. Were biblical scriptures recited from the beginning of the collection of books, the first scripture Muhammad would have heard would have been the early chapters of the book of Genesis. The fact that these verses are not carried over into the Qur'an speaks strongly against such a theory of copying.

To search the Qur'an for statements that, like those of the Bible, conflict with archeological, historical, or scientific evidence, proves frustrating. Muslims hold that no such conflicts exist, for they claim the Qur'an conforms perfectly not only with the sciences, but also with all fields of human knowledge, as should be expected of a book of God. That claim begins to look pretty good when the scientific evidence is examined. And while a full discussion of such claims is beyond the scope of this book, a small sample is in order. Those with deeper interests can examine the books: *The Bible, The Qur'an and Science*, by Dr. Maurice Bucaille; *The Universe Seen Through The Quran (Scientific Findings Confirmed)*, by Mir Anees-u-din M.Sc, Ph.D.; and a variety of smaller treatises available through Islamic bookstores. An especially good primer on this subject is *A Brief Illustrated Guide to Understanding Islam*.[111]

But now, let's take a look at a sampler of scientific evidence.

GEOLOGY

Mountains. We might well imagine that, to a desert Bedouin, a mountain would appear to be nothing more than an inconvenient beauty mark on the face of this Earth. To the caravan crews, farmers and sheepherders of Muhammad's time, mountains would likely have presented more difficulties than benefits. To have stopped and thought about them would have seemed odd, and to have found something good to say about them, odder.

Even in the present day, few people contemplate mountains beyond the recreational benefits they offer. A nice hike, an exhilarating ski, a peaceful picnic—such pleasantries would have meant nothing to a Bedouin faced with the inconvenience of having to detour a caravan around a mountain, plow an agricultural field uphill, or climb a steep, rocky hill to retrieve a wayward sheep.

What possible benefit could a desert Bedouin find in a mountain?

Only recently has modern geology recognized the greatest significance of mountains to the world as we know it: mountains possess roots. To quote Tarbuck and Lutgens, "The existence of these roots has been confirmed by seismic and gravitational data."[112] A three or four-mile-high mountain might project a root structure of continental crust thirty or forty miles deep into the surrounding mantle of the Earth.[113] This shaft of mountain-root serves to support the weight of the overlying mountain, thereby establishing equilibrium or, in the language of the geologist, an isostasy.[114] The eye of man sees nothing more than the relatively small nubbin of a mountain, while a forty-mile shaft of Earth's crust lies invisibly imbedded in the deeper, plastic asthenosphere, much like the head of a nail peeking above the surface of a block of wood, riding upon an imperceptible shaft of steel.

Or like a peg.

It is of interest, then, to note the description of mountains in the Holy Qur'an: "Have We not made the earth as a wide expanse, and the mountains as pegs?" (TMQ 78:6–7) Now where did *that* observation come from? From the mind of a Bedouin? Not likely.

In recent years geologists have surmised that mountains, because they arise at collision points between continental plates, stabilize the earth's crust. As such, they represent a weld between the colliding continental plates. In the absence of such a weld, the lithosphere plates would override one another, resulting in an earthquake every time a shift occurred to release accumulated strain. As all mountains represent such welds, the complete absence of mountains would destabilize the earth's surface.

Such knowledge developed following the study of plate tectonics in the late twentieth century, the relevant conclusion being that without the stabilizing influence of mountains, the Earth's surface would be in a frequent, if not continuous, quake. This information is considered revolutionary in the field of geology, but invites a 1,400-year-old yawn from a revelation that records, "And He has set up on the earth mountains standing firm, lest it should shake with you ..." (TMQ 16:15)

CREATION OF THE UNIVERSE

Origins of the Universe. One of the most undisputed principles of cosmology is that the universe was formed out of a hot, smoky mixture of gases and particulate matter.[115] The formation of stars can still be observed in the hearts of nebula (presumed to be remnants or imitators of the primordial dust-cloud) to this day. Relevant mention in the Qur'an is as follows:

> Moreover He [i.e., Allah] comprehended in His design the sky, and it had been (as) smoke. He said to it and to the earth: "You come together, willingly or unwillingly ..." (TMQ 41:11)

The heavens having been "as smoke" is an accurate description of the primordial dust cloud—"smoke" being a more apt description than "cloud," because clouds evoke the image of a cool, static mist, whereas smoke describes a swirling, hot gaseous mass choked with suspended particles. Astronomers encounter galaxies under formation in space to this day, and this is precisely what they look like.

The second line of the above quote mentions the "coming together," a remarkable comment on the necessary union of particle elements into a central core of condensed matter. It is the rupture of this super-dense central mass from which the "Big Bang" emanated, following which the universe expanded. Again, the Qur'an refers to the process:

> Do not the unbelievers see that the heavens and the earth were joined together (as one unit of Creation), before We clove them asunder?
>
> (TMQ 21:30)

An understanding of the origin of the universe, and in particular the concept of a common origin of the heavens and earth, has only been derived in the twentieth century. First proposed in 1920 by Alexander Friedmann and Abbé Georges Lemaître (and subsequently popularized by George Gamow and colleagues), the Big Bang supplanted creationist theory. And here's the point—if the creationist theory was all that was on the mind of man up until 1920, what an extraordinary achievement it would have been for a desert Bedouin to have conceived the Big Bang thirteen centuries earlier.

But, of course, he didn't.

He couldn't have.

The complexity of knowledge and technology required to derive the Big Bang theory (or the Hot Big Bang, as it is now known, since the temperature at 0.0001 seconds has been calculated to have been a cozy 10^{12} degrees Kelvin) boggles the mind.

Basically, the Big Bang theory required two major assumptions, the first being that Einstein's general theory of relativity accurately defined the gravitational interaction of matter, and the second being the cosmological principle, which is of such complexity as to be beyond the scope of this book. Suffice it to say that the theory was validated through the measurement of hydrogen, helium and lithium levels, as well as remnant microwave radiation, which itself was only discovered in 1965. *None* of this was available prior to the late twentieth century. In the early seventh century, all Muhammad had, other than revelation, was a clear view of the night sky.

Continental Drift. Around the year 1800, Alexander von Humboldt noted the near-perfect fit of the bulge of South America into the concave west coast of Africa. Based on this observation, he suggested that the landmasses bordering the opposite sides of the Atlantic were at one time joined.

Fifty years later, Antonio Snider-Pellegrini noted the consistency between von Humboldt's suggestion and the fossil record, which disclosed identical fossil plants in the coal deposits of North America and Europe.

Another half century later, in 1912, the German meteorologist, Alfred Wegener, proposed the concept of continental drift. He suggested that all of the landmasses were at one time joined together in one continent, which he called Pangaea. Based upon the geologic and paleontologic evidence, he proposed that Pangaea broke apart during the Triassic period (245 to 208 million years ago, give or take a long weekend). Separation and drift followed, to the present position of the world's landmasses (though according to modern measurements, these landmasses are still drifting).

In 1937 Alexander L. Du Toit refined Wegener's theory to include two original landmasses, Laurasia in the north and Gondwanaland in the south.

Congruency of continental shelves, evidence of shared glaciation, similarity of rocks and geologic structures, the paleontologic record,[116(EN)] the theory of seafloor spreading, and remnant magnetism[117(EN)] all support what is now accepted as the theory of continental drift. So ... continental drift appears to have been figured out. In the twentieth century. 1,400 years after the Holy Qur'an recorded the verse: "And it is He Who spread out the earth ..." (TMQ 13:3)

HEAVENLY BODIES

The Sun and the Moon. *Surah* 10, *ayah* 5 describes the sun and moon by two different words, both of which mean "light" in the Arabic language. However, the word *Dhi-yaa-an* describes the sun as a source of light while the word *noo-ran* describes the moon as giving light that originates from a source other than itself. Lane's *Arabic-English Lexicon* comments, "It is said that (*dui-yaa-an*) is essential, but (*noo-ran*) is accidental [light] …"[118] Although the Qur'anic and biblical descriptions differ (Genesis 1:16—"Then God made two great lights: the greater light to rule the day, and the lesser light to rule the night"), the Qur'an differentiates between the source of light of these two heavenly bodies.

Celestial Movement. The Qur'an describes rounded orbits of the celestial bodies, as well as rounded orbits of day and night: "It is He Who created the Night and the Day, and the sun and the moon: all (the celestial bodies) swim along, each in its rounded course" (TMQ 21:33). In addition, the Qur'anic verse of 39:5 describes the alternation between day and night by the verb *kaw-wa-ra*, which means to wind or coil, like wrapping a turban around the head (or, as per the example in Lane's *Arabic-English Lexicon*, "He wound the thing in a round form"). From this we understand the Qur'an to describe not only the rounded orbits of the planets and moon, but the spherical shape of the Earth itself. Furthermore, "And the Sun runs his course for a period determined for him …" (TMQ 36:38) hints at the fact that the entire solar system moves: as, in fact, it does. The sun may be the center of our solar system, but nonetheless it orbits in space around the axis of the Milky Way galaxy.

At a time when Western explorers were afraid to seek the horizon for fear of falling off, Qur'anic descriptions such as the above were centuries, if not more than a millennium, ahead of their time.

Solar and Lunar Orbits. *Surah* 36, *ayah* 40 reads: "It is not permitted to the Sun to catch up the Moon, nor can the

Night outstrip the Day: each (just) swims along in (its own) orbit (according to Law)." This description of separate, rounded orbits is unusual enough. However, what really shatters expectations is the statement that the sun and moon are not permitted to catch up to one another, for it was the common perception among ancient man, when viewing a solar eclipse, that the sun and the moon did just that—catch up with one another. Yet even though a solar eclipse occurred during Muhammad's life, this verse corrected the error of such primitive thinking.

PHYSIOLOGY

Cell Theory. Cells are the building blocks of all living things, and the main component of cells is water, to the tune of eighty to eighty-five percent. Life cannot exist without water, for a dry cell is a dead cell. And while these facts did not surface until the cell theory of the early nineteenth century, the Holy Qur'an states, "We [Allah] made from water every living thing" (TMQ 21:30).

Skin Renewal. All of the Abrahamic faiths stress the tortures of hellfire. However, the Qur'an goes one step further, for it states, "As soon as their skins are roasted through, We shall change them for fresh skins, that they may taste the penalty: for Allah is Exalted in Power, Wise" (TMQ 4:56). Now, only with electrophysiological testing, intracellular recording, and sophisticated microscopy techniques did mankind learn that pain and temperature receptors are restricted to the dermal layer of the skin. This is recent knowledge and yet, 1,400 years ago, in a time and place where research into human physiology had not even progressed to the stage of bodily dissection, revelation described that the key to maintaining the torture of hellfire is to renew the skin. Those who question Who had the power to dictate such punishment, and the wisdom to know this detail, are informed that "Allah is Exalted in Power, Wise."

The Frontal Lobes. The part of the brain located at the most anterior (i.e., the most forward) aspect of the brain are called *frontal* lobes for a reason: They ride up front. If we tap our foreheads, the part of the brain closest to our fingers is the pre-frontal region of the frontal lobes, the area of the brain concerned with personality and behavior. Science tells us, "The motivation and the foresight to plan and initiate movements occur in the anterior portion of the frontal lobes, the prefrontal area."[119] Surprisingly, we find oblique reference to this fact in the Holy Qur'an: "Let him beware! If he does not desist, We will drag him by the *naa-se-yah*, a lying, sinful *naa-se-ya-tin!*" (TMQ 96:15–16)

The word *naa-se-yah* (or *naa-se-ya-tin,* the genitive case of *naa-se-yah*), while often translated as "forelock," in fact deserves the longer and more accurate description of "fore {front} part of the head."[120]

Now, there is the story of the man who wanted to know which part of the body was responsible for thought. He decided that if he exercised his thought, the first part of his body to ache from fatigue would be the thinking part of his body. So he sat down and thought and thought and thought. After a while, the hard wooden stool that he sat upon began to take its toll, leading the man to focus his conclusion on the area of his ache.

It's a funny story, but it's not just for kids.

The point is that 1,400 years ago a Bedouin could hardly have known what modern medicine has only figured out in the present century. An illiterate Arab from the past would most likely think and talk in terms of "lying eyes," "lying lips" and "cheating hearts." Anyone who believes that a Bedouin of twelve centuries ago would have considered the prefrontal region of the frontal lobes of the cerebral cortex to be associated with conceiving sins and lies should be suspected of harboring a personal agenda. It wasn't common knowledge then, and it isn't even common knowledge now, except in scientific circles.

Inner Workings of the Body. Six hundred years before Ibn Nafis described the circulation of blood, and 1,000 years before William Harvey took the credit in his book, *Exercitatio Anatomica de Motu Cordis et Sanguinis in Animalibus* (The Anatomical Exercises Concerning the Motion of the Heart and Blood in Animals) in 1628, the Holy Qur'an alluded to the processes of digestion, absorption, blood circulation, and excretion as follows:

> And verily in cattle (too) will you find an instructive sign. From what is within their bodies, between excretions and blood, We produce, for your drink, milk, pure and agreeable to those who drink it.
>
> (TMQ 16:66)

The sciences of blood circulation, digestion, absorption, and glandular secretion remained mysteries up until the past few centuries. To encounter one verse that links all these processes together is to encounter a complex scientific anachronism.

BODIES OF WATER

The Holy Qur'an glorifies The Creator by mentioning some of the unique and unexpected characteristics of His creation. Take, for example, these two verses:

> It is He Who has let free the two bodies of flowing water:
> one palatable and sweet, and the other salt and bitter; yet
> He has made a barrier between them, a partition that is
> forbidden to be passed. (TMQ 25:53)

> He has let free the two bodies of flowing water, meeting
> together: between them is a barrier which they do not
> transgress: then which of the favors of your Lord will you
> deny? (TMQ 55:19–21)

Both quotes refer to a barrier between sweet and salt water found in an estuary. This zone of brackish water is well known. In the present day, that is. Whether Muhammad knew of it is hard to guess, but we can make some suggestive observations. To begin with, rivers are scarce in the Middle East. Furthermore, much of the well water in the Middle East is salty, so brackish water by the standards of modern developed nations was likely to have been considered potable in Muhammad's day.

In any case, should we contemplate a major river emptying into a sea, even in the present day, our minds tend to wonder that one day one of the two bodies of water will not win out over the other. Were a seventh-century man to investigate an estuary, he would likely have expected the force and volume of a major river such as the Nile or the Tigris-Euphrates to expand the region of brackish water and eventually dilute the entire sea. To bring up the point at all would have seemed strange to a desert-dwelling people not given to maritime adventures, yet it signifies the truth spoken by Muhammad. For were he a charlatan, why would he have brought up such an odd point in the first place? Even if he had known the fact (which is highly unlikely), what possible benefit could there have been in mentioning it?

The second of the above quotes may relate to the fact that oceans and seas vary in salinity, temperature, and density, and they meet at well-defined boundaries.[121] For example, the Mediterranean Sea meets the Atlantic Ocean in a stable and distinct border. The Mediterranean extends a dripping wet tongue of water, several hundred kilometers long, of higher temperature, higher salinity, and lower density over the Gibraltar Sill at a depth of 1000 meters.[122] The border with the colder, less salty, more dense Atlantic Ocean is relatively fixed and sharp, despite the strong currents, constant waves and regular tides that would be expected to blend these two bodies of water, or at least mix them where they meet. Is this an example of the "barrier which they do not transgress," mentioned in the quote? If so, it is all the more remarkable given the fact that this example is repeated at the borders of other seas and oceans.

Another oceanographic point is the mention of deep, internal waves. Such a mention may sound odd at first, and reasonably so, for this is a recent discovery, and not common knowledge even in present day.

Modern oceanography teaches that deep, internal waves "are found at an interface between water layers of different densities—for example, the pycnocline."[123] Internal waves behave just like surface waves, and may even break. However, unlike surface waves, they cannot be seen or studied without complex equipment, and certainly this was not the work of a desert people for whom the simple act of swimming was a rare ability.

There is a diagram in M. Grant Gross' book, *Oceanography, a View of the Earth,* that shows two levels of waves: one at the surface and the other internal, at the interface between the hyper-dense deep water and the less dense surface layer.[124] What is interesting is that this illustration corresponds perfectly with the Qur'anic passage,

Or (the state of a disbeliever) is like the darkness in a vast deep sea, overwhelmed with waves topped by waves, topped by dark clouds, (layers of) darkness upon darkness: if a man stretches out his hand, he can hardly see it! And he for whom Allah has not appointed light, for him there is no light (TMQ 24:40)[125].

Not only does this passage describe the layers of both superficial and deep waves, but it also refers to "darkness in a vast deep sea," darkness so complete that a person can barely see. Now, the absence of light at an ocean depth of 1,000 meters is recent knowledge, and could only be gained with the use of special equipment, for the human chest has the annoying habit of imploding at such depths.[126] Appreciation of any significant darkness requires a dive in excess of 50 meters, but an unequipped surface dive of more than 15 meters is beyond all but the rarest of human capabilities. Among those who have learned to swim in the first place, that is.

THE ATMOSPHERE

Altitude Sickness. Mountain sickness, or altitudinal shortness of breath, was clinically defined in 1937, and most likely was unknown prior to the late 1800s.[127] There are several reasons for this, but the most significant is that mountain sickness requires a rapid ascent, typically of 8,000 vertical feet or more. Prior to the twentieth century, such ascents were sometimes made, but almost never rapidly.

In fact, there was little, if any, motivation for lowlanders to climb mountains, and especially to a vertical scale of 8,000 feet or more. Recreational climbing was virtually unheard of, especially in the Middle East, where people exerted themselves to the fullest just to squeeze a bare existence out of an unsympathetic land. And prior to modern methods of rapid transportation, mountain folk acclimatized to the rarity of the atmosphere in which they lived. Those who sought higher altitudes in the process of pasturing their herds experienced such slow rises in elevation that their bodies adjusted.

Hence, up until two hundred years ago, mountain sickness was all but unknown, even in developed nations. In the Middle East, summits in the range of 8–10,000 feet are few and far between, so the likelihood of an Arab ever having experienced mountain sickness prior to the invention of the combustible engine is vanishingly small. Nonetheless, the Qur'an alludes to the constricted breathing experienced by those who venture into higher altitudes:

> He makes their breast closed and constricted, as if they had to climb up to the skies ... (TMQ 6:125)

Meteorology. Only recently have meteorologists described the formation of rain-generating cumulus clouds. In a nutshell, cumulus clouds migrate together and updrafts force the mass of vapor to extend vertically, like a haystack.[128,129] When a cloud grows tall enough the upper regions cool, condense, and fall as rain.

While meteorologists have required satellite photography, airplanes, weather balloons, computers and other sophisticated equipment to define the process, the Qur'an figured it out first:

> Don't you see that Allah makes the clouds move gently, then joins them together, then makes them into a heap? Then you will see rain issue forth from their midst. And He sends down from the sky mountain masses (of clouds) wherein is hail ..." (TMQ 24:43)

"Mountain masses (of clouds) wherein is hail"? Now *that's* interesting. The Qur'an describes the rain-generating clouds as heaps, but the hail-generating clouds as mountains. And, in fact, only when cumulonimbus clouds mass together like a mountain and extend from their altitudinal roots of 3–4,000 feet to a 25–30,000-foot ceiling do the upper layers generate hail through condensation and freezing.[130]

Once again, this is recent knowledge. For everybody but Muslims.

The Rain Cycle. It seems like a no-brainer for most people, but once again we have to step out of our twenty-first-century cone of silence to hear what people were saying about the rain cycle a thousand years ago. Or just a couple hundred years ago, for that matter.

The seventeenth-century philosopher René Descartes proposed that seawater seeped through underground channels into reservoirs underneath the tops of mountains, something like a natural water tower. Athanasius Kircher wrote in his 1664 *Mundus subterraneus* (Subterranean World) that seawater was driven by the force of tides into subterranean rifts, and eventually to outlets at springs. In his 1695 *An Essay Toward a Natural History of the Earth and Terrestrial Bodies*, the English geologist John Woodward endorsed the idea of a huge underground sea that communicated with the oceans and provided water through springs and rivers.

Bernard Palissy was the first to suggest that the sole source of springs and rivers was rainfall (*Discours Admirables,* 1580). The first experiments that supported his hypothesis were conducted in the basin of the river Seine toward the end of the seventeenth century.[131]

Amazingly, neither the people of Mount Waialeale, Hawaii, (despite having the world's highest average annual rainfall, at

1,168 centimeters per year) nor the Bedouins of the desert (despite having the greatest *need* for rain) ever seemed to have figured out the rain cycle on their own. One Qur'anic passage, however, presented the reality of the case over a thousand years before the rain cycle was conceived or tested:

> Don't you see that Allah sends down rain from the sky, and leads it through springs in the earth? Then He causes to grow, therewith, produce of various colors ... (TMQ 39:21)

ANATOMY AND EMBRYOLOGY

Correlation between Qur'anic statements and embryology are so accurate that they have stimulated books devoted to this subject. Complete summary in the format of this chapter, therefore, is doomed to inadequacy. However, some of the more salient features may be mentioned in brief, with a reference to more comprehensive books, should the reader wish to examine the topic in greater depth.

Conception. The concept of biparental inheritance was first proposed by Pierre-Louis Moreau de Maupertuis in his *Système de la Nature* in 1751. Before this, prevailing beliefs relied upon Aristotle's fourth century BC suggestion that embryos developed out of coagulation, or curdling, of menstrual blood, with "vapors" of semen acting as a catalyst. Aristotle's views may have made their way into the thoughts of at least one Bible author, for Job 10:10 records, "Did You not pour me out like milk, and curdle me like cheese ..." Even when discovered under the microscope by Antonie van Leeuwenhoek, spermatozoa were "proven" by the experiments of Lazzaro Spallanzani to be parasites in semen.

The theory of spontaneous generation was superseded by the theory of pre-formation—which proposed that a pre-formed fetus lived as a diminutive human in the head of the sperm (Jan Swammerdam, 1637–1680) or in the ovarian follicle (De Graaf, 1641–1693). This is turn gave way to the theory of biparental inheritance in the eighteenth century, which eventually lost the battle following Driesch's experiments at the beginning of the twentieth century. Yet, for the previous twelve centuries, the Holy Qur'an taught, "O mankind! We created you from a single (pair) of a male and a female ..." (TMQ 49:13) and "Verily, We created man from *Nutfah* (drops) of mixed semen (sexual discharge of man and woman) ..." (TMQ 76:2)

In the fourteenth century, Ibn Hajar Al Asqalani recorded the conflict between the fallacious opinions of the anatomists of his day and the revelation of the Holy Qur'an:

> Many of the anatomists claim that the semen of the male has no role in creation of the baby. Its role, they claim, is limited to curdling the menstrual blood from which man is born. The sayings of the Prophet deny what they say. The semen of the male actually participates equally to that of female in formation of the embryo.[132]

As an example of one such teaching, Muhammad was once asked, "O Muhammad! What is man created from?" The Prophet is recorded as having answered, "He is created from both: from the man's *Nutfah* (sperm) and the woman's *Nutfah* (ovum)."[133]

Remarkably, the story doesn't end there, for the Qur'an teaches that only a tiny element of semen functions in conception: "God made man's progeny from a quintessence of despised liquid" (TMQ 32:8). In a separate *hadith,* Muhammad is recorded as having said, "Not from the whole fluid (ejaculate), man is created, but only from a small portion of it."[134] This, in fact, wasn't realized by the scientific world until Hertwig described fertilization of an egg by a sperm in 1875.

Development. The embryo and fetus develop within the bouncy castle of the amniochorionic sac, suspended within the muscular uterus, itself encased within the ballooning abdominal wall. These three layers appear to be referenced in the passage, "He makes you, in the wombs of your mothers, in stages, one after another, in three veils of darkness" (TMQ 39:6).

Notably, the concept of the human embryo developing in stages was not recorded in scientific literature before the fifteenth century. According to the theories of pre-formation and spontaneous generation, the human was created complete, and just grew in proportion. Not until the fifteenth century was the staging of fetal development discussed, and not until the seventeenth century were scientists able to stage the development of chick embryos thanks to Van Leeuwenhoek's invention of the microscope. Staging of human embryos was first described in the twentieth century by Streeter, but by that time the Qur'anic concept of epigenesis (fetal development in stages) was thirteen centuries old and sporting a beard that would have put Rumpelstiltskin to shame. How complete are the Qur'anic descriptions of embryological staging? Judge for yourself:

> Then We placed him as (a drop of) *nutfah* (mixed drops of the male and female sexual discharge) in a place of rest, firmly fixed; then We made the *nutfah* into a clot of congealed blood; then of that clot We made a (foetus) lump; then We made out of that lump bones and clothed the bones with flesh; then We developed out of it another creature. So blessed be Allah, the Best to create! (TMQ 23:13–14)

From the scientific point of view, everything about this quote describing the initial stages of embryogenesis is twentieth-century knowledge: the drop-like appearance of the *nutfah* (i.e., the zygote, the earliest stage, formed by the union of sperm and ovum), and the firmly fixed adhesion of "the clot of congealed blood" (i.e., the blastocyst, formed by the splitting of the zygote, and which resembles a tiny blood clot under the microscope) in the "place of rest" (the uterus). The blastocyst develops chorionic villi that invade the uterine wall, resulting in adhesion as well as nutrition, for the chorionic villi become surrounded by microscopic lacunae ("lakes") of blood. At this stage, the blood is stagnant and there is no arterial-venous exchange, for the blastocyst is small enough to derive nutrition from seepage of nutrients. Hence, the blastocyst appears under the microscope to be a tiny blood clot. The Arabic word *alaqah* (translated "clot" in the above passage) in fact describes three qualities: a clot of blood, leech-like in appearance, and clinging.[135] And in fact, all three of these qualities apply. The appearance of the embryo at this stage of development is similar to that of a leech, both in form and physiology. Once again, this is twentieth-century scientific knowledge, predated by fourteen centuries by the Qur'anic description.

In regard to these Quar'anic passages dealing with human development, Dr. Keith L. Moore writes in his highly acclaimed embryology textbook, *The Developing Human,* that he was "astonished by the accuracy of the statements that were recorded in the 7th century AD, before the science of embryology was established."[136] Dr. Moore points out that the word *mudghah,* described in *surah* 23:14, actually means "a chewed lump." He correlates this description with somites, the curved, segmented masses of mesoderm in the embryo that resemble a mold of teeth marks.[137(EN)]

Furthermore, the above-quoted "Then We made out of that lump bones and clothed the bones with flesh" (TMQ 23:14) correlates precisely with the sequential development of the somites into cartilaginous skeleton, followed by the development of the muscles.

"Then We developed out of it another creature" (TMQ 23:14) may refer to the transformation in the eighth week from an indistinct embryo to a fetus bearing distinctive human characteristics. *Surah* 22:5 mentions, "Then out of a leech-like clot, then out of a morsel of flesh, partly formed and partly unformed ..."—which may refer to the fact that some tissues are differentiated at this stage, whereas others are not.

Moore's analysis is too lengthy for adequate discussion in a book not devoted to the subject.[138(EN)] But scientifically speaking, none of the above was known prior to Antonie van Leeuwenhoek's invention of the microscope in the seventeenth century, for none of this could be seen with the naked eye.

MISCELLANY

Honey. According to the Qur'an, honey is a substance "wherein is healing for men" (TMQ 16:69). Today, the medicinal benefits of honey are well-known and too numerous to mention here. High in antioxidants, vitamins and minerals, honey has antimicrobial, antifungal, and antiseptic properties that can speed the healing of burns, wounds, and sore throats.

Now, the point of interest is that Muhammad was recorded as having taught, "There is no disease that Allah has sent down except that He also has sent down its treatment."[139] Whether true or not, this is what he believed, so we would reasonably expect the Qur'an to contain a cookbook of home remedies—if, that is, Muhammad were the author. Such, however, is not the case. In fact, the Qur'an is conspicuously devoid of medicinal treatments.

Not so with Muhammad's teachings.

Sahih Al-Bukhari, one of the most respected and rigorously authenticated collections of *hadith,* contains fifty-eight entries in the chapter on medicine alone. So voluminous is the record of Muhammad's homeopathic and naturopathic remedies that books have been written on the subject. Medicine, it would seem, was very much on Muhammad's mind. However, as was the case with his wives and daughters, the Qur'an does not reflect Muhammad's interest. On the contrary, the only Qur'anic reference to a medicinal agent is to honey, and on this point, nobody disagrees.

Fingerprinting. The British scientific journal *Nature* described the uniqueness of fingerprints in 1880. Subsequently, Sir Francis Galton suggested a classification system that was developed, published, and adopted by Scotland Yard in the early 1900s. The Galton-Henry fingerprint classification system has since been adopted around the world.

Why is this interesting? Because whereas the uniqueness of fingerprints was scientifically recognized in the nineteenth century, the Holy Qur'an alluded to this fact over twelve centuries earlier. *Surah* 75:3–4 refers to the Day of Judgment and emphasizes Allah's perfect ability to resurrect mankind, *down to their fingertips*: "Does man think that We cannot assemble his bones? Nay, We are able to put together in perfect order the very tips of his fingers."

And now, for something completely esoteric.

Throughout the Qur'an, Allah refers to himself as "Lord of the East and the West." The casual reader might be struck by the fact that nowhere does Allah refer to himself as "Lord of the North and the South."

Perhaps we should consider that again and again, revealed scriptures emphasize the infinite perfection and powers of our Creator. Nowhere does a revealed scripture, be it the Old Testament, New Testament or the Holy Qur'an, place limitations upon God. So too with the above description.

Think about it. If we were told to travel north, and keep traveling north until we could travel north no further, we would reach the North Pole and stop, for to continue would be to turn south. Same with traveling south—once at the South Pole, one step farther would be in the direction of north. North has an upper limit, south a lower limit.

Now, what about east and west? If we were told to travel east (or west), and to keep traveling in that direction until we could travel no further, we would wind ourselves around the globe until we died. Or until eternity. And that's the point. To describe Allah as "Lord of the North and South" would place a limitation upon Him, whereas "Lord of the East and the West" bears the connotation of boundlessness.

Interesting it is, then, that the Qur'an identifies Allah as Lord of the East and West, and not of the North and South. Can we surmise that this choice was coincidental? Probably not, and for a very simple reason.

In *surah* 2:144, Allah redirected the Muslim prayer from Jerusalem to the sacred mosque in Makkah. Two *ayat* earlier, Allah told the believers how to answer objections to this change: "Say: To Allah belong both East and West ..." (TMQ 2:142)

Now, here's the rub. These verses were revealed when the Muslims were living in Madinah, in what is now known as Saudi Arabia. In Madinah, changing the direction of prayer from Jerusalem to Makkah constituted a reversal from praying

North-Northwest to due South. And yet, how were the Muslims instructed to answer objections? By saying, "To Allah belong both East and West." If ever there was a place to have said, "To Allah belong both North and South," this was it. What would a normal person have said? "Change the direction from North to South, for Allah is the Lord of North and South." What does the Qur'an say? "To Allah belong both East and West." Obviously, there is a deeper message, and if it is not the limitlessness of Allah's dominion, power and essence, we have to wonder what else that message could be.

One final point. During Muhammad's lifetime, the North and South poles and the axis of the Earth's rotation were unknown. For that matter, the Earth being round wasn't scientifically proven for centuries, if not a millennium. The Arabs lived in a postage stamp-sized area of the world where compass directions bore none of the connotations discussed above. So even had the Arabs wished to express Allah's limitlessness in this manner, they would not have been able to do so. Rather, we can well imagine that even the most intelligent, best educated and widely traveled Bedouin of fourteen centuries ago, who wanted to express Allah's supremacy, would have described Allah as the Lord of North, South, East, West and all points between. The fact that North and South are conspicuously devoid of mention may not prove divine origin of the revelation, but it certainly goes against what we would expect of a human author.

9
Summary of Evidence

Facts are stubborn things; and whatever may be our wishes, our inclinations, or the dictates of our passions, they cannot alter the state of facts and evidence.

—John Adams

The Qur'an claims to be the word of Allah, and as such is infallible: "No falsehood can approach it from before or behind it: it is sent down by One full of Wisdom, Worthy of all praise" (TMQ 41:42).

Non-Muslims claim the Qur'an was authored by Muhammad. However, as Dr. Maurice Bucaille points out, "It is easy to put forward the hypothesis of Muhammad as being a brilliant thinker, who was supposed to have imagined all on his own what modern science was to discover centuries later. In so doing however, people quite simply forget to mention the other aspect of what these geniuses of philosophical reasoning produced, i.e. the colossal blunders that litter their work."[140]

Not only is the Qur'an *not* littered with "colossal blunders," but it also appears to be devoid of even the smallest of errors. This is even more remarkable considering the wealth of information presented in it. Certainly many of the statements found in the Qur'an would have seemed peculiar during Muhammad's time, if not incomprehensible, and possibly unnecessary to the revelation. Should Muhammad be proposed an imposter, we have to wonder why he predicted future events and scientific truths that would remain unproven for centuries, if not for more than a millennium. And how did he get it all right? Without a single, solitary error?

In the words of Dr. Bucaille, "How could a man living fourteen hundred years ago have made corrections to the existing description to such an extent that he eliminated scientifically inaccurate material and, on his own initiative, made statements that science has been able to verify only in the present day? This hypothesis is completely untenable."[141]

In self-defense, some non-Muslims present "our book against yours" arguments, claiming that if the Qur'an contradicts Old or New Testaments, then it cannot be revelation. But this argument is only valid if the books under comparison possess the same authority, and this choice—the choice of which book is most reliable—is left to the reader.

Non-Muslims also sometimes argue on the basis of customs or traditions, but these issues bear no relation to the analysis of religion. Other issues, such as polygamy, the female headscarf, family roles, and food restrictions *are* religiously based, but foreign to Western lifestyles. As such these are not points of proof, but of preference, which is a dangerous basis for an evaluation, for "it is possible that you dislike a thing which is good for you, and that you love a thing which is bad for you. But Allah knows, and you know not" (TMQ 2:216). Personal preference, in other words, may be misleading.

Despite all philosophical arguments, the challenges remain to find a single falsehood or to compose a ten-word, three-line *surah* better than that of the Qur'an. Considering that these challenges have never been met and won, the Qur'an deserves our respect.

A statistician or a person who plays the odds will appreciate the fact that many of the Qur'an's predictions appear to have been bad bets in their day. Predictions such as those involving the battles of Rome versus Persia, and the condemnation of Abu Lahab, his wife and Al-Walid ibn Al-Mughirah would certainly fall into this category. The odds of such predictions coming true are incalculable, but even if each were given a likelihood of fifty percent, the sheer number of such predictions calculates out to an astronomically small chance of being correct in every instance.

For example, the likelihood of two predictions, each having a probability of fifty percent, both being correct is one out of four. Essentially there are three combinations of error (the first prediction is right and the second wrong, or the first is wrong and the second right, or both are wrong), and only one chance of both predictions being correct. One chance out of four, that is. The chance of three such predictions all being correct is one in eight, and with each additional prediction, the probability halves again. The likelihood of *every* prediction being correct is staggeringly small. There are over sixty such items of evidence cited in the previous chapters, and these represent only a fraction of the total cited by Islamic scholars. Yet if each of these sixty-plus pieces of evidence were assigned the conservative probability of fifty percent, the likelihood of all sixty-plus items proving correct on the basis of sheer chance would be $(1/2)^{60}$, which translates to less than one chance in 1,000,000,000,000,000,000. That's one in *one quintillion.* The fact that a popular religion surrounds a revelation that has such an infinitesimally small probability of coincidental correctness is hardly surprising. Indeed, the fact that so many stand in denial of such odds is the true wonder.

Despite the evidence, many Westerners complain that the Qur'an does not inspire them in the same way the Bible does.

We have to remember, however, that no translation does the Arabic justice. For this reason, we should respect the opinions of those who have mastered the Arabic language. A few such authors comment,

> All those who are acquainted with the Quran in Arabic agree in praising the beauty of this religious book; its grandeur of form is so sublime that no translation into any European language can allow us to appreciate it.[142]

> The truth is, I do not find any understanding author who controverts the elegance of the Alcoran, it being generally esteemed as the standard of the Arabic language and eloquence …[143]

> The Quran, in its original Arabic dress, has a seductive beauty and charm of its own. Couched in concise and exalted style, its brief pregnant sentences, often rhymed, possess an expressive force and explosive energy which it is extremely difficult to convey by literal word for word translation.[144]

Many Westerners may then despair over their inability to appreciate the Qur'an in the eloquence of the revealed Arabic. This difficulty can be compounded by the plethora of poor translations freely available through Western bookstores. The Abdullah Yusuf Ali translation of meaning (The Holy Qur'an), that of Saheeh International (The Qur'an), of the combined effort of Muhammad Al-Hilali and Muhammad Khan (The Noble Qur'an), and of Marmaduke Pickthall (The Glorious Qur'an) are among the best. Other respected translations exist, but those of Alexander Ross, George Sale, Rev. J. M. Rodwell, Edward Henry Palmer, and Richard Bell are certainly to be avoided.

What remains, then, is for people to read the Qur'an, understanding that the emotive qualities of Arabic are lost in translation. Having said that, the message and the messenger are inseparable, and many find they appreciate the scripture best when they study the life of the man who conveyed it.

PART II
MESSENGERS

All cats are gray in the dark.

—Vietnamese Proverb

As it is with the messengers. So let's shed some light upon them.

Not all prophets are the same. Some received revelation, some claimed divine inspiration, and these two groups are not necessarily mutually inclusive. For example, Jesus Christ claimed to have been of the first category, and Paul of the second. Jesus' claim was concrete; Paul's was mystical.

Who, if anybody, should we trust?

In the history of religion, one fact that quickly becomes apparent is that Judaism, Christianity, and Islam were all founded upon a remarkably consistent core message. During the period of their origins, all three of these religions taught the unity of God, the humanity of His prophets, and a set of laws that showed only slight modification from one revelation to the next.[145(EN)]

Equally apparent is the fact that mysticism eventually invaded each of these religions and corrupted the beliefs from those held during the period of origins, creating a kaleidoscope of deviant sects from the original. At the center of each of these deviant sects was always an "inspired prophet."

Hence, Orthodox Judaism has become largely overshadowed by the more permissive Reform Judaism; the strict monotheism and commitment to Old Testament law that typified early Christianity became corrupted by the Trinitarian formula and the lawlessness of Paul's concept of justification by faith; and orthodox Islam has been eroded by the many "reform," "modern" and "mystical" movements that have attempted to rewrite the laws of Islam. At the head of each deviant sect is a man, woman or group who seduced a following by offering greater religious permissiveness, typically in combination with the promise of a near-effortless salvation. Some people choose to follow scripture and the prophets who conveyed it; others trust the teachings of mystically "inspired" leaders.

The fact that the teachings of these "inspired" leaders typically contradict the teachings of the true prophets has not gone unnoticed. Neither has the fact that the true prophets refused to fashion revelation to suit the desires of their followers. If piety were a party, everyone would attend. But it's not. Whereas charlatans (and their followers) frequently live in luxury and ease, true prophets (and *their* followers) are better known for having suffered poverty and persecution, but with evidence of divine protection. Relief was near, but always came following a period of trial.

For example, God recompensed Joseph's unwavering faith, despite enslavement and subsequent imprisonment, with liberation and a position of authority. He rewarded Job's patient suffering with the return of his health, wealth, and position, Noah's loyalty with salvation from both the disbelieving people and the flood, and Moses' perseverance with position of leadership among the Jews. The list goes on and the pattern is consistent. False prophets enjoy high style in this worldly life in reckless disregard of the punishment that awaits them in the hereafter. True prophets, on the other hand, prove their sincerity through forbearance of trial, and in the end are rewarded for their faith and perseverance.

"What about Jesus Christ?" some might ask. "What about his crucifixion and suffering? What about his *passion?*" Yes, well, if Jesus Christ was not crucified, then God saved him and *there was no passion.* Should such have been the case (the evidence of which is discussed in the first book of this series, *MisGod'ed*), God saved Jesus by raising him up from this worldly life, and close to the Day of Judgment will return him to Earth in a position of authority.

Another commonality is that all true prophets were sent to correct transgressions from previous scripture. Throughout the history of revelation some embraced the teaching, others perverted the message, and still others denied it outright. The diversity of religious sects is a direct result of this collage of human nature. The main themes of divine unity and God's laws run through the foundation of all revealed religions, whereas core values of mysticism and self-serving theology run through the deviant sects. Religious trends, it would seem, don't change much.

Most people consider themselves capable of differentiating true prophets from false, and pure revelation from corrupt, but it is a painful fact that for every prophet there have been those who considered him deluded, and for every deluded babbler there have been those who considered him a prophet. Fortunately, indicators exist to clarify any candidate's claim to prophethood, and it is these indicators that demand examination.

1
Adam to Moses

One man with courage is a majority.

—Andrew Jackson

J udaism, Christianity and Islam all describe the chain of prophethood from Adam to Moses, and recognize each prophet as having stood relatively alone in the field of righteousness during his day. The Bibles of the Jews and Christians, as well as the Holy Qur'an, all mention the following (with the Arabic names, where different, in parentheses): Adam, Noah (Nuh), Lot (Lut), Abraham (Ibrahim), Ishmael (Isma'il), Isaac (Ishaq), Jacob (Yaqoub), Joseph (Yusuf), Aaron (Harun), Moses (Musa), David (Dawood), Solomon (Sulaiman), Job (Ayyub), Ezekiel (Zulkifl), Jonah (Yunus), Elias (Ilyas), and Elisha (Al-Yasa').

While the Old Testament, New Testament and Holy Qur'an all acknowledge these prophets, they differ in the details of their lives. For example, all three scriptures affirm that the people of Lot were obliterated as punishment for their "backward" ways, the prophet Jonah slipped both directions on the slick waterslide of a whale's throat, and David made a stunning first (and last) impression on Goliath.

However, there are significant differences.

Islam records that Allah forgave Adam and Eve for their sin of having eaten the forbidden fruit, closing the door on the concept of Original Sin. The Holy Qur'an does not attribute incest, drunkenness, contracting prostitution and murder to certain prophets, in stark contrast to Old Testament descriptions of Lot, Noah, Judah, and David, respectively. Rather, Islam teaches that the prophets exemplified, rather than contradicted, the righteous conduct they were sent to convey.

In addition, the Holy Qur'an mentions Hud, sent to the people of 'Ad (TMQ 7:65); Salih, sent to the people of Thamud (TMQ 7:73); and other prophets, though not necessarily by name.

Now, while we can establish continuity in the chain of major prophets, the pattern of prophethood remains somewhat elusive in the Jewish and Christian scriptures. Certainly, the genealogy of the human race appears to have been agreed upon: Adam had a wife, they had children, and from them the human race arose. The two sons of Adam established the tradition of sibling rivalry to no small degree, while at the same time representing the opposite poles of righteousness and impiety. And men have been beating each other's brains out ever since.

A series of known prophets followed in well-spaced sequence, with other, anonymous prophets as offshoots from the main lineage. But why? What is the overall scheme?

Certainly, some prophets followed in the footsteps of others, such as the seemingly endless succession of prophets sent to the wayward Jews. However, what about those cultures that grew, prospered, and died off without ever having a Moses or Christ to steer the population toward salvation? What happened to *those* people? Within the confines of Judeo-Christian teachings, the only answers to this question lie in speculation.

Islam, on the other hand, teaches that no population was ever left without guidance. As the Holy Qur'an states, "Verily,

We have sent you [Muhammad] in truth, as a bearer of glad tidings, and as a warner: and there never was a people, without a warner having lived among them (in the past)" (TMQ 35:24).

Somewhere in time, God bestowed the blessing of written language to mankind, and subsequent revelation was recorded in hard copy. The Suhuf (Sheets) were revealed to Abraham, the Zaboor (Psalms) to David, the Tawraat (Torah) to Moses, the Injeel (Gospel) to Jesus and the Qur'an to Muhammad.

With the advent of written records, each revelation enjoyed greater duration and circulation, with reduced need for human reminders. However, the early scriptures were manipulated and corrupted (as discussed in *MisGod'ed*), and demanded renewed revelation to set the record straight. After all, what would be the need for another prophet if the previous scripture were above reproach?

Because the Old Testament scriptures were corrupted, Jesus Christ was needed to restore the purity of revelation. This purity, however, did not last, and the New Testament bears ample witness to its adulteration. Hence the need for a final prophet—as predicted by both Old and New Testaments—and for a divinely protected final revelation.

Who is this final prophet? And what is the final revelation? According to Islam, Muhammad and the Holy Qur'an. However, in order to appreciate that claim, we first have to examine the lives and messages of Moses and Jesus.

2
Moses

He who speaks the truth should have one foot in the stirrup.
—Hindu proverb

Who was the Moses of the Old Testament? A human Trojan Horse in the house of Pharaoh, a self-imposed exile after having accidentally slain an abusive slavemaster, a man of honor and integrity returning to Pharaoh's court, fearless of consequences, to satisfy the command of his Creator, and a prophet struggling against adversity, both from without and from within the rebellious body of refugees rescued from slavery by the will of God—this was the man Moses. He was a prophet rejected by most in his homeland, repeatedly defied by those he was sent to save, who struggled until the end of his days to instill some sense of piety in a people who, time and again, openly rebelled against God's commandments.

And yet he persisted.

He fell from a lofty royal office to the lowest position of anonymity, only to be granted the gift of revelation, given credence by a series of supportive miracles. And in this he appears to have succeeded, for he left this earth having fulfilled what was commanded of him. A few of his followers remained obedient to the dictates of Old Testament law, and a large number did not. Most peculiar, however, is that the revelation Moses transmitted admonished the Jews for their transgressions and yet, again and again, the only message many of them seem to have retained is the concept of having been "chosen." The importance of fidelity to the mandates of God became secondary, in many of their minds, to the simplistic concept of racial elitism, and this despite the Old Testament verses that criticize or condemn the Jews.

For example, Moses went through some pretty thick hieroglyphics for the sake of bearing his message of revelation. Yet he couldn't even take a forty-day leave of absence to commune with the Creator without his followers reverting to paganism. Even though they had witnessed the miracles— walking between the walls of seawater, given shade by a pillar of cloud during the day and warmed by a pillar of fire at night, subsisting on manna and quail and drinking water from the rock of twelve springs, all by the grace of God—when Moses stepped out of the picture for a little communion with The One who saved and protected them all, they set about making a useless idol of a flop-dropping quadruped! (Neh 9:9–18)

God's reaction? To advise Moses:

> Arise, go down quickly from here, for your people whom you brought out of Egypt have acted corruptly; they have quickly turned aside from the way which I commanded them; they have made themselves a molded image …I have seen this people, and indeed they are a stiff-necked people. Let Me alone, that I may destroy them and blot out their name from under heaven …(Deuteronomy 9:12–14)

The Old Testament continues by recounting the Jews' rebellion against God's commandments (Deuteronomy 9:22–24), their stubbornness and wickedness (Deuteronomy 9:27), their breaking of their covenant and God's resultant anger (Deuteronomy 31:16–21), with Moses effectively summing up:

> Take this Book of the Law, and put it beside the ark of the covenant of the lord your God, that it may be there as a witness against you; for I know your rebellion and your stiff neck. If today, while I am yet alive with you, you have been rebellious against the lord, then how much more after my death? Gather to me all the elders of your tribes, and your officers, that I may speak these words in their hearing and call heaven and earth to witness against them. For I know that after my death you will become utterly corrupt, and turn aside from the way which I have commanded you. And evil will befall you in the latter days, because you will do evil in the sight of the lord, to provoke Him to anger through the work of your hands (Deuteronomy 31:26–29).

In Deuteronomy 32:21, God is recorded as having said,

> They have provoked Me to jealousy by what is not God;
> They have moved Me to anger by their foolish idols.
> But I will provoke them to jealousy by those who are not a nation;
> I will move them to anger by a foolish nation.

This last line concerning "who are not a nation … a foolish nation" may strike a chord of interest, for who in the land of the Israelites were more divided than the Ishmaelites, or in other words, the Arabs? An uneducated and ignorant ("foolish," if you will), disparate and divided group of desert-dwellers in the pre-Islamic Period of Ignorance, they were so much "not a nation" that Alexander the Great, the Persian Empire, the

Roman Empire, and the Egyptians all passed them by. Why? Because there was no Arabian nation to conquer. They were so divided and spread out, so unorganized and tribal, that there was no national identity to address and no crown jewels to covet.

Yet, following the revelation of the Holy Qur'an, these people became united for the first time in history, rose up to develop the greatest intellectual institutes of their day, spread their territorial boundaries from Spain to the edge of China to establish, in the short span of twenty-five years, an empire that held dominion over more kingdoms and countries than the Roman Empire ever did in eight hundred years. In addition to which they subjugated the Jews, to effectively "move them to anger by a foolish nation."

And God foretold of even greater punishments:

> I will heap disasters on them;
> I will spend My arrows on them.
> They shall be wasted with hunger,
> Devoured by pestilence and bitter destruction;
> I will also send against them the teeth of beasts,
> With the poison of serpents of the dust.
> The sword shall destroy outside;
> There shall be terror within
> For the young man and virgin,
> The nursing child with the man of gray hairs ...
> Vengeance is Mine, and recompense;
> Their foot shall slip in due time;
> For the day of their calamity is at hand,
> And the things to come hasten upon them.
> (Deuteronomy 32:23–35)

And yet, despite God's repeated punishments, chastisements, curses, and condemnation, how often do we encounter Jews who contemplate the significance of such harsh statements of censure, as opposed to boastfully parroting the phrase of "chosen people"? The error is regrettable, for it has misguided many to disregard the Old Testament predictions of three prophets to follow. The Jews of Jesus' time understood this prediction, and that is why the Pharisees inquired into the identity of John the Baptist:

> Now this is the testimony of John, when the Jews sent priests and Levites from Jerusalem to ask him, "Who are you?" He confessed, and did not deny, but confessed, "I am not the Christ." And they asked him, "What then? Are you Elijah?" He said, "I am not." "Are you the Prophet?" And he answered, "No" (John 1:19–21).

After John the Baptist's evasive answer, the Pharisees persisted by inquiring, "Why then do you baptize if you are not the Christ, nor Elijah, nor the Prophet?" (John 1:25)

Christ, Elijah, and "the Prophet," clearly mentioned not just once, but twice. By the scripture, John the Baptist wasn't the Christ, although he may have been Elijah—despite John's alleged denial, Jesus Christ identified him as Elijah in Matthew 17:11–13. Inconsistencies aside, the critical issue is the identity of the third messenger. Who is "the Prophet"?

Since the Jewish scholars of John the Baptist's time anticipated three messengers to follow, we can reasonably expect to find evidence in the Old Testament, for from what other source would the Pharisees have known to expect three divinely appointed guests?

And, in fact, the Old Testament teems with predictions and descriptors of messengers to follow. Those passages aligned with John the Baptist and Jesus Christ are well known. Predictably, however, several passages do not fit the description of these two prophets—as we might expect, considering that the Jews anticipated a third. Among these predictors is Isaiah 42, in which the prophet in question is twice referred to as a messenger to the Gentiles (Isaiah 42:1 and 42:6), unlike Jesus Christ, who claimed not to have been sent "except to the lost sheep of the house of Israel" (Matthew 15:24).

Furthermore, consistent with other Old Testament predictors of an Ishmaelite prophet (Genesis 17:20, 21:13 and 21:18), Isaiah 42:11 describes the predicted prophet as an Ishmaelite in the line of Kedar—that is, the line of Muhammad's ancestry.

Relevant to this topic, the names Isaac and Ishmael might have been switched in the biblical scripture out of religious prejudice. This suggestion is not unreasonable, for other elements of the Old Testament story fit together like a square peg in a round hole.[146(EN)]

Why is this important? Because Isaiah 42 is not the only chapter in the Old Testament that predicts a prophet other than John the Baptist or Jesus Christ. Furthermore, as we shall soon see, there is reason to suspect this final prophet arose not from the line of the Jews, but from the line of the Ishmaelites.

And how will we know this final prophet? Jeremiah 28:9 states, "As for the prophet who prophesies of peace, when the word of the prophet comes to pass, the prophet will be known *as* one whom the lord has truly sent." If we accept this verse as a criterion by which to judge a prophet, Muslims are quick to point out that Muhammad prophesied peace. Furthermore, as we have discussed earlier, every prediction within the Holy Qur'an has either been fulfilled or, at the very least, remains unassailable. The "word of the prophet," it would seem, has "come to pass."

An additional point is that the Hebrew word for "peace" in Jeremiah 28:9 is *shalom,* the Arabic equivalent of which is *salam,* or "Islam." Hence, should the above verse be translated into Arabic, it would read, "As for the prophet who prophesies of *salam* ..." or "As for the prophet who prophesies of Islam ..."

Most significantly, however, Jesus Christ does not appear to have been the prophet mentioned in Jeremiah 28:9. True, Christians speak of Jesus Christ as the "Prince of Peace," but what did Jesus say? Something quite different: "Do not think that I came to bring peace on earth. I did not come to bring peace but a sword" (Matthew 10:34) and "Do *you* suppose that I came to give peace on earth? I tell you, not at all, but rather division" (Luke 12:51). So who is the predicted prophet who would prophesy peace (*salam,* or Islam), if not Jesus?

Let's ask Jacob. In Genesis 49:10, Jacob is recorded as having said,

> The scepter shall not depart from Judah,
> Nor a lawgiver from between his feet,
> Until Shiloh comes;
> And to Him *shall be* the obedience of the people.

Oookay. Who, or what, is "Shiloh?" A person, a place, an ideology? It doesn't much matter. Could "Shiloh" refer to Jesus Christ? Most certainly not, for he was born in the bloodline of Judah, from whom this verse predicts the scepter to depart. Could "Shiloh" refer to Islam, since both *Shiloh* and Islam mean peace? Well, maybe. But maybe not. Again, it doesn't much matter. What does matter is that the loss of the power of legislation and prophethood in the line of Isaac is foretold. It's a done deal. If the Old Testament is to be respected it either has happened, or will happen. After all, what is the entire book of Malachi about, if not the transfer of revelation from the wayward Israelites to the line of the Gentiles?

So what are we saying? That the Old Testament predicted a final prophet to follow Jesus—and not just a final prophet, but one in the line of the Ishmaelites?

Uh, yes, that's exactly what we're saying.

But if that were the case, wouldn't we expect Moses and Jesus to have spoken about this matter?

In fact, it appears that they did. According to Deuteronomy 18:18, Moses conveys God's revelation in these words: "I will raise up for them a Prophet like you from among their brethren, and will put My words in His mouth."

So who might be the prophet "like Moses"? It does not appear to have been Jesus Christ, for his lineage was through the line of Isaac, and the prophet in question was foretold to arise from among the brethren of the Israelites, which we cannot be faulted for understanding to mean the Ishmaelites. But let's be clear on this point. Does "brethren" mean "brothers," as seems intuitive, or does it mean offspring and relatives, as some authors propose?

Let's ask the Bible.

Genesis 16:12 teaches that Ishmael "shall dwell in the presence of all his brethren." Now, at the time this verse was revealed, Ishmael did not have offspring (for that matter, he wasn't even born yet). So let's give him fourteen years to mature, a year for his first child, another fifteen years for the first child to mature and blend bloodlines with that of an outsider, another fifteen years to maturity—nearly fifty years would have had to pass before Ishmael's bloodline could be diluted to twenty-five percent. So who could the brethren, in whose presence Ishmael would dwell, have been, if the only other Ishmaelites, for the next fifty years or so, would be his very own children and grandchildren? If the passage refers to his offspring, we would expect that to have been made clear. After all, to call a person's own offspring "brethren" is to snap and splice a few branches off the old family tree. The only remaining candidates for Ishmael's brethren, then, were his brothers, the Israelites.

So if we understand the foretold prophet to originate in the line of Ishmael, who might he be? Who was the prophet "like Moses"?

Let's list what we know of Moses, and see how this compares with Jesus Christ.

1. Moses was born of both father and mother, whereas Jesus was born by Virgin Birth, which is to say, without a father.

2. Moses married and had children, while Jesus was unmarried and celibate.

3. Moses, though initially rejected by his people, was eventually accepted, while Jesus to this day is rejected by the people to whom he was sent (i.e., the Israelites).

4. Moses was a king to his people, holding the power to assign capital punishment (Numbers 15:35–36), while Jesus held that "My kingdom is not of this world ..." (John 18:36). Furthermore, Jesus refused to assign capital punishment, as recorded in the story of the adulterous woman (John 8:3–7).

5. Moses conveyed a new law whereas Jesus professed the old.

6. Moses led his people to freedom in a mass exodus from the land of their persecution. There is no such parallel in the historical record of Jesus.

7. Moses was victorious over his enemies, whereas the biblical record claims that Jesus was the opposite—a victim of his enemies.
8. Moses was held by his people to have been a prophet, but a mortal man. Jesus is held by Christians to be God, a son of God, and/or partner with God.
9. Moses died a natural death and was buried. Christians claim Jesus was crucified and his body raised up to heaven.
10. Once dead, Moses stayed dead, whereas Christians claim Jesus was resurrected.

Now, what about Muhammad? He was born "from among the brethren" of the Israelites, in the lineage of Ishmael's second son, Kedar. And since Jesus fails to match Moses on the above criteria, let's see how Muhammad measures up:

1. Both Moses and Muhammad had fathers.
2. Both married and had children.
3. Both were initially rejected by their people, but were eventually accepted and elevated to hold the power of kings.
4. Having the power of kings, both had the power to assign capital punishment and direct the people to warfare.
5. Both conveyed modifications to the previous law, while maintaining unchanged the essential elements of monotheistic creed.
6. Moses led his people to freedom in a mass exodus from the land of their persecution; Muhammad did the same in directing his people from Makkah to Medina in the *hijra* (migration).

7. Both Moses and Muhammad were victorious over their enemies.
8. Both were held by their people to be prophets, but mortal men.
9. Both died natural deaths and were buried.
10. Neither suffered apotheosis, and neither was resurrected.

Whereas there are few significant parallels between Jesus and Moses, either in their worldly lives or prophetic missions, it is a challenge to find one single element of importance in the life of either Muhammad or Moses that does not have a close parallel in the life of the other.

Muhammad, unlike Jesus, was very much "like Moses."

Furthermore, Muhammad satisfies the full description of Deuteronomy 18:18–22, as follows (with the author's comparison in brackets):

I will raise up for them a Prophet like you [like Moses] from among their brethren [the Ishmaelites, from whom Muhammad takes his lineage], and will put My words in His mouth, and He shall speak to them all that I command Him [Muhammad claimed an oral revelation transmitted by the angel of revelation]. And it shall be *that* whoever will not hear My words, which He speaks in My name, I will require *it* of him. But the prophet who presumes to speak a word in My name [there was no doubt in whose name Muhammad claimed to speak, for all but one of the 114 *surahs* of the Holy Qur'an begin with the dedication, "In the name of Allah, most Gracious, most Merciful."], which I have not commanded him to speak, or who speaks in the name of other gods, that prophet shall die. [Muhammad transmitted the revelation of the Qur'an over a period of twenty-three years, without suffering the death promised to false prophets.]

And if you say in your heart, "How shall we know the word which the lord has not spoken?"—when a prophet speaks in the name of the lord, if the thing does not happen or come to pass, that *is* the thing which the lord has not spoken; the prophet has spoken it presumptuously; you shall not be afraid of him. [Nothing in the revelation of the Qur'an has ever failed to come true, and nothing has ever been proven false, contrary to the promised fate of false prophecies.]

So who believes the prophet predicted in Deuteronomy 18:18–22 is the same as "the prophet" foretold in John 1:21? Well, Christians, for one. Look up John 1:21 in any Bible containing cross-references (e.g., the New International Version Study Bible), and you will find Deuteronomy 18:18 cross-referenced. Christian scholars believe these two passages both predict the same final messenger.

Muslims claim that Muhammad fulfills all the Old Testament predictors of the foretold prophet, and wonder why the commandment, "Him you shall hear" is ignored by those who claim to keep the commandments of God. Christians, however, assert that the biblical prediction of a final prophet remains unfulfilled. In this manner, Muslims compare the Christian denial of Muhammad with the Jewish denial of Jesus. In their minds, both Christian and Jewish cases defy conclusive evidence, and both postures reveal more devotion to doctrine than to divinity.

For Christians, confirmation or refutation of this embarrassing charge should be found in what Jesus had to say on the subject.

3

Jesus Christ

Pressed into service means pressed out of shape.
—Robert Frost, "The Self-Seeker"

Who was Jesus Christ? That question has haunted the world of Christianity for two millennia. The historical Jesus is so shrouded in mystery as to have invited thousands of books on the subject, with nothing approaching a consensus of opinion. Many authors have stitched together comfortable pillows of conjecture upon which popular opinion reclines, whereas others rip the seams open and pull out the stuffing in an attempt to sort out the conflicting evidence. The German theologian Heinz Zahrnt builds one such convincing argument, which concludes:

> Once the biblical history had been divested of dogma, the Christ proclaimed by the Church seemed in unavoidable conflict with Jesus himself. There was a manifest contradiction between what historical investigation discovered about Jesus of Nazareth and what the Church said of him in its preaching, between what Jesus himself originally proclaimed and did and what the Church afterwards made of him.[147]

Regarding the deficiencies of the historical record, Zahrnt states the problem bluntly:

This was the reason why those who studied the life of Jesus could never escape from their predicament. How are the gaps to be filled in? In the worst instances this was done with clichés, in the best with historical fantasy ...
The image of the historical Jesus which was now being developed was not in fact simply drawn from the historical sources. It was largely governed by the presuppositions entertained by the writers themselves.[148]

Another German theologian, Martin Kähler, draws this conclusion:

The Jesus of the "Lives of Jesus" is nothing but a modern variation of the products of human inventive art, no better than the discredited dogmatic Christ of Byzantine Christology; both are equally far removed from the real Christ.[149]

The shock in reviewing such literature is not in discovering how little is known of the *private* life of this great messenger of God, but in learning how little is known of his *public* life, and just how freely people speculate on the unknown. Scant knowledge exists of the man who taught in the synagogues, lectured on the mount, and organized the guidance and feeding of the masses. For a man who toured the countryside, reportedly turning water into wine, calming storms, walking on water, exorcising demons, healing lepers, curing the blind, raising the dead—he must have attracted a lot of attention and made quite an impression. Why, then, is the historical record on Jesus so meager? And why has the little that *has* been passed down in the historical record been buried beneath conflicting dogmas, to the point that, "the discontinuity between the historical Jesus and the Christ of the Church became so great that it was almost impossible to recognize any unity between the two figures"?[150]

The critical question, then, becomes whether Jesus was the Christ of scripture or the Christ of Pauline (that is, Trinitarian) theology. The Christ of scripture spoke of a final prophet to follow. The Christ of Pauline theology spoke of no such thing, cancelling the primacy of seeking the final prophet by promising salvation based on faith alone—the Christian analogue of the Jewish concept of being "the chosen people." The Jews consider themselves chosen; Pauline Christians consider themselves forgiven. Neither viewpoint was endorsed by the prophets of scripture, and both prove destructive through inviting a false sense of spiritual security, religious elitism, and closed-mindedness. Who's going to seek the final prophet when they already consider themselves saved?

Similarly, the Christ of scripture spoke of himself as a "son of man," yet Pauline theology painted him to be "son of God." The Christ of scripture spoke of One God; the religious reformers partitioned the One God into three metaphysical plots. Jesus focused on God; Pauline Christians focus on Jesus, or even more oddly, on his mother. Jesus spoke of not changing the law; Paul discarded it. Jesus spoke of the final prophet and the angel of revelation; Pauline theologians twisted his words to imply an esoteric "holy spirit." Instead of seeking the final prophet foretold by Jesus, Pauline Christians focus their priorities upon embodying the "holy spirit," of whom their preachers claim to possess exclusive distribution rights.

Once the stark conflict between the Christ of scripture and the Christ of Pauline theology is recognized (see *MisGod'ed* for deeper discussion of this subject), Christians must rationally conclude that they can have one, but not both.

A person can fairly expect certain qualities from a prophet, including humility, honesty, benevolence, gentleness, kindness, and manners. We expect a prophet to be preoccupied with worship, rather than worldly pursuits. And, for the most part, the biblical sketch of Jesus Christ satisfies these expectations. But not always.

Cursing a fig tree for not bearing fruit (Matthew 21:19, Mark 11:20–21), likening Gentiles (and don't look now, but that is most of mankind, most of this book's audience, and most Christians) to dogs (Matthew 15:26, Mark 7:27) or swine (Matthew 7:6), and rebuffing his own mother, as if she were not of those who "does the will of my Father in heaven" or who "hear God's word and put it into practice" (Matthew 12:48–50, Mark 3:31–35, Luke 8:20–21)—these accounts drag one wheel on the soft shoulder of the road of lofty expectations. The resultant dust cloud is slightly off-putting, especially when pelted by the loose gravel of the claim that Jesus Christ lost faith in his Creator, questioning divine decree with the sacrilegious words, "My God, my God, why have you forsaken me?" (Matthew 27:46). History boils over with examples of righteous men and women who endured equal or greater suffering, persecution, and death in the path of what they believed to be obedience to Almighty God. The tales of such martyrs dying with staunch and intact faith are copious. Yet we are to believe that Jesus Christ died questioning the decree of his Creator? Socrates died without a word of impatience or despair.[151] Michael Servetus and Joan of Arc were burned to death with more honor, dignity, and unwavering faith. Once again, either the words attributed to Jesus are wrong, or the authors quoted the wrong man.

So what should we make of the above quotes? If they are to be believed, a more human (and less divine) Jesus emerges. And perhaps that is the point. On the other hand, if the above quotes are not to be believed, we return to the question of what part of the Bible *can* be trusted.

Having said that, the thrust of this book is to derive conclusions based upon a chain of accepted evidence, and not to throw one more straw of opinion onto the mountainous haystack of speculation. If the needle of truth regarding the historical Jesus has not been laid bare for analysis by the present age, it likely will remain buried until such time as he returns.

All the same, most Christians accept what the Bible says Jesus said. And it is from this perspective that those who await the foretold final prophet analyze the scripture and wonder, as the Jews did with Moses, what Jesus Christ had to say on the subject.

Concerning the assertion that the final prophet would arise from the line of Ishmael, Jesus is quoted as having taught the parable of the vineyard, the lesson of which is that God would replace those who defy Him with those who would "render to (God) the fruits in their seasons" (Matthew 21:41). Following this parable, Jesus reportedly said:

> Have you never read in the Scriptures:
> "The stone which the builders rejected
> Has become the chief cornerstone.
> This was the Lord's doing,
> And it is marvelous in our eyes"?
> Therefore I say to you, the kingdom of God will be taken from you and given to a nation bearing the fruits of it. And whoever falls on this stone will be broken; but on whomever it falls, it will grind him to powder.
> (Matthew 21:42–44)

The reaction of the chief priests and Pharisees? They "perceived that he was speaking of them" (Matthew 21:45).

Note that Jesus did not *threaten* that the kingdom of God (i.e., prophethood and revelation) would be taken away. A threat, by definition, is conditional, along the lines of, "If you don't do this, then such-and-such will happen." That is a threat. But the above is not a conditional threat; it is an unconditional decree. It was over. The decision had been made. It was going to happen. And furthermore, any who opposed the revelation when it came would either be broken or ground to powder.

Yee-ouch.

So here is a passage that prophesies the transfer of "the kingdom of God" from the Israelites to a "nation bearing the fruits of it." Not just a faithful nation, but one which would "become the chief cornerstone." Exactly whom this passage refers to is the subject of unrelenting debate. However, what defies debate is the fact that these verses predict transfer of prophethood outside the line of the Israelites. So who are the "stone which the builders rejected?" Who are slated to receive revelation? Ask a hundred Christians. Ask a thousand Jews. Ask Paul of Tarsus. The answer is always the same: the "rejected" are the Ishmaelites.

In the first book of this series, the "paraclete" Jesus Christ predicted to follow his ministry was analyzed, so repetition here is unnecessary. Suffice it to say that Jesus Christ was described as a "paraclete" in the First Epistle of John 2:1, and four passages of the Gospel according to John (14:16, 14:26, 15:26, and 16:7) foretell the coming of *another* paraclete. This foretold prophet is expected to be "the Spirit of truth" and to "abide with you forever" (John 14:16–17), to convey a comprehensive revelation, to revere Jesus Christ (John 14:26 and 15:26), and yet be rejected by the majority of mankind (John 14:17). One renowned scholar, after listing the evidence, concluded, "The Paraclete therefore is a parallel figure to Jesus himself; and this conclusion is confirmed by the fact that the title is suitable for both. It is clear from 14.16 that the source taught that there were two sendings of two Paracletes, Jesus and his successor, the one following the other."[152]

The concept of an unfulfilled prophecy leaves Christians with a blank scriptural check. Muslims, on the other hand, claim the final prophet *has* come. Regarded by his followers as "the Spirit of truth," Muhammad's honesty was unchallenged even by his enemies,[153(EN)] and he bore the distinctive reputation of having told the truth even when joking. The details of his life are preserved in extensive *hadith* records, which "abide" with mankind to the present day. Furthermore, the Holy Qur'an reveres Jesus Christ and clarifies his teachings. At the same time, the Qur'an is a comprehensive revelation accepted by over a billion Muslims, but rejected by the majority of mankind.

Why? What is so appealing to some and so distasteful to others about Muhammad and the revelation he conveyed? And do those who pass judgment upon Muhammad even know the man?

Those who reject Muhammad commonly do so based upon personal dislike of the man, his message, or both. Unfounded Western propaganda, which is overwhelmingly negative, frequently plays a role. The opinions and conclusions of non-Muslims based upon objective study are rare, but with that purpose in mind, we enter the next chapter.

4
Muhammad

In matters of style, swim with the current;
In matters of principle, stand like a rock.

—Thomas Jefferson

So who was Muhammad?

Several good biographies have been written, the most highly acclaimed in the English language being *Muhammad, His Life Based on the Earliest Sources*, by Martin Lings, and *When the Moon Split*, by Safi-ur-Rahman al-Mubarakpuri.[154(EN)] A full biography is not within the limits of this book, but some salient points can be introduced.

Muhammad ibn Abdullah[155(EN)] was born in Makkah into the powerful tribe of Quraysh in or about 570 CE. The time, place, and culture of his birth were dominated by idol worship and heathen practices. Muhammad's father died before he was born, and his mother passed away when he was six years old. The orphan Muhammad was raised by a Bedouin family who taught him the caravan trade and shepherding. Over time he became known for a high standard of ethics and honesty, gentleness, fairness, sobriety and a deep contemplative spirituality. He rose to wealth and high social position upon marriage to one of the most eligible widows of Quraysh, Khadijah, at the age of twenty-five. She was fifteen years his senior, yet he remained faithful to her throughout their loving marriage, unto her death.

By the age of forty he had secured a successful life, having been happily married with children, wealth, and high social position. Yet it was at this point that he began receiving revelation, in a terrifying upset to his accustomed peace and tranquility, and he sacrificed virtually everything of this world for the sake of conveying the message revealed through him. It was at the conclusion of that purpose that he passed from this worldly life in 632 CE.

The monotheism of the revelation made enemies of his tribesmen, whose religion required many idols, and of those Jews, Christians, and pagans who rejected his message. Forced first to flee and later to fight, the small band of early Muslims grew against remarkable odds. With time, Islam revolutionized life throughout the Arabian Peninsula, abolishing idol worship and other pagan practices, liberating women from the oppression of tribal custom, and establishing a noble code of conduct, morality, and social justice. More profound than any other accomplishment, the revelation established a religion in which worship was directed to the One God: a faith that has since grown to provide guidance and inspiration to one-fifth of the world's population.

The seventeenth-century Scottish writer Alexander Ross, though no friend of the Islamic religion, nonetheless neatly outlines Muhammad's purpose as follows:

> He did not pretend to deliver any new religion to them, but to revive the old one, which God gave first to Adam; and when lost in the corruption of the old world, restored it again by revelation to Abraham, who taught it his son Ismael their ancestor, and then he, when he settled first in Arabia, instructed men in the same; but their posterity degenerating into idolatry, God sent him now to destroy it, and restore the religion of Ismael. He allow'd both of

the Old and New Testament, and that Moses and Christ
were prophets sent from God; but that the Jews and
Christians had corrupted these Holy Writings, and that
he was sent to purge them from those corruptions, and to
restore the Law of God to that purity in which it was first
deliver'd …[156]

During his lifetime, Muhammad came to be respected in
his roles as father, friend, husband, neighbor, merchant, teacher,
preacher, judge, lawgiver, commanding general, statesman,
ruler and social and religious reformer. He was one of the most
influential men in history, yet he was illiterate and lived a life
of self-imposed poverty.

Muhammad's person and life is well-documented, from
physical appearance to traits, habits, teachings, and endorsements.
From the late 1800s, in a time and place where such compliments
to the Prophet were scant indeed, if not frankly condemned by
an oppressive Anglican Church, we read,

Mohammad was of middle height, rather thin, but broad
of shoulders, wide of chest, strong of bone and muscle.
His head was massive, strongly developed. Dark hair,
slightly curled, flowed in a dense mass almost to his
shoulders; even in advanced age it was sprinkled with
only about twenty gray hairs, produced by the agonies
of his "Revelations." His face was oval-shaped, slightly
tawny of colour. Fine long arched eye-brows were divided
by a vein, which throbbed visibly in moments of passion.
Great black restless eyes shone out from under long
heavy eyelashes. His nose was large, slightly acquiline.
His teeth, upon which he bestowed great care, were well
set, dazzling white. A full beard framed his manly face.
His skin was clear and soft, his complexion "red and
white," his hands were as "silk and satin," even as those

of a woman. His step was quick and elastic, yet firm as that of one who steps "from a high to a low place." In turning his face he would also turn his whole body. His whole gait and presence was dignified and imposing. His countenance was mild and pensive. His laugh was rarely more than a smile.

In his habits he was extremely simple, though he bestowed great care on his person. His eating and drinking, his dress and his furniture retained, even when he had reached the fullness of power, their almost primitive nature. The only luxuries he indulged in were, besides arms, which he highly prized, a pair of yellow boots, a present from the Negus of Abyssinia. Perfumes, however, he loved passionately, being most sensitive to smells. Strong drink he abhorred.

He was gifted with mighty powers of imagination, elevation of mind, delicacy and refinement of feeling. "He is more modest than a virgin behind her curtain," it was said of him. He was most indulgent to his inferiors, and would never allow his awkward little page to be scolded whatever he did. "Ten years," said Anas his servant, "was I about the Prophet, and he never said as much as 'uff' to me." He was very affectionate towards his family. One of his boys died on his breast in the smoky house of the nurse, a blacksmith's wife. He was very fond of children; he would stop them in the streets and pat their little heads. He never struck anyone in his life. The worst expression he ever made use of in conversation was, "What has come to him? May his forehead be darkened with mud!" When asked to curse someone, he replied, "I have not been sent to curse, but to be a mercy to mankind." "He visited the sick, followed any bier he met, accepted the invitation of a slave to dinner, mended his own clothes, milked the goats, and waited upon himself," related summarily another tradition. He never first withdrew his hand out of another man's palm, and turned not before the other had turned.

He was the most faithful protector of those he protected, the sweetest and most agreeable in conversation. Those who saw him were suddenly filled with reverence; those who came near him loved him; they who described him would say, "I have never seen his like either before or after." He was of great taciturnity, but when he spoke it was with emphasis and deliberation, and no one could forget what he said.[157]

Even Muhammad's greatest enemies, from the period of his life to contemporary times, admitted his virtues. George Sale filed a statement that documented abject hatred, buffered by admiration of Muhammad's personal virtues. In his preface "To the Reader" in his 1734 translation of the Holy Qur'an, Sale states,

For how criminal forever Mohammed may have been in imposing a false religion on mankind, the praises due to his real virtues ought not to be denied him; nor can I do otherwise than applaud the candour of the pious and learned Spanhemius, who, tho' he owned him to have been a wicked impostor, yet acknowledged him to have been richly furnished with natural endowments, beautiful in his person, of a subtle wit, agreeable behaviour, showing liberality to the poor, courtesy to every one, fortitude against his enemies, and above all a high reverence for the name of God; severe against the perjured, adulterers, murderers, flanderers, prodigals, covetous, false witnesses, etc. a great preacher of patience, charity, mercy, beneficence, gratitude, honouring of parents and superiors, and a frequent celebrator of the divine praises.[158]

Islamic history records a *hadith* in which Hind ibn Abi Hala, the son (by previous marriage) of Muhammad's wife, Khadijah, offers his own perceptive observations:

> The Messenger of Allah was of consecutive sorrows, continuous thought, never finding rest, long in silence. He did not speak without cause. He spoke with his full mouth (was not arrogant), and spoke concisely. His speech was just, with neither excess nor deficiency. He was not pompous, nor denigrating. He exalted all blessings no matter how small and never belittled a single one. He would never praise his food nor criticize it. He was never angered by matters of this life nor that which was associated with it. However, if justice was transgressed nothing could stand up to his anger until justice was established. He never became angry for his own self nor sought retribution for himself. If he gestured, he did so with his whole palm. If he was amazed, he overturned it. If he spoke, he struck with his right palm the inside of his left thumb. If he became angry he turned away, and when he was happy he lowered his gaze. The majority of his laughter was (restricted to) smiling.[159]

Similarly, Ali ibn Abi Talib, cousin to the prophet and one of the earliest caliphs of Islam, noted:

> He was not vulgar nor did he condone vulgarity, and he was not one to shout in the market place. He did not reward evil with evil, rather, he would forgive and overlook. He never in his life struck anything with his hand except when he was fighting in the name of Allah. He never struck a servant nor a woman, and I never saw him taking revenge for an injustice dealt him, except if the prohibitions of Allah were transgressed. For if the

prohibitions of Allah were transgressed he was among the strongest of them in anger. He was never given a choice between two matters but he chose the simplest of the two. If he entered into his home he was a man like any other, cleaning his own garment, milking his own goat, and serving himself.

He was continually smiling, gentle in manners, soft in nature. He was not severe, harsh-hearted, loud, abusive, or miserly. He would disregard that which he disliked, and no one ever despaired of him. He never responded to disparagement or evil words. He forbade himself three things: argument, arrogance, and that which did not concern him. And he relieved the people of three: He would not degrade any among them or abuse them, he would not search after their honor or private matters, and he would not speak except in matters which he hoped to be rewarded for. When he spoke his attendees would lower their heads as if birds had alighted upon them. Once he finished they would speak. They would not vie with one-another in his presence to speak, but when one would talk in his presence the rest would listen until he finished. Speech in his presence was that of the first among them. He would laugh with them, and wonder with them. He had patience with the strangers when they were gruff in speech and requests, to a degree that his companions would fetch them to him. He would say: "If you see someone in need, fetch him to me." He would not accept praise except from those who were balanced and not excessive. He would not interject into someone's speech unless they transgressed, in which case he would either rebuke them or else leave.[160]

One of the most beautiful and succinct comments recorded in the *hadith* literature reads: "He was the most generous of heart, truthful of tongue, softest in disposition, and noble in relationship."[161]

These quotes provide a peek through a small window into Muhammad's life and character. In striking contrast to the fuzzy profile of the historical Abraham, Noah, Moses and Jesus, Muhammad's character is brought into sharp focus by the many volumes of authenticated *hadith* that catalogue the most intimate descriptors of appearance and manners, character and conduct. As a result, those who choose to do so can view Muhammad's life in fine focus. In this regard, the English archeologist and scholar D.G. Hogarth wrote:

> Serious or trivial, his daily behaviour has instituted a canon which millions observe at this day with conscious mimicry. No one regarded by any section of the human race as Perfect Man has been imitated so minutely. The conduct of the Founder of Christianity has not so governed the ordinary life of his followers. Moreover, no founder of a religion has been left on so solitary an eminence as the Muslim Apostle.[162]

Paradoxically, Christians rarely imitate the little we know of Jesus Christ. In fact, as discussed in *MisGod'ed*, we are surprised to find the example of Jesus better preserved in the practices of Muslims than Christians. Choose an issue. "Rabbi" Jesus adhered to the strict "life for a life" Old Testament law. He grew his beard, wore flowing robes (and, for that matter, his mother wore the head scarf), avoided pork and usury, and abstained not just from fornication but also from the slightest extramarital physical contact with women. He prayed in prostration, spoke with humility, and taught the unity of God and his own humanity in prophethood. Rarely do Christians preserve these values. In fact, those who do are frequently disparaged by their own co-religionists, who not infrequently label them "Jesus freaks," as if there were something wrong with emulating a prophet.

As a model for emulation, Muhammad's character is well-documented:

He was sober and abstemious in his diet, and a rigorous observer of fasts. He indulged in no magnificence of apparel, the ostentation of a petty mind; neither was his simplicity in dress affected; but the result of a real disregard to distinction from so trivial a source …

His military triumphs awakened no pride, no vainglory, as they would have done had they been effected for selfish purposes. In the time of his greatest power, he maintained the same simplicity of manners and appearance as in the days of his adversity. So far from affecting regal state, he was displeased if, on entering a room, any unusual testimonial of respect were shown him. If he aimed at universal dominion, it was the dominion of the faith: as to the temporal rule which grew up in his hands, as he used it without ostentation, so he took no step to perpetuate it in his family.

The riches which poured in upon him from tribute and the spoils of war, were expended in promoting the victories of the faith, and in relieving the poor among its votaries; insomuch that his treasury was often drained of its last coin. Omar ibn Al Hareth declares that Mahomet, at his death, did not leave a golden dinar nor a silver dirhem, a slave nor a slave girl, nor anything but his gray mule Duldul, his arms, and the ground which he bestowed upon his wives, his children, and the poor. "Allah," says an Arabian writer, "offered him the keys of all the treasures of the earth, but he refused to accept them.[163]

The relevant question, however, is not whether we like, admire or respect Muhammad, but whether he was the prophet he claimed to be. In order to evaluate this claim, several challenges arise. Obviously, we must overlook slanders and abstain from prejudice, both positive and negative. We must begin our quest to establish the reality of Muhammad's case with a mental and emotional blank slate, for emotions frequently lead mankind astray. The facts, and only the facts, must be our guide.

Let us begin, then, by evaluating the commonly accepted criteria of prophethood. The biblical prophets have all passed this test, and so should the final prophet.

PART III
PROOF OF PROPHETHOOD

The best way to suppose what may come, is to remember what is past.

—George Savile, Marquis of Halifax

Many biblical prophets were predicted in previous scripture. Christian scholars link John the Baptist with the book of Malachi, and Jesus Christ with multiple predictions scattered throughout the Old Testament. Old and New Testament predictors, as discussed in *MisGod'ed*,[164] and in the preceding chapters on Moses and Jesus in this book, can easily be linked with Muhammad with equal or greater congruency. No wonder, then, that the *New Catholic Encyclopedia* remarks, "There is reason to believe that many Jews, expecting the imminent advent of a messiah in Arabia, showed special interest in him [i.e., Muhammad]."[165]

1
Miraculous Signs

A miracle is not the breaking of the laws of the fallen world.
It is the re-establishment of the laws of the kingdom.
—André Borisovich Bloom, *Living Prayer*

There are two kinds of miracles—those which surround a person and those which are channeled *through* a person. The first kind of miracle, which I'll call "miraculous signs," is the subject of this chapter and the second, which I'll call "miracles performed," is the subject of the next.

Examples of miraculous signs include God saving Daniel from the lions, Jonah from the whale, Abraham from the fire, and Moses from Pharaoh and his army. Certainly, the Virgin Birth of Jesus and the miracle of the star in the East rank high as well. Less known to Westerners is the miracle of the star that signaled the birth of another prophet. Hassan ibn Thabit, the legendary Muslim poet and a member of the *Sahaba* (Muhammad's companions), is but one witness. On the day of Muhammad's birth in Makkah, he was in Madina, over two hundred miles away, where he heard a Jew screaming at the top of his voice, "O my Jewish community, tonight the star of Ahmad (i.e., the foretold prophet, Muhammad) in which he was born upon, has arisen."[166] In a separate *hadith*, Zaid ibn Amr ibn Nufa'il related that on the day of Muhammad's birth he was in Syria, and a respected Jewish scholar told him, "A prophet has appeared in your country, or he is going to appear, because his star has arisen. Go back (to your country)! Believe in him, and follow him."[167]

There were other signs: a popular tradition among Muslims relates that when Muhammad was born, the "eternal" flame of the fire-worshiping Zoroastrians in Persia was miraculously extinguished. Many other incidents suggest that Muhammad enjoyed divine protection. As previously mentioned, Muhammad survived multiple attempts upon his life through divine intervention. In one case, a disbeliever accosted Muhammad when the Prophet was undressed for his afternoon rest. He took a sword Muhammad had hung from a tree and threatened him, asking, "Who will save you now?" When Muhammad replied, "Allah," the disbeliever's hand was instantly paralyzed and he dropped the sword.[168]

Abu Jahl approached Muhammad as he prayed, intending to crush his head with a boulder while he was in prostration. However, a vision of a vicious camel, which none of his companions could see, repelled him.[169]

Abu Lahab's wife (whose condemnation to hell is told in Part I, Chapter 7 of this book) once sought Muhammad for the purpose of stoning him. When she found his companion, Abu Bakr, she inquired about Muhammad's whereabouts, even though he sat directly next to Abu Bakr. Her eyes were apparently blinded to his presence.[170]

On other occasions Muhammad claimed to have been informed, either by miracle or by the angel of revelation, of plots to kill him. In this manner he avoided being poisoned,[171] pushed off a mountainside,[172] and crushed by a boulder dropped from a height.[173]

What makes this history compelling is not only that every plot of which Muhammad claimed to have received foreknowledge did in fact turn out to be true, but that there were no false alarms. Not a single time, throughout his life, did Muhammad claim a plot that did *not* prove true. He was not in the habit of refusing food out of suspicion of poison, changing his travel route to avoid being pushed off a cliff, or changing seats out of suspicion that he was being set up for a boulder-drop. He had every reason to be paranoid, and yet, he boldly forged forward upon his purpose, without taking what most people would consider to be sensible precautions. Only occasionally was his otherwise incautious schedule interrupted by a premonition or actual revelation of an attempt upon his life. And in those few instances, he was never wrong.

Muhammad, as previously mentioned, discharged his bodyguards upon receiving revelation that "Allah will defend you from men (who mean mischief)" (TMQ 5:67). He did not have a food taster, even though poisoning was a frequent threat to rulers of his time, and yet he was not plagued with suspicions or paranoia. Rather, he calmly approached each day and each circumstance with confidence that "God was with him." His behavior, in fact, displayed a confidence that speaks of his depth of trust in divine protection. Faced with the most hazardous of circumstances, he cultivated an almost superhuman calm.

For example, on the night of his planned emigration from Makkah to Medina, a mob of assassins surrounded Muhammad's house. Muhammad's response? Instead of furtively hiding, attempting to slyly creep past or to make a mad dash for freedom, he simply trusted in the protection of his Creator, supplicated Allah and recited from the Holy Qur'an. Then, he strode out of his residence and through the midst of his enemies whom he found miraculously to be struck senseless, and out of Makkah.

Later, when evading his pursuers en route to Medina, he and his companion, Abu Bakr, hid in a small cave on Mount

Thawr. When their pursuers approached the mouth of the cave, Muhammad stilled Abu Bakr's fears with the soothing reminder that Allah was their protector. Although they sat no more than a few steps inside the cave, the pursuers left without entering. When Muhammad and Abu Bakr investigated, they found the cave's entrance obstructed by an acacia tree, a large spider's web, and a dove upon a newly-built nest. The pursuers had turned back, confident that no one could have entered the cave without disturbing such wonders. Yet the tree, the web, and the nest had not been there when Muhammad and Abu Bakr had entered the cave.

Similarly, when Suraqah ibn Malik caught up with the two on open ground, Abu Bakr recognized the great warrior. However, Muhammad's confidence remained unshaken as he calmed Abu Bakr's fears, saying, "Don't be downcast, verily, Allah is with us."[174] As we shall see in the following pages, Suraqah's attempts to apprehend the two were frustrated by similarly supernatural events, and Muhammad and Abu Bakr were able to continue to their planned destination.

At the decisive Battle of Badr, the Muslim army of three hundred faced thirteen hundred Quraysh. The Muslims had two horsemen, the Quraysh, one hundred. The Muslims had few weapons; six hundred of the Quraysh wore protective chain mail. What did Muhammad do? Order retreat? Organize guerrilla warfare? No. In a symbolic gesture, he threw a handful of dust and gravel at the distant enemy and supplicated, "Confusion seize their faces!" Immediately, a violent sandstorm sprang up in the faces of the enemy, and Allah revealed, "When you threw (a handful of dust), it was not your act, but Allah's ..." (TMQ 8:17). The end of the battle saw seventy of the Quraysh dead, a similar number captured, and a scant fourteen Muslims killed, despite the fact that the

Muslims were under-equipped and outnumbered more than four-to-one. Following the battle, both sides testified to having seen angels fighting in the ranks of the Muslims.[175,176]

These are only a few of the incidents in which forces of nature were recruited to serve Muhammad. On another occasion, the Makkan pagans drafted a pact to boycott the Muslims until Muhammad renounced his claim to prophethood or was ostracized by his clan. After three years of lethal starvation, some of the pagans sought an end to the suffering of their Muslim relatives. As the pagan Quraysh debated, Muhammad had a revelation that ants had eaten the parchment on which the unholy pact had been written, except for the words glorifying Allah. Muhammad's uncle, Abu Talib, conveyed this revelation to the pagans, and promised to surrender Muhammad to them if the revelation proved false. When the pagans retrieved the pact, they found ants had eaten everything but the words, "In the name of Allah." They conceded that the proclamation was cancelled by Allah, using ants as His agents, and cancelled the boycott.[177]

In addition, Muhammad's caravan companion, Maisara, reported that the Prophet was followed by clouds in the desert, providing shade. Bahira, the Nestorian monk of Syria, noted the same phenomena when Muhammad was a child of twelve, passing through the Basra market with the caravan of his uncle, Abu Talib. After questioning Muhammad, Bahira became increasingly certain that he was the foretold final prophet and physically examined him. He found what he was looking for: a birthmark he claimed to be the seal of prophethood described in scriptures of old as a mark of the final prophet.[178]

The most dramatic example of this class of miracle was the mystical nighttime journey described by Muslims as *Al-Isra' w'al-Mir'raj* (i.e., the journey and ascension). Tradition relates that angel Gabriel transported Muhammad through the sky from Makkah to Jerusalem, from where they then ascended through the heavens. When Muhammad reported this miracle to the people of Makkah on the morning of his return, his claim met with understandable consternation. How could Muhammad possibly have traveled to Jerusalem—a one-way journey of not less than twenty days, ascended through the seven heavens, and returned to Makkah—all in one night? And yet, when challenged, Muhammad described Jerusalem in exquisite detail to those who knew the city well, even though he had never been there.[179]

Furthermore, the second century AH[180(EN)] Islamic historian, Ibn Hisham, narrated that while upon this heavenly journey, Muhammad reported he had seen a Bedouin on caravan seeking a lost camel, and had directed him from his vantage point in the sky to the camel visible from his lofty perspective. Muhammad described the approaching caravan as two days distant, and included in his description the distinctive markings of the lead camel. He described how one camel had broken its leg, as well as the features of all the other riders and their camels.

Pretty wild claims, a person might have thought.

And yet, not only did the caravan arrive in two days, complete with the distinctive lead camel and all other riders outfitted as described, but one of the Bedouins confirmed he had been guided to his lost camel by a voice from the nighttime sky.[181]

2
Miracles Performed

A miracle is an event which creates faith.
That is the purpose and nature of miracles.
—George Bernard Shaw, Saint Joan

When we consider the qualities that define a prophet, one of the things we think of are miracles. Miraculous events distinguish the prophets from other mortals, whereas miracles performed by the prophets themselves convey not only divine favor, but authority. Those miracles associated with Moses and Jesus are well known, and those associated with Muhammad are so numerous as to warrant another book entirely.

This point is not an exaggeration. Many books have been written, in English as well as in Arabic, upon just this subject.[182] The miracles attributed to Muhammad include everything from predictions to physical feats, but by far the greatest miracle is the Qur'an itself. The unmatched eloquence, consistency with prior (unknown) revelation, confirmation of previously unknown history, precocious statements of scientific fact, predictions, unconquered challenges and much more, have all been discussed above. When taken in total, we are left with a revelation of unmatched perfection. And if that is not a miracle, then what is?

Nonetheless, we have reason to question what miracles Muhammad is recorded as having performed.

The answer is, a lot.

An exhaustive list is not practical within the limits of this chapter, but those desiring greater detail can read the aforementioned biographies, as well as *Ash-Shifa*, by Al-Qadi 'Ayad (now available in English translation), and the many collections of *hadith*. Within the covers of these books, we encounter a wealth of miracles beyond easy cataloguing. We also encounter a methodology of historical authentication and record-keeping that puts Western archives of *any* period to shame.

We find stories of Muhammad, through invoking blessings from Allah, bringing milk to the dry udders of non-productive sheep, energizing camels virtually too weary to walk into the fastest of the bunch, feeding and watering the masses from miniscule quantities, and transforming a stick of wood into a sword for a soldier, Ukashah ibn Mihsan Al-Asdi, whose weapon had broken at the Battle of Badr.

Scores of the hungry poor were fed from a bowl of milk that appeared sufficient for only one. An army numbering over a thousand was fed from a measure of flour and pot of meat so small as to be thought sufficient for only ten persons at the "Battle of the Trench," after which the meal seemed undiminished. Another army of fourteen hundred, headed for the Battle of Tabuk, was fed from a few handfuls of mixed foodstuffs, over which Muhammad invoked blessings, and the increase was sufficient to fill not only the stomachs of the army, but their depleted saddlebags as well.

An expedition of eighty men on one occasion, and an army of fourteen hundred (en route to settle the Treaty of Hudaibiya) on another, were provided enough water for drinking and making ablution from mere handfuls of water less than sufficient for one.

Evil spirits (*jinn*) were exorcised, the broken leg of Abdullah ibn 'Ateeq and the war-wounded leg of Salama ibn Aqua'a healed on the spot, the inflamed eye of Ali ibn Abi Talib cured, the bleeding wound of Al-Harith ibn Aws cauterized and healed, the poisonous sting of Abu Bakr's foot quieted, and the vision of a blind man restored. On another occasion, Qutadah ibn An-Nu'man was wounded in the Battle of Badr so severely that his eye prolapsed onto his cheek. His companions wanted to cut off the attachments but Muhammad supplicated over the eye, replaced it, and from that day on Qutadah could not tell which was the injured eye and which not.

Until the Battle of Uhud, that is.

At the Battle of Uhud an arrow struck Qutadah in the eye socket while he was defending Muhammad, and when they tried to remove the arrow, the eye came with it. But Muhammad supplicated, "Allah protect his eye as he protected my face, and make this eye the best eye he has, and the strongest eye he can see with." Muhammad replaced the once-orphaned eye in its socket, and thereafter it became Qutadah's strongest eye.[183]

Muhammad once called for rain from a cloudless sky in a time of drought, whereupon the sky filled with clouds and the earth was painted with rain until, one week later, he was requested to ask Allah for an end to the deluge. In response, Muhammad prayed for the rain to be "around us, but not upon us," whereupon the city became surrounded by rain but spared the damaging effects of the prolonged downpour.

Many times Muhammad received revelation that, though not included in the Holy Qur'an, proved prophetic. All such information proved to be transmitted by other than temporal means. On one occasion Muhammad advised messengers from Persia, upon arrival in Madina, that their emperor had been murdered during their absence. When the messengers returned to Yemen they were met with a letter, just received from the new ruler of Persia, that confirmed the news. Since there was no way Muhammad could have known of the assassination, other than through revelation, the Persian governor of Yemen and his subjects accepted Islam on this evidence alone.[184]

Similarly, Muhammad predicted, "Yamama is bound to give rise to a liar who will arrogate prophethood to himself but he will subsequently be killed."[185] The prediction came true when a man named Musailimah falsely claimed prophethood in Yamama. Though Muhammad advised him, "You are doomed. Even if you repented and stopped what you were doing, Allah appointed that you would be slain,"[186] Musailimah persisted and, true to the promise, was slain during the caliphate of Abu Bakr.[187]

Another false prophet, Al-Aswad al-'Ansi, was killed in Yemen one day before Muhammad died. Yet Muhammad informed Al-Aswad's delegates that news of his death had reached him through divine revelation. Following Muhammad's demise, the veracity of his statement was confirmed from sources in Yemen.[188]

Amir's martyrdom at the battle of Khaibar was foretold, as was the condemnation of one of the Muslim soldiers, who later committed the unforgivable sin of suicide.[189] In one of the boldest predictions ever, Muhammad related, "When Khusraw [i.e., Chosroes—the emperor of Persia] is ruined, there will be no Khusraw after him; and when Caesar is ruined, there will be no Caesar after him. By Him in Whose Hands my life is, you will spend their treasures in Allah's cause."[190]

Indeed, the Muslims did capture the lands of Chosroes, as well as those of Heraclius, the Eastern Roman emperor. The lines of these two emperors came to an end and the wealth of their treasuries was spent in the Muslim cause.

When asked by the pagan Quraysh to provide a miracle, Muhammad directed their vision to the nighttime sky and showed them the moon split in two. The moon split in two? Pretty farfetched, to the minds of many. But others acknowledge that all creation is subject to the Creator. If God could divide a sea for Moses, so too could he split the moon for Muhammad.

When called to wrestle Rukanah, an unbeaten champion, Muhammad won miraculously. Merely touching Rukanah on the shoulder, the champion fell down, defeated. In a rematch, the miracle was repeated. A third challenge brought the same result.

When asked to call for rain, he did, and rain fell. When requested to feed the people, his supplications brought sustenance; from where, the people did not know. When interceding as a healer, wounds and injuries simply disappeared.

In short, Muhammad's supplications brought relief and blessings to the believers. And yet, whether being humiliated amidst his tribe and loved ones, stoned in Ta'if, starved in Makkah or beaten beside the Kaba, Muhammad faced his personal trials, of which there was an abundance, with patience, persistence, and forbearance.

We learn something interesting about Muhammad in this regard. Whereas he readily beseeched Allah to relieve the believers' suffering, rarely did he seek divine intervention for himself. Considering the tumultuous time in which he lived, it is this quality of selfless patience and constancy that intrigues us to learn more of this great man's character.

3
Character

Some people strengthen the society just by being the kind of people they are.

—John W. Gardner

Close your eyes and think of Abraham, Ishmael or Isaac, and what do you see? Not much, I bet. Now close your eyes and think of Noah, Moses, Jesus, and what do you see? Movie clips, perhaps an image you saw in a stained glass window, a mural or painting, a magazine cartoon or even an illustrated children's book. You see more, but is any of it accurate?

Intuitively, we know that all prophets exhibited exemplary character. However, we have a hard time reconciling this with the biblical stories of Noah stripped naked and passed out drunk, of Lot committing incest (albeit unknowingly) while intoxicated, and of David contracting a murder. Our consternation increases when we read of Judah committing fornication and of Jesus cursing a fig tree, degrading the Gentiles and rebuking his mother.

These stories don't jibe with our expectations.

Furthermore, our desire for details remains frustrated. The paucity of information regarding the biblical prophets, speckled with unseemly inconsistencies such as those mentioned above, mix together to form a collage of blurred, Picasso-like portraits. The curve of one concept skirts the shadow of another, less seemly design. Details necessary to bring this conflict into focus are largely lacking. What was Abraham like? Well, you know, he was a prophet. Yes, but I want details. Oh, sorry, can't help you there.

Whereas the situation with the biblical prophets seems irresolvable, the good news is that similar difficulties do not exist in the case of the prophet Muhammad. The image we gain from books of history and *hadith* is remarkably clear, consistent, and compelling.

For one thing, Muhammad appears to have been nothing if not an example of piety. Scanning opinions of the past, we find comments such as,

> The essential sincerity of his (Muhammad's) nature cannot be questioned; and an historical criticism that blinks no fact, yields nothing to credulity, weighs every testimony, has no partisan interest, and seeks only the truth, must acknowledge his claim to belong to that order of prophets who, whatever the nature of their physical experience may have been, in diverse times and in diverse manners, have admonished, taught, uttered austere and sublime thoughts, laid down principles of conduct nobler than those they found, and devoted themselves fearlessly to their high calling, being irresistibly impelled to their ministry by a power within.[191]

And:

> His readiness to undergo persecution for his beliefs, the high moral character of the men who believed in him and looked up to him as leader, and the greatness of his ultimate achievement—all argue his fundamental integrity. To suppose Muhammad an impostor raises more problems than it solves. Moreover, none of the great

figures of history is so poorly appreciated in the West as
Muhammad. Western writers have mostly been prone
to believe the worst of Muhammad, and, wherever an
objectionable interpretation of an act seemed plausible,
have tended to accept it as fact. Thus, not merely must we
credit Muhammad with essential honesty and integrity of
purpose, if we are to understand him at all; if we are to
correct the errors we have inherited from the past, we must
in every particular case hold firmly to the belief in his
sincerity until the opposite is conclusively proved …[192]

Muhammad lived a life, acknowledged by both Muslims
and non-Muslims alike, devoted to the delivery of the message
he claimed to be that of revelation. Worldly comforts were of
little or no concern to him. On the contrary, his life is recorded
as having been so abstentious that, for normal people, it would
have overloaded tolerances and tripped the circuit breaker of
the bearable.

History relates that Muhammad lived in single room,
dirt-brick apartments comparable in size to a small bedroom
of modern dimensions. He dressed in common clothing,
slept on a rough leather mat stuffed with date-palm fiber, ate
whatever was available during times of hardship, and partook
of unrefined foods, in moderation, during times of plenty.

On occasion, Muhammad survived for months on nothing
but dates and water, with an occasional treat of camel's milk.
He abstained from luxuries from the first day of revelation
until the day he died, to the point of refusing bread made
from finely milled flour. He routinely prayed two thirds of the
night, fasted in all seasons, and gave away any gifts or profits
he received to those in need. He was described as having been
shyer than a virgin in her boudoir, yet the most stalwart of
fighters in battle. Ali, himself famous for combat bravery,

related, "Whenever the fight grew fierce and the eyes of fighters went red, we used to resort to the Prophet for succor. He was always the closest to the enemy."[193]

Muhammad's generosity was legendary, his manners exemplary, his comportment inspiring. He died, as he lived, a pauper, having given his weapons to the Muslims and the last seven dinars in his possession to charity. He left behind, at the height of his success, a riding mule, his armor (which was mortgaged to a wealthy Jew), and a piece of land designated for charity. To the nine wives who outlived him, he left behind Allah's promise to provide for His servants: a promise history reveals to have been handsomely fulfilled. To his one surviving daughter, Fatimah, he left the glad tidings that she would be the first of his family to join him in the afterlife: news in which she rejoiced. Six months later, and despite Fatimah's youth compared with that of Muhammad's surviving wives, his word was proven true, even after death.

Anything but a self-centered sample of pampered royalty, Muhammad used to milk his own goat, mend his own clothes, cobble his own shoes, serve his family in their home, and attend to the poor and ailing. When manual labor was called for, he would haul two stones when all others carried one. In raising the Quba mosque in Medina, he was the first to lay bricks and stones. At the "Battle of the Trench" he dug beside his followers, in one instance shattering a boulder his companions, working together, had been unable to budge. Asking no one to do what he would not do himself, Muhammad refused his companions' offers at the Battle of Uhud to combat a challenger (Ubai ibn Khalaf) in his stead and, facing the horseman on foot, dealt him a mortal wound.

Aristotle defined the doctrine of the golden mean as the existence of virtue at the middle point between the opposite extremes of self-indulgence and self-renunciation. Similarly, the Islamic religion stresses the virtue of taking the "middle path" with regard to permissible things. There is a time for work and a time for play, but then again there is a time for prayer and contemplation—acts that demand physical and psychological commitment, but that bring the reward of inner peace. Islam teaches, in most circumstances, to partake of food in moderation. However, when breaking fast, Muslims may feast. Money is neither to be hoarded in the manner of a miser, nor wasted in the manner of a spendthrift. And although the virtues of charity are stressed, the only obligation upon the Muslim is to pay the *zakat*, or poor-due.[194(EN)] Worldly pleasures are to be enjoyed, but not to the point of transgression. On the opposite side of the scale, self-denial is not condemned unless practiced to an extreme. The ideal Muslim, in other words, is neither epicurean nor ascetic. However there is nothing wrong, and actually a great deal to be admired, in being *zahid*.

The Arabic word *zahid* has no English equivalent, but is probably best translated as "stoic." Like the stoics, who assert that happiness depends upon inner peace rather than outward circumstance, *zahids* consider material comforts to be nice but not necessary, and find their pleasure from within. Once such an overriding peace is discovered, material comforts tarnish into insignificance.

Unlike the maladjusted, dissatisfied wealthy, *zahids* take the Creator, and not the material elements of His creation, to be their focus. If money, comforts, and sensual pleasures enter their lives, well, that's great. But if not, well, that's okay too, for patience and piety are the true keys to peace and satisfaction.

To make a long story short, Muhammad was a *zahid*. Whether suffering deprivation, beatings and abuse or surrounded by the wealth of an expanding empire, he remained constant in his convictions, unattached to material goods, and patient in suffering. Although his living conditions were outwardly those of an ascetic, he was not an ascetic at all, for he did not practice self-denial. Rather, he was indifferent to wealth, and freely gave whatever he had to others. He preferred to divest himself of anything that distracted him from the practice of his religion, so we encounter stories of Muhammad giving away a colorful garment on one occasion, and the last of his money on another.

A religious leader who shunned glorification, an emperor who eschewed finery and distinction, a ruler who toiled beside his followers, a general who fought at the front of his army—Muhammad was all these things. He was a man who reformed a nation, established a state, and conveyed a revelation destined to guide over one-fifth of mankind in the present day. And yet, his sober demeanor and admirable humility cast a cloak of commonality over this completely uncommon man, sufficient to inspire the love of his followers.

> "I have seen," said the ambassador sent by the triumphant Kuraish to the despised exile at Medina; "I have seen the Persian Chosroes and the Greek Heraclius sitting upon their thrones, but never did I see a man ruling his equals as does Muhammad."
> Head of the State as well as of the Church, he was Caesar and Pope in one; but he was Pope without the Pope's pretensions, and Caesar without the legions of Caesar. Without a standing army, without a body-guard, without a palace, without a fixed revenue, if ever any man had the right to say that he ruled by a right Divine, it was Mohammad; for he had all the power without its instruments and without its supports.[195]

We have seen how Muhammad's honesty was unquestioned, to the point where even non-believers trusted his word. When he met Suraqah ibn Malik during his emigration from Makkah to Medina, his companion, Abu Bakr, recognized the great warrior. However, Muhammad's confidence remained unshaken as he calmed Abu Bakr's fears, saying, "Don't be downcast, verily, Allah is with us."[196] Enticed by the reward of one hundred camels, offered by the pagan Quraysh for Muhammad's return, Suraqah was the only Quraysh'ite warrior to have intercepted the two, alone and unarmed. However, he ran into a slight difficulty.

Upon drawing near, Suraqah's horse stumbled and threw him. This was sufficiently unusual for this noted horseman that he stopped to reconsider. As was the pagan Arabs' habit in such circumstances, he drew lots in order to divine whether or not to continue, and found the divination unfavorable. Nonetheless, he allowed his caution to be trampled by his lust for the hundred fuzzy, ill-tempered humps of reward, and so returned to the chase. His horse stumbled again, and he fell. Suraqah remounted. Stumbled and fell. Remounted. The combination of the unpropitious divination and the repeated insults to his body and pride served to awaken him to the stark peculiarity of this chain of events. With considerably more prudence, he approached close enough for Muhammad to call out and promise that if Suraqah would abandon his pursuit, one day Suraqah would wear the bracelets and crown of Chosroes, the emperor of Persia.

Even though he was not a Muslim, upon hearing such a promise from a man known to him as "As-Saadiq Al-Ameen" (the truthful; the trustworthy), Suraqah gave up the chase and returned to Makkah, confident that one day the promise would be fulfilled.

Now, Suraqah eventually accepted Islam, outlived Muhammad by more than a decade, survived multiple military campaigns against sizeable (if not unbelievable) odds, participated in the defeat of the Persian Empire and lived to wear the crown and bracelets of Chosroes.

Wow. Amazing prophecy.

Yes, but that's not the most important point to be made.

At the time Muhammad made his prophecy to Suraqah, he was the spiritual leader of a tiny group, numbering in the hundreds, and running for their lives from the pagan Quraysh. And yet the non-Muslim Suraqah accepted Muhammad's assurance that one day this meager group of outcasts, who had failed to establish Muhammad's authority in the small desert town of Makkah, would grow to overthrow the major world power of Persia. And furthermore that he, Suraqah, would wear the crown and bracelets of the monarch.

It's not hard to imagine the thoughts that would have flashed through an average Bedouin's mind upon hearing such a seemingly outrageous prophecy:

"Get that funky dung beetle out of here! You expect me to believe ..."

"Here, try these on for size."

"What? Oh, hey, this crown pinches a tad, but the bracelets fit just ..."

To have accepted such a promise demanded conviction, if not in the divine role of the messenger, then in Muhammad's honesty. And there's the startling incongruity: Many of Muhammad's contemporaries refused the message of Islam, but nonetheless trusted him to the letter of his word. Dramatic examples speak for themselves, beginning with the unanimous consensus of the entire population of Muhammad's native city of Makkah.

Muhammad first declared his appointment to prophethood

by assembling the people of Makkah and announcing the fact. However, prior to making his announcement, he tested their trust by asking if they would believe him, should he state that an army was approaching from the other side of the mountain. One of the populace responded that they had never caught him lying, and not a single person objected. And they had known him for forty years.

When Muhammad followed this vote of confidence by proclaiming his prophethood, the people refused his message but not his honesty.[197]

How do we make sense of this? Let's ask Abu Jahl.

Abu Jahl was one of the greatest enemies to Muhammad and the message of Islam. As you may remember, he once swore he would crush Muhammad's head with a boulder, only to fail in the attempt. Not to go home empty-handed, he spent the remainder of his life persecuting Muhammad's followers. In one case of horrific brutality, he killed a defenseless Muslim woman, Sumaya bint Khibat, by thrusting a spear into her genitals. Eventually he was killed while leading the Quraysh'ite army against the Muslims in the Battle of Badr.

He was no soft-spoken critic.

Nonetheless, it is written that Abu Jahl repudiated Muhammad's correctness, but not his honesty, with the words, "We do not accuse you of being a liar, but verily we reject what you have come with."[198]

Following this exchange, the verse was revealed, "We know that you, (O Muhammad), are saddened by what they say. And indeed, they do not call you untruthful, but it is the verses of Allah that the wrongdoers reject." (TMQ 6:33)[199]

Interestingly enough, although this would have been one of the easiest verses for the disbelievers to contest, none of them ever did.

So how deep did this confusing conviction go? Deeper than Ubai ibn Khalaf's wound, that's for sure.

Here's the story: Ubai once threatened to kill Muhammad, who stated that no, it would be *he* who killed Ubai instead. The two fought at the Battle of Uhud, and Muhammad inflicted a wound upon Ubai that appeared to be no more than a small scratch on the neck. Nonetheless, Ubai's confidence in the word of a man of whom he had never witnessed a lie or an unfulfilled promise was such that he told his companions, "He [Muhammad] had already told me when we were in Makkah: 'I will kill you.' By Allah, had he spat on me, he would have killed me."

Perhaps Ubai's wound was deeper than reported, and he died of an internal injury. Perhaps he died of a panic-induced stroke or heart attack. Either way, Muhammad killed him, as promised. More significantly, Ubai's fellow warriors ascribed the severity of his affliction not to his wound, but to his depth of trust in Muhammad's promise, for they counseled Ubai, "By Allah you are scared to death."[200] And die he did.

An isolated event?

No, not really.

On another occasion, a disbeliever named 'Utaibah ibn Abi Lahab made the poor career choice of abusing the prophet, whereupon Muhammad supplicated, "O Allah! Set one of Your dogs on him."

Some time later, when traveling in Syria, 'Utaibah and his companions spotted a lion nearby.[201] Remembering Muhammad's words, 'Utaibah said, "Woe to my brother! This lion will surely devour me just as Muhammad supplicated. He has really killed me in Syria while he is in Makkah." Even though 'Utaibah had been forewarned, the beast rushed into the group and crushed his head.[202]

Perhaps the most impressive story is encountered in *Sahih al-Bukhari,* one of the two most respected and rigorously authenticated collections of *hadith.*[203(EN)] This story relates Heraclius' interrogation of Abu Sufyan. Now, we should note that Abu Sufyan was anything but a friend to Muhammad. Prior to the Muslim conquest of Makkah, Abu Sufyan was a member of the elite alliance of powerful Quraysh'ites devoted to defaming Muhammad and destroying the Islamic message. These were men who stooped to the lowest tactics and the vilest deeds to undermine the growth of Islam. Yet, although they would not refrain from lying about Muhammad when they could get away with it, they were reticent to propagate lies that would have been condemned by their people. For the Makkan Arabs knew Muhammad's character and would have rejected slanders upon his person.

Unlike those who slander Muhammad today (all the while knowing little or nothing about him), those who lived with him, walked and talked with him, managed affairs with him and, in short, knew him through intimate, life-long relations, refused to call him a liar.

The tradition relates:

Allah's Messenger (peace be upon him) wrote to Caesar and invited him to Islam. Allah's Messenger (peace be upon him) sent Dihyah al-Kalbi with his letter and ordered him to hand it over to the Governor of Busrah who would forward it to Caesar, who as a sign of gratitude to Allah, had walked from Hims to Ilya (i.e. Jerusalem) when Allah had granted him victory over the Persian forces.

So when the letter of Allah's Messenger (peace be upon him) reached Caesar, he said after reading it, "Seek for me any one of his people, if at present here, in order to ask him about Muhammad." At that time Abu Sufyan ibn Harb was in Sha'm with some men from Quraysh who had come (to Sham) as merchants during the truce that had been concluded between Allah's Messenger (peace be upon him) and the pagans of Quraysh.

Abu Sufyan narrated, "Caesar's messenger found us somewhere in Sha'm so he took me and my companions to Ilya (Jerusalem). We were admitted into Caesar's court, to find him sitting in his royal court wearing a crown and surrounded by the senior dignitaries of the Byzantines.

"He said to his interpreter, 'Ask them who among them is a close relation to the man who claims to be a prophet.'"

Abu Sufyan said, "I replied, 'I am the nearest relative to him.' He asked, 'What degree of relationship do you have with him?' I replied, 'He is my cousin.' And there was none of Banu Abdul Manaf[204(EN)] in the caravan except myself. Caesar said, 'Let him come nearer.' He then ordered my companions to stand behind me near my shoulder and said to his interpreter, 'Tell his companions that I am going to ask this man about the man who claims to be a prophet. If he tells a lie, they should give me a sign.'"

Abu Sufyan added, "By Allah! Had it not been shameful that my companions label me a liar, I should not have spoken the truth about Muhammad when Caesar asked me. But I considered it shameful to be labeled a liar by my companions. So I told the truth.

"Caesar then said to his interpreter, 'Ask him what kind of family does Muhammad belong to.' I replied, 'He belongs to a noble family among us.' He said, 'Has anybody else among you ever claimed the same before him?' I replied, 'No.' He said, 'Had you ever known him to tell lies before he claimed that which he claimed?' I replied, 'No.' He said, 'Was anybody amongst his ancestors a king?' I replied, 'No.' He said, 'Do the noble or the poor follow him?' I replied, 'It is the poor who follow him.' He said,

'Are they increasing or decreasing?' I replied, 'They are increasing.' He said, 'Does anybody among those who embrace his religion become displeased and then renounce his religion?' I replied, 'No.' He said, 'Does he break his promises?' I replied, 'No, but we have now a truce with him and we are afraid that he may betray us.'" Abu Sufyan added, "'Other than the last sentence, I could not work in a single word against him.' Caesar then asked, 'Have you ever waged war with him?' I replied, 'Yes.' He said, 'What was the outcome of your battles against him?' I replied, 'The result varied; sometimes he was victorious and sometimes we were.' He said, 'What does he order you to do?' I said, 'He tells us to worship Allah alone, not to worship others with Him, and to discard all that our forefathers used to worship. He orders us to pray, give in charity, be chaste, keep our promises and return that which is entrusted to us.'

"When I had said that, Caesar said to his interpreter, 'Say to him: I asked you about his lineage and your reply was that he belonged to a noble family. In fact, all messengers of God came from the noblest lineage of their nations. Then I questioned you whether anybody else among you had claimed such a thing, and your reply was in the negative. If the answer had been in the affirmative, I should have thought that this man was following a claim that had been made before him. When I asked you whether he was ever known to tell lies, your reply was in the negative, so I took it for granted that a person who did not tell a lie about people could never tell a lie about God. Then I asked you whether any of his ancestors was a king. Your reply was in the negative, and if it had been in the affirmative, I should have thought that this man sought the return of his ancestral kingdom.

"'When I asked you whether the rich or the poor people followed him, you replied that it was the poor who followed him. In fact, such are the followers of the messengers of God. Then I asked you whether his followers were increasing or decreasing. You replied that they were increasing. In fact, this is the result of true faith until it is complete (in all respects). I asked you whether there was anybody who, after embracing his religion, became displeased and renounced his religion; your reply was in the negative. In fact, this is the sign of true faith, for when its blessedness enters and mixes in the hearts completely, nobody will be displeased with it.

"'I asked you whether he had ever broken his promise. You replied in the negative. And such are the messengers of God; they never break their promises. When I asked you whether you fought with him and he fought with you, you replied that he did, and that sometimes he was victorious and sometimes you. Indeed, such are the messengers of God; they are put to trials and the final victory is always theirs.

"'Then I asked you what he commanded of you. You replied that he ordered you to worship Allah alone and not to worship others along with Him, to leave all that your forefathers used to worship, to offer prayers, to speak the truth, to be chaste, to keep promises, and to return what is entrusted to you. These are the qualities of a prophet who I knew (from the previous Scriptures) would appear, but I did not know that he would be from amongst you. If what you say is true, he will very soon capture the land under my feet, and if I knew that I would reach him definitely, I would go immediately to meet him; and were I with him, then I would have certainly washed his feet.'"

Caesar then collected his nobles and military leaders and asked them what would their response be if he were to accept Muhammad's request. The whole court was thrown into a great uproar, the officers became extremely restless raising their voices in objection and their eyes grew wild. When he saw this he quickly interjected and claimed that he had only asked that question in order to test their resolve and their firm stance. So he renounced his previous resolve and refused Muhammad's message.[205]

The above is a long tradition, with a great many morals. With regard to the present topic two points stand out, the first being, once again, that Muhammad's enemies testified to his honesty. Not only did Abu Sufyan affirm Muhammad's honesty, but none of his companions contradicted his claim.

Now, how likely is *that*? Muhammad was inviting Heraclius, the ruler of one of the greatest world powers, to Islam. Had Heraclius converted, he could have rolled the Roman Empire over the Quraysh like a Mack truck over an ant. Abu Sufyan and his companions must have been desperate to disparage Muhammad and his message of Islam. But they didn't. And we have to wonder why, if not due to their sincerity.

The second point is the recurring paradox of recognizing Muhammad's honesty but refusing his message. On one hand Heraclius said, "I took it for granted that a person who did not tell a lie about people could never tell a lie about God" and, "such are the messengers of God; they never break their promises." On the other hand, when he saw the seeds of sedition in his court, he "renounced his previous resolve ..."

Here is a man who not only recognized Muhammad's claim to prophethood, but who explained his reasoning. Yet, when forced to choose between his religious convictions and worldly concerns, he crumbled.

This incongruity is witnessed on multiple occasions, one remarkable case being that told by Safiyah, a Jewess who later married Muhammad. Her father, Huyayi, and her uncle, Abu Yasir, were two Jewish leaders who visited Muhammad when he came to Quba. Safiyah described that her father and uncle

...did not return until sunset when they came back walking lazily and fully dejected. I, as usually, hurried to meet them smiling, but they would not turn to me for the grief that caught them. I heard my uncle Abu Yasir say to Ubai and Huyayi, "Is it really he (i.e. the foretold prophet)?" The former said, "It is he, I swear by Allah!" "Did you really recognize him?" they asked. He answered, "Yes, and my heart is burning with enmity towards him."[206]

Yeah, that makes sense. He's the foretold prophet, let's despise him.

Well, it's not the first time truth fell sacrifice to convenience. The point is, however, that even those who hated Muhammad acknowledged his honesty.

The Qur'an itself mentions this paradox, for the disbelievers witnessed Muhammad's life-long honesty, yet denied his message of revelation: "A whole life-time before this I have tarried among you: will you not then understand?" (TMQ 10:16) Furthermore, Muhammad was consoled with the revelation: "We know indeed the grief which their words do cause you: it is not you they reject: it is the Signs of Allah which the wicked disdain" (TMQ 6:33).

Once again, we should note that no one who knew Muhammad denied this verse. To quote the *New Catholic Encyclopedia*, "His adversaries, among whom were many Jews and Christians, watched eagerly for indications of fraud; and Mohammed was able successfully to assume a remarkable self-assured attitude toward any accusations of that sort."[207]

4

Persistence and Steadfastness

God Almighty hates a quitter.

—Samuel Fessenden, 1896

Whether ridiculed for constructing an ark in a waterless desert, pursued by a vindictive pharaoh or flogged and condemned to crucifixion, the prophets suffered more than any imposter could reasonably be expected to have endured. And it is this extraordinary persistence that casts a cloak of credibility over true prophets' claims of divine appointment.

History suggests Muhammad was a member of this noble company. Over a span of twenty-three years, he delivered a revelation that infuriated his antagonists to ostracize, assault, torture and even murder its believers. Muhammad was himself threatened, humiliated, beaten, stoned, and driven out of his home and city. His beloved wife, Khadijah, died in exile imposed by the pagan Quraysh. Attempts on his life were numerous. Yet through all periods of stress and hardship, Muhammad stood in prayer at night until his body rebelled.

On one occasion, revelation stated that Allah had forgiven Muhammad for his sins, past, present and future (TMQ 48:2).

Muhammad's response?

To sit back and take it easy?

Anything but. Despite the guarantee of paradise, Muhammad stood two-thirds of the night in prayer, until his feet swelled and cracked. When asked, "Hasn't God forgiven you that which is before you and that which is behind you?"— Muhammad replied, "Should I not be a thankful servant?"[208]

Now, charlatans pamper themselves, and then claim divine dispensation as an excuse to escape the rigors of worship. Muhammad did neither. Rather, like the prophets before him, he suffered to convey the message of revelation. And then he honored that message more than any of his followers, to the day he died.

Similarly, no true prophet misused his position for self-serving ends. For one thing, no true prophet ever claimed to be more than a man. As discussed in *MisGod'ed*, the apotheosis of Jesus was not *his* idea, but that of his misguided followers. Mindful of this danger, Muhammad took every precaution to prevent such a deviation from developing in the minds of the Muslims. He discouraged preferential treatment, and responded to gestures of respect with admirable humility. His servant Anas related,

> No one was more beloved to us than the Messenger of Allah (peace be upon him), [however], if we saw him we would not stand up for him for we knew how much he disliked [for us to do so]. And on one occasion someone called to him saying: "O best of mankind ..." He replied: "That is Abraham, peace be upon him."[209]

On another occasion a man said, "God and You (O Muhammad) have willed this," in reference to a certain matter, and Muhammad rebuked him by asking, "Have you made me equal to God?"[210]

Muhammad stressed the distinction between God and His prophets by teaching, "Do not over-praise me as the Christians over-praised [Jesus] the son of Mary. For I am only His [God's] servant, so say: 'Allah's servant and messenger.'"[211]

Consistent to the very end, even when suffering a terminal illness, Muhammad warned his companions not to make his grave a focus of worship.[212]

Many other events illustrate Muhammad's humility. In one dramatic example, the sun eclipsed on the day Muhammad's son, Ibraheem, died. Out of love of their prophet, the Muslims began to say, "The sun has eclipsed for the death of Ibraheem."

Muhammad's response?

Stop.

Think about it.

What would a charlatan have said? Liars and confidence artists seize such opportunities and distort them for personal gain.

On the contrary, Muhammad advised his followers, "Verily, the sun and the moon are two signs of the signs of Allah; they do not eclipse for the death of anyone nor for his birth, so if you see that (an eclipse) then supplicate to God, reverence His name, pray and give charity."[213]

Okay, but wait. Where's the "That's right, the sun eclipsed for the death of my son, so dig deep and donate?" If ever Muhammad had an opportunity for self-glorification, that was it. Yet he seized the opportunity not for his own design, but to glorify God.

Muhammad repeatedly demoted his significance in the eyes of his followers, teaching them, "Say: 'I tell you not with me are the Treasures of Allah, nor do I know what is hidden, nor do I tell you I am an angel. I but follow what is revealed to me'" (TMQ 6:50), and "Muhammad is no more than a messenger ..." (TMQ 3:144)

We encounter many circumstances Muhammad could have manipulated for self-serving ends, had he been so inclined. When, after a decade of exile, the Muslim army reoccupied Makkah in a peaceful and virtually bloodless takeover, the populace requested clemency.

Again, put yourself in the picture.

For the past twenty years, the Makkan pagans beat, tortured, and killed your followers. For the past ten, they made open war upon you. They starved many of the Muslims literally to death, among them your beloved wife. They killed your uncle in battle—well, loses are to be expected in war—but then mutilated his corpse and chewed his liver. When you made a treaty with them, they broke it by murdering your followers.

What did they do to you personally? They beat you, starved you, stoned you till you bled, dumped camel guts over you while you prayed, attempted to kill you on multiple occasions and eventually drove you from your home, tribe and town. Not to mention the insults, slanders and humiliation which, to a Bedouin, are worse than any wound.

And they've been doing this to you for *twenty years*.

So now that you've got the upper hand, what are you going to do?

Okay, maybe not *you*. Maybe you're too nice. Or too unrealistic. Maybe you're sitting in a cushioned chair with a chilled Frappuchino in your hand, soft music in the background, and no matter how hard you try, you *can't* put yourself in the picture.

But the people of that period sure could. It was a time of rape and plunder, raze-to-the-ground and stack-the-heads-in-the-town-square conquests. That was the standard of the times, even when there were *no* vindictive emotions involved. A "You killed my wife, uncle and followers, stole our homes, property and possessions, and dared to 'dis' me? Well, the shoe is on the other foot now" attitude would in no way violate reasonable expectations. Revenge would not just be understood, but expected. Encouraged, even.

However, Muhammad was not a man driven to violence or revenge. He conformed to the mold of men guided by a higher calling than passions. Despite the list of atrocities calling for justifiable retribution, he exhibited a patience and generosity that bespoke the sincerity of his prophetic mission. Measuring his munificence against that of other conquerors of their time, the entire populace of Makkah embraced Islam, without the slightest compulsion.

The sincerity of this mass conversion is proven by the fact that the Makkans did not revert from their new faith when Muhammad died a short time later.

Two classic comments summarize this event as follows:

The day of Mohammad's greatest triumph over his enemies was also the day of his grandest victory over himself. He freely forgave the Koreysh all the years of sorrow and cruel scorn in which they had afflicted him, and gave an amnesty to the whole population of Mekka. Four criminals whom justice condemned made up Mohammad's proscription list when he entered as conqueror to the city of his bitterest enemies. The army followed his example, and entered quietly and peacefully; no house was robbed, no women insulted. One thing alone suffered destruction. Going to the Kaaba, Mohammad stood before each of the three hundred and sixty idols, and pointed to it with his staff, saying, "Truth is come, and falsehood is fled away!" and at these words his attendants hewed them down, and all the idols and household gods of Mekka and round about were destroyed.

It was thus that Mohammad entered again his native city. Through all the annals of conquest there is no triumphant entry comparable to this one.

The taking of Mekka was soon followed by the adhesion of all Arabia.[214]

And this excerpt from Arthur Gilman's 1890 classic, *The Saracens:*

It is greatly to his [Muhammad's] praise that on this occasion, when his resentment for ill-usage in the past might naturally have incited him to revenge, he restrained his army from all shedding of blood, and showed every sign of humility and thanksgiving to Allah for His goodness ...

The prophet's first labor was the destruction of the idol-images in the Kaaba, and after that had been done he ordered his original muezzin to sound the call to prayer from the top of the Kaaba, and sent a crier through the streets to command all persons to break in pieces every image that they might possess.

Ten or twelve men who had on former occasion shown a barbarous spirit, were proscribed, and of them four were put to death, but this must be considered exceedingly humane, in comparison with the acts of other conquerors; in comparison for example, with the cruelty of the Crusaders, who, in 1099, put seventy-thousand Moslems, men, women and helpless children, to death when Jerusalem fell into their hands; or with that of the English army, also fighting under the cross, which, in the year of grace, 1874, burned an African capital, in its war on the Gold Coast. Mohammed's victory was in very truth one of religion and not of politics; he rejected every token of personal homage, and declined all regal authority; and when the haughty chiefs of the Koreishites appeared before him he asked:

"What can you expect at my hands?"

"Mercy, O generous brother."

"Be it so; you are free!" he exclaimed.[215]

Perhaps the greatest example of Muhammad's steadfastness is that, though fallen from wealth, power, and high social standing, and despite the extreme violence and prejudice he faced, he refused to forsake the message of revelation. During a peak period of Muhammad's persecution, Muhammad's uncle appealed to him to cease his preaching, to which the Prophet replied, "O my uncle! By Allah if they put the sun in my right hand and the moon in my left on condition that I abandon this course, until Allah makes me victorious or I perish therein, I would not abandon it."[216]

The test of Muhammad's commitment came shortly thereafter, when the leaders of the pagan Quraysh offered him just such a ransom:

> If you (O Muhammad) are doing all this with a view to getting wealth, we will join together to give you greater riches than any Quraysh'ite has possessed. If ambition moves you, we will make you our chief. If you desire kingship we will readily offer you that. If you are under the power of an evil spirit which seems to haunt and dominate you so that you cannot shake off its yoke, then we shall call in skilful physicians to cure you.[217]

Muhammad's refusal testified to his sincerity and selfless devotion. But then why did he suffer the tortures and indignities that accompanied his claim to prophethood, if not for wealth or power? The answer, for Muslims, is that he strove not for the comforts of this temporal world, but for the rewards of the next.

Over a decade later, the Muslims reoccupied Makkah and subdued the same population that had offered Muhammad their wealth and kingship.

Um, so what's the point? That Muhammad wouldn't accept their wealth and throne over a decade earlier, and free of worldly charge, but felt he had to spend the rest of his life in privation and war in order to earn it?

Hardly.

The point is that Muhammad did not fight to establish *himself* in authority, but to establish the religion. Had he wanted wealth or kingship he could have accepted the Quraysh leaders' offer to buy him off with these things long before. But that would have required him to abandon the revelation. Instead, he fought to establish to word of Allah, and in the end achieved victory both for Islam and for himself.

End of story?

Nope. What is truly interesting is what happened next.

Once in power, most charlatans pull out a wish list of "revealed" paybacks, and then start filling the order. Muhammad did nothing of the sort. In fact, he did the opposite, transmitting the revelation:

> This day have I perfected your religion for you, completed My favor upon you, and have chosen for you Islam as your religion.
>
> (TMQ 5:3)

This revelation signaled completion. Completion, among other things, of "My favor upon you." At a time when any charlatan in the world would consider himself perfectly poised to begin "revealing" verses inclined to self-gratification, Muhammad transmitted revelation that spoke of an end of Allah's favor upon him. Not only that, but he conveyed revelation that commanded him to "Celebrate the praises of your Lord, and pray for His forgiveness ..." (TMQ 110:3)

The latter verse was revealed nine nights before Muhammad died.[218] Of course, he could not have anticipated his death by earthly means. In other words, if he was not a prophet he could not have anticipated his death, but if he was a true prophet and knew of his impending death through revelation then he was ... um ... stay with me here: a true prophet.

But the point is this: The final verses Muhammad conveyed as revelation emphasized his sincerity. Rather than "revealing" a legacy for family and loved ones, injecting some final words of personal wisdom or glorifying himself with the promise of salvation, the final verses of the Holy Qur'an completed not only his life, but also the revelation.

And what was the final verse? The last verse revealed counseled Muhammad:

> And fear the Day when you shall be brought back to Allah. Then shall every soul be paid what it earned, and none shall be dealt with unjustly (TMQ 2:281).

Where other conquerors bask in self-veneration and die of the poisons of their excesses, Muhammad transmitted a series of verses that bade him to glorify the Creator and seek His forgiveness. He died as he had lived, impoverished in worldly terms but successful in his religion. His death was not tainted by the whim of self-glorification, the satiation of long-suppressed lusts or the satisfaction of a thirst for revenge.

Rather, Muhammad died wealthy only in sincerity and piety, as he had been for the preceding twenty-three years of his prophethood.

We close this chapter with tributes paid by three renowned writers. First, British socialist H.M. Hyndman:

> Even to-day, with all the details of his early life and subsequent career laid bare by men of our own race, who have studied the whole extraordinary story of the noble Arabian, it is no easy matter to comprehend the character, or to account for the marvelous success of Mohammed in the early part of the seventh century. Never claiming divine powers at any period of his mission ... this very human prophet of God made his first converts in his own family, was able, after almost hopeless failure, to obtain control in his own aristocratic *gens* [clan], and had such remarkable personal influence over all with whom he was brought into contact that, neither when a poverty-stricken and hunted fugitive, nor at the height of his prosperity, did he ever have to complain of treachery from those who had once embraced his faith. His confidence in himself, and in his inspiration from on high, was even greater when he was suffering under disappointment and defeat than when he was able to dictate his own terms to his conquered enemies. Mohammed died as he had lived, surrounded by his early followers, friends and votaries: his death as devoid of mystery as his life of disguise.[219]

Washington Irving, essayist, biographer and author, had this to say in his *Mahomet and His Successors:*

> Even in his own dying hour, when there could be no longer a worldly motive for deceit, he still breathed the same

religious devotion, and the same belief in his apostolic mission.[220]

And finally, a revisit to the impressions of Thomas Carlyle:

His last words are a prayer; broken ejaculations of a heart struggling up, in trembling hope, towards its Maker ... He went out for the last time into the mosque, two days before his death; asked, If he had injured any man? Let his own back bear the stripes. If he owed any man? A voice answered, "Yes, me, three drachms," borrowed on such an occasion. Mahomet ordered them to be paid: "Better be in shame now," said he, "than at the Day of Judgment" ... Traits of that kind show us the genuine man, the brother of us all, brought visible through twelve centuries ...[221]

5
Lack of Disqualifiers

We search coal for diamonds, but we search diamonds for flaws.

—L. Brown

True prophets are rarer than diamonds, and like diamonds, are not expected to be perfect. Certainly we expect prophets to be human, complete with the occasional sin or error in judgment. We don't expect them to be angels, just … better than the rest of us.

What we shouldn't accept, however, are charlatans who claim divinity, manipulate revelation for personal gain, or who show signs of unreliability, such as lying or mental instability. Intuitively, we tend to disqualify all such claimants.

As we have seen, Muhammad did not exhibit any of the above disqualifiers. He never claimed divinity or manipulated revelation, and was never known to have told a lie. So how can we challenge Muhammad's claim to prophethood?

That is a difficult question. Evidence forces us to abandon the claims of epilepsy, lying, or delusion. So what possibilities remain?

Aside from true prophethood, little or nothing. Or nothing of substance, that is. Since the more blatant charges are easily dismissed, those who attack Muhammad's character are forced to focus upon purely emotional issues, which in fact have little or nothing to do with validating his claim to prophethood.

Some of these issues, such as Muhammad having sins (albeit few, and of a minor nature), are true, whereas others, such as the slander that Muhammad was a voluptuary, driven by hunger for sensual pleasures, are not, as we shall soon see. In both cases the emotional argument boils down to Muhammad's critics saying he could not have been a prophet because he had sinned, waged war, endorsed polygamy, required women to cover their hair, outlawed alcohol, or whatever.

Huh, what a surprise: people don't like his actions, or the revelation he conveyed. But wait, isn't that how we would expect most people to react to a true prophet? Weren't all true prophets greeted more with rebellion than acceptance? The fact is that virtually all true prophets were initially rejected by the majority of their populace. No surprise there—it is not the mark of a prophet, but of a charlatans, to gather followers by telling them what they want to hear. And let's ask ourselves, why did God send prophets, anyway? To pat everyone on the back and tell them they're doing everything right, or to guide mankind away from our wayward desires and back to the path of His design, whether to our liking or not?

Perhaps there is no more emotional issue in revelation than the commandment to fight, and interestingly enough, the Holy Qur'an mentions just this: "Fighting is prescribed for you, and you dislike it. But it is possible that you dislike a thing which is good for you, and that you love a thing which is bad for you. But Allah knows, and you know not" (TMQ 2:216). Now let's think about this: Is there any greater test of love than fighting for it? Love deepens when someone sticks up for us, whether it is our parent, child, friend, spouse, or colleague. Fighting is the ultimate test of love, and whereas a war of words may be sufficient in most circumstances, nothing shows true commitment like putting one's life on the line.

Similarly, out of love of God, Old Testament prophets led their people to war again and again to establish the supremacy of God's law on Earth. The crusaders and colonialists have given Christianity its share of fighting, ostensibly under the banner of God, as well. Jesus Christ may never have waged war, but then again he wasn't in a position to do so. However, he did declare his purpose: "Do not think that I came to bring peace on earth. I did not come to bring peace but a sword" (Matthew 10:34), and "Do *you* suppose that I came to give peace on earth? I tell you, not at all, but rather division" (Luke 12:51). Was it for no reason that Jesus reportedly told his disciples, "He who has no sword, let him sell his garment and buy one" (Luke 22:37)?

War has been guided and misguided, used for good and for evil, in righteousness and impiety, but fighting was a test of the faithful of old and continues to be a test of the righteous today. And yet, there are those who dismiss Muhammad's claim of prophethood on this one most emotional of issues. Where, then, does that leave the long list of biblical prophets who led their people to war in the name of God?

One common emotional polemic is that Muhammad beheaded hundreds[222(EN)] of his enemies following the "Battle of the Trench." But wait. Did he? Let's set the record straight. Before the Battle of the Trench, the Muslims forged cooperative treaties with three neighboring Jewish tribes. However, during the battle, the tribe of Bani Qurai'tha betrayed their treaty and offered a gap in the Muslim defenses to the attacking pagan Quraysh, through which the Quraysh could assault the Muslims from an undefended side. The plan failed, however, and the Muslims imprisoned the Bani Qurai'tha for treason.

Contrary to what Christian polemicists would have us believe, it was not Muhammad who condemned the prisoners.

Rather, Bani Qurai'tha requested to be judged by one of the tribes friendly to them. Muhammad agreed, and offered them the chief of the Aws tribe, a Muslim named Saad ibn Mu'ath. Bani Qurai'tha agreed to Saad's judgment, for the Aws and Bani Qurai'tha tribes had been close confederates for generations, and they could expect clemency from them. However, contrary to their expectations, Saad condemned the Bani Qurai'tha men to death, and the women and children to slavery. Why? Because friends or no friends, fair is fair, and that was the punishment for treason at that time and place.[223]

Contrast this with more recent British law. Why were the signatories of the American Declaration of Independence considered unusually brave? Why did Benjamin Franklin quip that if they didn't hang together, they would hang separately? Because the British punishment for treason was to hang traitors until nearly dead, then cut them down, disembowel them alive, burn their entrails in front of their eyes, and then draw and quarter them. In this context, beheading would have been considerably more humane than the torture meted out by the British "defenders of the faith," "the faith" being the Church of England.

So where does this bring us? Back to the point that emotional issues are not valid criteria by which to evaluate any man's claim to prophethood. Even if Muhammad *had* condemned the Bani Qurai'tha, he would have acted within the military standard of his day. More importantly, if we were to dismiss Muhammad's claim to prophethood on this basis, what should we say about Moses, who ordered the Jews to slaughter (and I do mean to literally cut their throats) those among them who had made and worshipped the idol of a calf during Moses' forty-day communion with God. And how many were these heretics, who Moses ordered slaughtered? They numbered in the thousands.

A less bloody example of emotional ploys can be found in the Holy Qur'an, where Allah forgave Muhammad for his sins (TMQ 48:2). Many Christian detractors jump on this *ayah* and point out that Islam teaches that Muhammad had sins, while Jesus Christ was sinless. Similarly, Christian polemicists frequently state that Abraham, Noah, Moses, and Muhammad all died and were buried, but Jesus Christ was raised up from the dead.

Okay, buuut ... so what? These my-prophet-is-better-than-yours arguments don't work, for a number of reasons. To begin with, there is no contest between Jesus Christ and Muhammad in the Islamic religion—both are recognized as prophets, with the former having predicted the latter, and with the pure teachings of both having been the teachings of Islam (i.e., God is One, I'm His prophet, and here are His laws. Now, *follow* them). Secondly, the moral of the biblical parable of the lost sheep is,

> What do you think? If a man has a hundred sheep, and one of them goes astray, does he not leave the ninety-nine and go to the mountains to seek the one that is straying? And if he should find it, assuredly, I say to you, he rejoices more over that sheep than over the ninety-nine that did not go astray (Matthew 18:12–13).

Or Luke 15:7: "There will be more joy in heaven over one sinner who repents than over ninety-nine just persons who need no repentance."

The moral of the parable of the lost coin is the same: "There is joy in the presence of the angels of God over one sinner who repents" (Luke 15:10). And let us not forget the moral of the parable of the prodigal son—that there is more rejoicing over the repentance of the sinful son than over the one who never went astray to begin with (Luke 15:11–32).

What's the point? That Christian detractors argue the "My prophet is better than yours" line on the basis of Jesus having been sinless. However, according to the biblical parables we've just quoted, this priority should be reversed, for "there will be more joy in heaven over one sinner who repents than over ninety-nine just persons who need no repentance."

Finally, nowhere in the Bible is a prophet disqualified for having sinned, or from having died and been buried. Now, no doubt Jesus Christ was a hard act to follow, but if having sins or having died and been buried excludes a person from prophethood, then we have to disqualify all the other biblical prophets as well. And since we're not going to do that, what is the point of the argument?

One point that *can* be made, however, is that Muhammad persisted in his mission despite his human shortcomings. He never attempted to either excuse or conceal his sins or his humanity. On the contrary, he conveyed a revelation that immortalized these facts, following which he continued to persevere, in the manner of the prophets before him.

Just as Muhammad did not identify any one prophet as better than another, he did not elevate his own status above that of the prophets who preceded him.

Not so with other religions.

Maimonides' Thirteen Principles of Jewish Faith teaches that Moses was the greatest of the prophets.[224] And look where that attitude got the Jews: so enamored with Moses that they deny not only Muhammad, but John the Baptist and Jesus Christ as well. On the other hand, Christians elevate Jesus Christ to divinity and consider the chain of prophethood to end with him, despite both the Old Testament and Jesus

Christ himself predicting a final prophet to follow. This is not so much a matter of people having blind faith as it is of a peoples' faith blinding them.

Now, Muhammad could just as easily have made such claims, and a group of his followers would have believed. They had already believed Muhammad to be the foretold final prophet, and they had witnessed the long list of miracles that occurred both through him and around him, so they most likely would have honored a claim to divinity. After all, they had previously reverenced the 360 statues in the Kaba at Makkah as gods. Heck, the Arabs of that period used to mould statues out of *dates*, call the confectionary *a god*, and then *eat it*. What's the chance they *wouldn't* have considered Muhammad a god, had he made such a claim?

But he didn't.

Instead, he transmitted a revelation that proclaimed all the prophets to have been men, no one of whom is to be considered superior to any other:

> We believe in Allah, and the revelation given to us, and to Abraham, Isma'il, Isaac, Jacob, and the Tribes, and that given to Moses and Jesus, and that given to (all) Prophets from their Lord: we make no difference between one and another of them, and we bow to Allah (in Islam) (TMQ 2:136).

Perhaps the most common claim against Muhammad is that he was a voluptuary, led around by his lusts. Interestingly, this is a modern claim. The disbelievers of Muhammad's time, though eager to attack his character, never made this claim. They would have been laughed out of town if they had.

Although Muhammad didn't deny himself life's pleasures, he lived a most frugal existence. He distributed whatever wealth he had, passed on any gifts he received to others, and even shared his food. He rejected the prestige and finery of success, and always placed the needs and desires of his followers ahead of his own. He loved perfumes and honey, but enjoyed them sparingly. And in any case, nobody ever embarked upon a religious quest for honey.

So what about wine, women, and song?

Prior to the revelation, Arabic society permitted prostitution, temporary marriage contracts, and limitless polygamy. Music and alcohol were ubiquitous, and the entire society was given to gambling, feasting, fighting, cursing, drunkenness, lying, licentiousness, and laziness. If those were the things Muhammad desired, he could have had them without speaking a word of revelation. Instead, it is difficult to find anything the Arabs liked that the Islamic revelation didn't forbid or restrict.

Take the above issues one by one. Extramarital relations? Forbidden. Music? Curtailed. Alcohol, gambling, lying, licentiousness? Forget it. Feasting was replaced with fasting, fighting with forgiveness, cursing with supplication (i.e., if you don't like something don't curse it, which accomplishes nothing, but ask Allah to change it for the better), and laziness with the duties of worship.

What's left? Polygamy? Now, Muhammad's many wives were never an issue before modern times, and there is a very good reason why.

No, wait, that's wrong. There isn't just *one* good reason, there are *many*.

To begin with, had Muhammad been a voluptuary with regard to women, we would expect his desires to have been evident in his youth, when a man's sexual drive is at its peak. However, throughout Muhammad's youth he only had one wife, Khadijah. They were married for twenty-five years, and throughout that period he was unwaveringly faithful, despite the fact that she was fifteen years his senior. Yet Muhammad's detractors propose that, at the age of fifty, with the energy of his youth behind him, he set a flock of wives as his goal in life?

Unlikely.

And even if that premise were true, never in history did a man suffer so much for something he could have had anyway. For if this is what Muhammad had wanted, he could have had any number of wives, concubines, sex slaves and prostitutes, even from his youth. The laws of the society in which he lived were ... well ... were that there *were* no laws. He could have fornicated freely and let his lusts run wild in the pasture of sexual permissiveness. But he didn't. Despite the sexual freedoms that must have tempted any man of youth and vigor, Muhammad remained chaste until his first marriage, at the age of twenty-five. His reputation was one of temperance, not licentiousness.

So why did Muhammad eventually marry so many wives?

For the most part, for practical reasons. Through his marriages he cemented inter-tribal ties, sheltered orphaned widows and divorcees, and demonstrated Islamic marital limits. Far from being the powerful ruler who handpicked the choicest maidens for his personal enjoyment, Muhammad's wives were not known for their youth, beauty, wealth, or high social standing.

In fact, just the opposite.

Only one wife, A'ishah, was a virgin.[225] The rest were either old, divorced, widowed, or a combination of the above. For example, Muhammad married Mai'moona when she was fifty-one years old. Another of his wives could have been

Mai'moona's mother (or, considering the age at which women married back then, her grandmother), for Muhammad married Um Salama when she was eighty-two. His first wife, Khadijah, was a widow. Another wife, Zainab bint Jahsh, bore the social stigma of having been divorced from a freed slave. We can dismiss lust as a factor in most of Muhammad's marriages, not only for the reasons just given, but also because he never consummated the marriage with a number of his wives.[226]

So the accusation that Muhammad died poor but with a stable of wives as one of his life's objectives is an insult not only to the man, but to reason. Spiritual leader, commander of the faithful, king of the realm—no law was beyond his design, had he acted beyond divine constraints. Others instituted manorial laws ranging from legalized prostitution to the infamous *droit du seigneur*, whereby medieval feudal lords assumed first right to bed the bride of their vassals. And yet, nowhere did Muhammad betray the lusts of a voluptuary.

If nothing else, Muhammad's example falls well within biblical limits. With fewer wives than Solomon (ahem ... far, *far* fewer), less transgression than David (who, the Bible tells us, lusted so much for Bathsheba that he ordered her husband's death), and more restraint than Judah (who is recorded as having had relations with Tamar, believing her to be a prostitute), Muhammad's claim to prophethood cannot be contested on the charge of voluptuousness unless accepted biblical prophets are charged as well.

So what teaching did Muhammad convey regarding women and marriage? The permissibility of polygamy, to be sure. However, we should remember that polygamy was permitted in the Old Testament as well.[227] Furthermore, although not explicitly condoned in the New Testament, neither was polygamy forbidden.

On the other hand, the revelation Muhammad conveyed required, for the first time in history, that women be respected and married with necessary formality. Thirteen centuries before the developed West awarded women their rights to inheritance, property, marital choice and equality in education and religion, the Holy Qur'an commanded such rights. The most revolutionary concept, perhaps, was the recognition of women possessing souls and equal prospects as men in the afterlife, two concepts openly debated in Christian circles up to the turn of the twentieth century, after which the debate was moved behind closed church doors for the sake of political correctness.

But the point is that, in Islam, this issue … never *was* an issue.

It was perhaps to the disbelievers that Thomas Carlyle addressed the following:

> Mahomet himself, after all that can be said about him, was not a sensual man. We shall err widely if we consider this man as a common voluptuary, intent mainly on base enjoyments,—nay on enjoyments of any kind. His household was of the frugalest; his common diet barley-bread and water: sometimes for months there was not a fire once lighted on his hearth. They record with just pride that he would mend his own shoes, patch his own cloak. A poor, hard-toiling, ill-provided man; careless of what vulgar men toil for. Not a bad man, I should say; something better in him than *hunger* of any sort—or these wild Arab men, fighting and jostling three and twenty years at his hand, in close contact with him always, would not have reverenced him so! They were wild men, bursting ever and anon into quarrel, into all kinds of fierce sincerity; without right worth and manhood, no man could have commanded them.[228]

But command them he did. And it is the nature of what Muhammad commanded that is of the utmost interest.

6
Maintenance of the Message

If you wish to preserve your secret, wrap it up in frankness.
—Alexander Smith, *Dreamthorp*

According to Islam, the core message of revelation never changed. The Islamic monotheism of Adam was the same Islamic monotheism conveyed by all prophets: Moses, Jesus, and Muhammad included. Logically, it cannot be any other way, for to change the creed conveyed through revelation is to change the Creator Himself. To say that "God is One" gave way to "God is three in one and one in three" is to claim that God's essence changed. And that is exactly what Trinitarian Christianity proposes.

But let's be clear on this point: that is what *Trinitarian* Christianity proposes, but not what *Christ* proposed. If the first book in this series, *MisGod'ed*, exposes no other fact, it exposes this: Jesus Christ taught the monotheism and laws of the Old Testament. Trinitarian Christianity was not so much the product of the teachings of Jesus Christ as it was of those who followed in his name: men like Paul and the subsequent Pauline theologians.

Again, this cannot be stressed enough: Jesus Christ's followers and those who followed in Jesus' name are *not* the same group of people. The former group adhered to his teachings and, as a result, became strict monotheists adhering to Old Testament law: a relatively small subset of Unitarian Christians.[229(EN)] However, among those who followed in Jesus' name were the Trinitarians, who proposed a construct of God that Jesus never taught.

Back to the point.

The point is that Jesus Christ taught the unity of God, the humanity of God's prophets (himself included), and God's requirement to adhere to the laws laid out in revelation. And that is what all prophets taught, up to and including Muhammad.

So that's the message, and therein lies the test. A true prophet would maintain that message, consistent with the teachings of the prophets who preceded him. Charlatans, on the other hand, corrupt that message for personal gain, to one degree or another.

Now, what do we find in the case of Muhammad?

To begin with, as discussed in the previous chapter, we find no evidence of Muhammad having done *anything* for personal gain, much less corrupt the message of revelation. He lived and died a pauper, so we find no evidence of personal gain, period.

Next, not only does the Holy Qur'an preserve the previous prophets' message of divine unity but, excepting the Sabbath, Islam maintains the Ten Commandments. The essential creed, in other words, is preserved unchanged. So too are the laws taught by Moses and Jesus, with little variation.

But what about that "little variation"? Isn't that significant?

Depends on your perspective. We can easily understand why the true creed of the eternal God cannot change, but what about God's laws? Are those fixed as well?

The answer is that with the final revelation, yes, God's laws became fixed. However, prior to this, there are examples of God having changed some laws from one revelation to the next.

In the Old Testament, God allowed the sons and daughters of Adam to marry. Only later did He forbid this. In Noah's time, people could eat all kinds of meat and animals. Only later did God reveal the restrictions of Mosaic Law. At one time a man could marry two sisters; later this practice was forbidden. A most rapid reversal of God's commandments is to be found in the story of Abraham. First, God commanded Abraham to sacrifice his son, but He rescinded the command when Abraham was about to do so.

Christians do not claim that one or two of the Ten Commandments were abolished, but that the entire law was repealed. Not only has Old Testament law been displaced by the doctrine of justification by faith, but Trinitarian Christians claim God Himself transformed from the wrathful and harsh God of the Old Testament to the all-forgiving God of the New Testament. And yet, Christians effectively argue, "We say God Himself is transformed and all previous laws are repealed. But Islam says alcohol is now forbidden? That's ridiculous!"

Hmm. Islam teaches that Allah delayed certain restrictions and commandments until mankind became capable of satisfying them. Earlier restrictions would have placed a burden upon humans greater than they could have borne. Mankind, in other words, wasn't ready; it needed to grow up. Just as we instruct children according to their level of maturity, Allah had to wean the human race gradually, until it was ready to accept the restrictions of revelation.

So if the restrictions of the Sabbath were recalled here, and the permissibility of alcohol annulled there, it should be no surprise.

In summary, what do we encounter in the Islamic religion? The Oneness and preeminence of Almighty God, as taught by all preceding prophets,[230] and a comprehensive book of laws.

And what do we *not* find? We don't find Muhammad having modified religious conventions for personal gain, or having manifested any of the many symptoms of false prophethood. In particular, he never claimed to have been a saint or Christ returned, as so many deceivers have. Furthermore, he transmitted a revelation that corrected, rather than reinforced, popular Jewish and Christian misconceptions. This would have been a decidedly strange way of gathering a following, to have told the Jews and Christians that the opinions they held (and hold to this day) are wrong, and then set about teaching them their own scripture. It is strange to face such an uphill battle with no apparent worldly incentive. Strange for all but a true prophet, that is.

So was Muhammad the final prophet, as predicted in both Old and New Testaments? If so, one thing is certain, and it is that the revelation he transmitted upset a lot of people. Surprising? Maybe not. There is no greater hatred than that of the impious for a righteous good example. Furthermore, prophethood was never a popularity contest, but a test of sincerity and endurance, commitment and correctness. And, right in line with the parable of the wedding feast, which concludes with the lesson, "For many are called, but few are chosen" (Matthew 22:14), it was always the minority who followed.

To close this chapter, let's view Muhammad's teachings through the testimonies of others. Ja'far (the son of Abu-Talib, the Prophet's uncle and protector) testified to Najashi (Negus), the Christian king of Abyssinia as follows:

> O King of Abyssinia, we used to be a people of ignorance, worshipping idols, eating dead animals, performing indecencies, casting off family bonds, doing evil to our neighbors, and the strong among us would eat the weak.

This remained our common trait until God sent to us a messenger. We knew his ancestry, his truthfulness, his trustworthiness, and his chastity. He called us to Allah that we might worship Him alone and forsake all that which we had been worshipping other than Him of these stones and idols. He commanded us to be truthful in speech, to keep our trusts, to strengthen our family bonds, to be good to our neighbors, to avoid the prohibitions and blood, and to avoid all indecencies, lying, theft of the orphan's money, and the slander of chaste women. He further commanded us to worship Allah alone, not associating anything in worship with Him. He commanded us to pray, pay charity, and fast (and he listed for him the requirements of Islam). So we believed him, accepted his message, and followed him in that which he received from Allah, worshipping Allah alone, not associating any partners with Him, refraining from all prohibitions, and accepting all that which was made permissible for us.[231]

Some, like the Christian king of Abyssinia, were impressed with this statement, and followed. Others viewed the bearer of such teachings with such distaste that they sought to kill the messenger, the message, or both—much like the ungrateful invitees to the king's wedding feast in Jesus' parable (Matthew 22: 1–14). And look at what happened to them.

Throughout history, many scholars found ample cause to attribute greatness to Mohammad. The great French poet and statesman, Alphonse de Lamartine, wrote eloquently about the Prophet's influence and greatness:

If greatness of purpose, smallness of means, and astounding results are the three criteria of human genius, who could dare to compare any great man in modern history with

Muhammad? The most famous men created arms, laws and empires only. They founded, if anything at all, no more than material powers which often crumbled away before their eyes. This man moved not only armies, legislations, empires, peoples and dynasties, but millions of men in one-third of the then inhabited world; and more than that, he moved the altars, the gods, the religions, the ideas, the beliefs and souls. On the basis of a Book, every letter of which has become law, he created a spiritual nationality which blended together peoples of every tongue and of every race. He has left us as the indelible characteristic of his Muslim nationality the hatred of false gods and the passion for the One and immaterial God. This avenging patriotism against the profanation of Heaven formed the virtue of the followers of Muhammad; the conquest of one-third of the earth to his dogma was his miracle; or rather it was not the miracle of a man but that of reason. The idea of the Unity of God, proclaimed amidst the exhaustion of fabulous theogonies, was in itself such a miracle that upon its utterance from his lips it destroyed all the ancient temples of idols and set on fire one-third of the world. His life, his meditations, his heroic revilings against the superstitions of his country and his boldness in defying the furies of idolatry, his firmness in enduring them for fifteen years at Mecca, his acceptance of the role of public scorn and almost of being a victim of his fellow countrymen; all these and, finally, his flight, his incessant preaching, his wars against odds, his faith in his success and his superhuman security in misfortune, his forbearance in victory, his ambition, which was entirely devoted to one idea and in no manner striving for an empire; his endless prayers, his mystic conversations with God, his death and his triumph after death; all these attest not to an imposture but to a firm conviction which gave him the power to restore a dogma. This dogma was twofold, the unity of God and the immateriality of God; the former telling what God is, the later telling what God is not; the one overthrowing false Gods with the sword, the other starting an idea with the words.

Philosopher, orator, apostle, legislator, warrior, conqueror of ideas, restorer of rational dogmas, of a cult without images; the founder of twenty terrestrial empires and of one spiritual empire, that is Muhammad. As regards all standards by which human greatness may be measured, we may well ask, is there any man greater than he?[232]

PART IV
THE UNSEEN

There is no good in arguing with the inevitable.
—James Russell Lowell, 1884

The preceding chapters discussed the material reality of the prophets and the books of revelation. Now we shift to the unseen: the intangible entities and concepts that have long been part of classical comparative religion. While preceding chapters expose corroborating evidence suggesting a continuity of revelation from Judaism to Christianity to Islam, this present section demonstrates the commonality of ethereal concepts. Differences do exist, of course, but these differences are primarily the result of human caprice. Central core values, meaning those we encounter in revelation, are remarkably harmonious.

1

Angels

Angels: they're there. Any questions?

At least, that is the view of all three Abrahamic faiths. We like to believe in things we can see and touch, and so we are frustrated that angels are not available for individual analysis, scientific research, and talk shows. They are one of God's unseen creations, as are the devils, heaven, hell, and other ethereal entities.

Judaism and Islam both view angels in a practical manner. Mankind may consider itself the supreme being, but no human is more than a tiny dot of protoplasm, precariously perched on the brink of a frail mortality. Each of us occupy borrowed real estate on a pinhead-sized mud-ball called Earth, spun into orbit 150 million kilometers from the nearest yellow dwarf of spectral class G2 solar hand-warmer, largely ignorant of our Milky Way galaxy neighbors. These neighbors span a scant eighty thousand light-years in diameter, and lie buried in what is known as a Local Group of over thirty galaxies occupying a cylinder of space five million light-years in diameter. This Local Group is *itself* only an insignificant speck cloistered within the Local Supercluster of scores of clusters called "galaxy clouds," some containing close to two hundred galaxies, and laying claim to yet another insignificantly small cylinder of space 150 million light-years in diameter. All this is neatly tucked into the heart of the known universe—a daunting forty billion light-years in diameter (each light-year being roughly six trillion miles).[233] All in all, it's a long drive, and Planet Earth is the last rest stop.

The Islamic understanding is that we are not alone. Certainly, mankind is not the supreme being. The only human quality approaching 240 sextillion (that's 240 followed by 21 zeros) miles in diameter, containing 140 billion known galaxies and expanding at greater than ninety percent of the speed of light is some people's egos. As Rudyard Kipling wrote, "You haf too much Ego in your Cosmos."[234] God created mankind, but He also created angels and jinn (i.e., spirits), and each of these elements of creation have different properties and powers, many of them far superior to our own. Mankind and jinn possess free will. Some are evil, some merely mischievous, some righteous and devout. Angels, on the other hand, have no free will. They are God's functionaries and are absolutely obedient. They worship God, convey revelation to the prophets, record each person's deeds, support the righteous when Allah so decrees, collect the souls of the dying, direct the weather, guard the heavens and hell, and perform other duties. The best-known angel is Gabriel, the angel of revelation (also known in the Islamic religion as the "holy spirit.")

The question periodically arises: Why didn't God make all mankind faithful and good, and grant every person paradise? One answer is that He certainly could have, had He so desired. However, Allah already had the angels, who are perfectly obedient. Why would Allah create mankind in the same mold? Unlike angels, God gave human beings a choice. We can be *better* than angels, by being obedient of our own free will, or we can be worse than devils. Angels have no choice in the matter. But then again, it's the human race and not the angels who will face judgment in the hereafter, and receive either the blessings of paradise or the punishment of hellfire.

In contrast to the Jewish and Muslim understanding, Christians believe in a host of imaginary angels whose existence is unsubstantiated by scripture. Furthermore, Christians have done what Jews and Muslims refuse to do, which is to portray likenesses of the angels. This may seem harmless, but the religious purist is quick to recall the commandment, "You shall not make for yourself any carved image, or *any* likeness of *anything* that is in heaven above, or that is in the earth beneath, or that is in the water under the earth ..." (Exodus 20:4). Ask people what they think an angel looks like, and ninety-nine percent of the time they will recall a likeness created by those who violated this commandment.

Of course, this issue may at first seem unimportant, unless taken in the context of God's commandments. But adhering to God's commandments, of course, is what religion is all about.

2
Day of Judgment

You never get a second chance to make a good first impression.
—Old Proverb

True belief earns a reward in the hereafter. Disbelief does too, buuuut ... you don't want it. Such has been the message of all the prophets: each and every one of them.

How can we justify an afterlife? Well, where else can the injustices of this life be rectified, if not in an afterlife? If God did not offset the injustices of worldly life with appropriate rewards and punishments in the hereafter, it would be a poor reflection upon His sense of fairness. Some of the worst-of-the-worst enjoy some of the most luxurious and carefree lives. Meanwhile, some of the best-of-the-best suffer terribly. For example, which prophet had an easy time of it? Which prophets lived pampered lives of splendor to match that of a mafia boss, drug lord or tyrannical ruler, either of our time or theirs? If we are to trust in the mercy and justice of our Creator, we cannot believe He restricts the rewards of piety and the punishments of transgression to this worldly life, for the inequities of life are clear.

So there will be a Day of Judgment, we'll all be there, and it will be a bad time to start thinking about changing our lives for the better. Because ... now stay with me here ... because our lives will be, in a word, *over.* It'll be too late. The record of our deeds will be done. And there's no going back.

Mankind will be sorted according to beliefs and deeds. The faithful will be vindicated, the disbelievers condemned, and the transgressors (if not forgiven) punished according to the severity of their sins.

Jews declare paradise to be a birthright of the "chosen people," Christians claim "not to be perfect, just forgiven," and Muslims believe that all who die in submission to the Creator are eligible for redemption. Those who followed the revelation and prophet of their time will be successful, whereas those who forsook the revelation and prophet of their day did so to the compromise of their souls.

According to Islam, the believing Jews were upon the truth right up until they rejected the prophets who followed (i.e., John the Baptist and Jesus Christ) and their teachings, not to mention the revelation Jesus conveyed. In this manner, the Jews lived in submission to God not on *His* terms, but on *their* terms. When God sent prophets or revelation they didn't like, they chose to stick with the religion of their forefathers rather than that of God. In this way they fell into disobedience and disbelief.

Similarly, Jesus' followers followed the truth, right up until they rejected the final prophet, Muhammad. Again, Jesus' followers submitted to God, but only on their terms. And that's not good enough. When called upon to acknowledge the prophet Muhammad and the final revelation of the Holy Qur'an, they rejected and fell into the same disobedience and disbelief as their Jewish cousins.

According to Muslims, the religion of truth has always been Islam, since Islam's core message of submission to the will of Allah is what all prophets taught. However, submission to Allah's will demands adherence to the final revelation and teachings of the final prophet. Hence, the only group that submits to God's religion in the present day is the Muslims.

Those who know Islam and reject it will be condemned. Those who know of Islam and willfully duck the responsibility of studying the religion will likewise be condemned. However, those who die neither knowing of Islam nor willfully avoiding investigation thereof will be tested on the Day of Judgment, to prove what they would have done, had they known. And on that basis, Allah will judge them.

In this manner, if it can be imagined that there are Jews who died without having known of the prophets who followed, and Christians who died ignorant of Muhammad and the Holy Qur'an, they are not to be condemned. Rather, Allah will judge them according to their submission to the revelation to which they had been exposed during their lifetimes, and test their faith and obedience. So, too, with those who die ignorant of revelation as a whole; if they die sincerely seeking the religion of truth, they have hope for salvation. The same, however, cannot be said for those who willfully ignore the truth.

3
Divine Decree

Man proposes, God disposes.

—Thomas à Kempis

Predestination, or fate, cannot be proven. We all know that. What *can* be proven, however, is the commonality of the concept. For unbeknownst to most Jews and Christians, predestination is an article of faith common to all three of the Abrahamic religions.

We have already discussed the Jewish concept of being God's "chosen people." However, aside from this supremely optimistic thought, very little is written in the Old Testament about predestination. *Holman's Bible Dictionary* comments,

> From time to time the children of Israel were tempted to presume upon God's gracious favor, to assume, for example, that because the Lord had *placed* His temple at Jerusalem, they were exempt from judgement. Again and again the prophets tried to disabuse them of this false notion of security by pointing out the true meaning of the covenant and their mission among the nations (Jer. 7:1–14; Amos 3:2; Jonah).[235]

Even Jesus Christ was recorded as having lamented,

> O Jerusalem, Jerusalem, the one who kills the prophets and stones those who are sent to her! How often I

wanted to gather your children together, as a hen gathers her chicks under *her* wings, but you were not willing! (Matthew 23:37)

Which raises the question, "Chosen for what? To kill the prophets and stone the messengers?" Hardly a sensible formula for salvation, one would think. But then again, how often can rational argument penetrate the armor of elitist conceit?

Surely the Israelites were the "chosen people" for as long as they honored their prophet and the revelation he conveyed. However, they broke their covenant with God when they rejected the prophets foretold by their own scripture. Through their obstinate defiance, they nullified God's promise of salvation. *Encyclopedia Judaica* comments:

> The covenant relationship defined in this manner carries with it responsibilities, in the same way that chosen individuals are responsible for certain tasks and are required to assume particular roles ... Israel is obligated by this choice to "keep His statutes, and observe His Laws (Ps. 105:45).[236]

In other words, contract broken, contract cancelled. Let's move on.

The New Testament suggests foreknowledge and predestination in Romans 8:29—"For whom He foreknew, He also predestined ..." Ephesians 1:3–14 either explicitly or implicitly describes predestination ten times, and Acts 4:27–28 reads, "For truly against Your holy Servant Jesus, whom You anointed, both Herod and Pontius Pilate, with the Gentiles and the people of Israel, were gathered together to do whatever Your hand and Your purpose determined before to be done." 1 Peter 1:1–2 contributes, "To the pilgrims of the Dispersion in Pontus, Galatia, Cappadocia, Asia, and Bithynia, elect according to the foreknowledge of God the Father ..." with the fourth verse adding, "to an inheritance incorruptible and undefiled and that does not fade away, reserved in heaven for you ..."

Jesus Christ appears to have taught predestination when he said, "Come, ye blessed of my Father, inherit the kingdom prepared for you from the foundation of the world" (Matthew 25:34), and, "but rather rejoice, because your names are written in heaven" (Luke 10:20).[237]

From this scriptural foundation, a plethora of theories have grown.

Catholic theology proposes God's infallible foreknowledge of who will be saved, who will not, and why. According to *The Catholic Encyclopedia,* "predestination is in some way to be explained by God's foreknowledge of man's conduct."[238] Furthermore, God will save the blessed in precisely the manner He foreordained.[239]

The Protestant Reformation ushered in the theories of Martin Luther and John Calvin, which were equally uncompromising. Both Luther[240] and Calvin[241] claim God pre-destined each and every one of us either to eternal salvation or everlasting perdition. Whereas Luther proposed belief in Christ as the trademark of the elect, Calvin proposed that, as man was either saved or doomed from the time of creation, the "elect" were physically incapable of nullifying their salvation and the "doomed" were incapable of achieving redemption.

Into this fray walked the engagingly named Jacobus Arminius. Born in 1560 CE, fourteen years following Martin Luther's death and four years preceding Calvin's, Arminius grew to contest Calvin's proposal of unconditional election and irrevocable grace. Arguing the incompatibility of the injustice of irrevocable condemnation with the absolute justice of the Creator, Arminius proposed that God's comprehensive knowledge encompasses the will of man. Hence, though God neither wills people to specific actions nor predestines them to a particular fate, he knows their spiritual design and moral substance from before they are born. By way of His infinite knowledge, God knows what each and every human will think and do, how he or she will turn out, and what end they will earn in the hereafter.

Arminius' theory is of interest, because he harmonized human free will with divine omniscience and the fate of man. Nonetheless, the Reformed Church condemned his theories at the Synod of Dort in 1618–19. Different Protestant denominations subsequently set their sails to prevailing opinion and tacked back and forth between the theories of Luther, Calvin and variations upon those of the Catholics. In modern times, most Protestant sects have drifted to the twentieth century weld of predestination and Christology.

None of these theories have achieved unanimous acceptance, and so the subject remains very much alive in Christian circles.

Predestination is perhaps less debated within the Islamic religion, for the simple reason that all religions have mysteries of faith, and Islam considers this one of them. Furthermore, the Islamic teachings discourage Muslims from debating what is recognized to be a problematic topic given the limits of human intellect.

As with Arminius' theory (or perhaps we should say that Arminius' theories, as with those of Islam, since the Islamic principles predated Arminius' birth by roughly a thousand years), Islam acknowledges both divine predestination and human free will, and harmonizes these elements through Allah's omniscience.

Nonetheless, Islam teaches that Allah has predetermined everything we do.

In a relevant *hadith*, a Bedouin asked Muhammad if everything we do has been preordained, or if we do it of our own free will. Muhammad replied, "Rather, it has been preordained." The Bedouin then asked, "In that case, why don't we give up doing any acts, and rely upon what has been preordained for us?" Muhammad answered, "Nay, rather, act (i.e. do what you wish), for every person will find it easy to do what he was created for."[242]

Another tradition that clarifies the Islamic understanding is the *hadith* in which Muhammad taught,

> There is not one among you for whom a seat in Paradise or Hell has not been allotted and about whom it has not been written down whether he would be a miserable person or a happy one. A man said, "O Apostle of Allah, should we not then depend upon our destiny and abandon our deeds?" Thereupon the Messenger of Allah said, "Whoever belongs to the company of happiness, he will have good works made easier for him, and whoever belongs to the company of misery, he will have evil acts made easier for him." Then he recited, "So he who gives (in charity) and fears (Allah), and (in all sincerity) testifies to the Best, We will indeed make smooth for him the path to Bliss. But he who is a greedy miser and thinks himself self-sufficient, and gives the lie to the Best, We will indeed make smooth for him the path to Misery" (TMQ 92:5–10).[243]

Attempting to rectify human free will with predestination invites no end of controversy. However, unlike speculation over other secrets of the unknown, such as the nature of angels, spirits, the Day of Judgment, heaven, hell, et cetera, argument over predestination might lead to disbelief. Perhaps for this reason, Islam discourages Muslims from debating this issue.

To illustrate the point, Muhammad once caught a group of his companions debating predestination. Some quoted verses from the Qur'an that prove that Allah wills everything; others quoted verses that prove human free will. When Muhammad learned the topic of discussion, he became angry and said,

> Is this what you have been commanded to do? Is this why I have been sent to you? Verily, the people before you were destroyed when they argued amongst themselves regarding this matter. I caution you not to differ about it.[244]

Those who heed Muhammad's warning continue with their effort in life and religion, all the while accepting that "The pens have been lifted and the pages have dried"[245]—a philosophy very much in line with the old proverb, "Pray to God, but keep hammering."

PART V
CONCLUSIONS

Wisdom is knowing what to do next. Virtue is doing it.
—David Starr Jordan

The greatest deductions in life usually result from a sequence of smaller cognitive steps. The following three chapters in this section represent the steps this author deems necessary to arrive at the most balanced and correct conclusion as concerns the subject of this book.

1
The "Deviant" Religion

What is truth? said jesting Pilate; and would not stay for an answer.

—Francis Bacon, *Essays*

Many years ago a Christian bigot described Islam to me as "a deviant religion." That challenge was the impetus for these books. Opinionated oratory can have fleeting emotional appeal, but evidence argues a lasting truth.

This particular Christian parroted a common Western slander. But for those who exercise their intellect, religious propaganda fails to override what people deduce for themselves. More and more, people recognize that once we lift the veil of slanders from the face of a much-maligned institution, we frequently encounter a reality of such exquisite appeal as to dispel all false preconceptions.

These two books, *MisGod'ed* and *God'ed?*, were written to lift that veil of slanders and expose the underlying truth. Now let us examine the charge of deviancy.

To begin with, the analysis of deviation requires us to establish a stable frame of reference. Until we establish this reference, we will never be able to answer the question "Deviation from what?" With regard to religion, there is simply no argument. The measure of religious correctness can be none other than compliance with the directives of Almighty God.

Should we presume to find correctness in a man-made religious canon, we risk measuring in reference to the wrong standard. Each group of soldiers standing out of rank and file will consider all others to deviate from their misaligned standard, if they are blind to the possibility of being misaligned themselves. Unfortunately, most religious sects foster just such a cognitive paralysis, instilling an uncompromising "us against them" attitude of spiritual elitism.

Breaking through this barrier of committed ignorance is often not possible. However, this is the second ingredient necessary for the determination of deviancy. We must analyze objectively and embrace the truth, whether it confirms opinions we consider distasteful or conflicts with concepts we hold dear.

Some may measure deviation in reference to accepted norms, but this methodology is also error-prone. If majority opinion is the standard by which truth should be measured, then the concepts of the planets orbiting around the sun, the earth being round, and the germ theory of disease were incorrect at the time they were conceived.

Similarly, it was always the minority who accepted the prophets of their day. If majority rules, the prophets were wrong.

And that's the point.

Social norms and absolute truth do not necessarily skip hand-in-hand down Reality Lane. So let's measure by the only reliable standard, which in the case of religion is the will of our Creator.

Muslims claim to bow to the will of Allah in Islam, as conveyed through Muhammad and the Holy Qur'an. Those who claim to bow to the will of Allah in Judaism or Christianity must face the evidence presented in this book. According to the evidence, which religion is on the straight path of our

Creator's design, and which deviate therefrom? Which group bows to the word of God, and which to an error-ridden creed constructed by fallible and scripturally manipulative men?

The information presented in these two books should allow most people to answer these questions for themselves. However, in a sense, the answer doesn't matter, and I'll tell you why. If you are Jewish, the Jewish Bible (that is, the Old Testament) bids you to accept the foretold prophets. And where does that lead? First to Jesus and then to Muhammad. On the other hand, if you are Christian, Jesus Christ bade his followers to seek the foretold final prophet. And that also leads to Muhammad.

All roads, it would seem, lead to Islam.

Perhaps it is better to say that *one* road leads to Islam, or at least the one road we have been discussing in these books—the road of revelation.

Whether or not people act upon this insight depends upon each person's willingness to surrender to the indisputable evidence.

2
Surrender

Swift gratitude is the sweetest.

—Old Proverb

To surrender to God, on the face of it, should not be difficult, yet most people "surrender" only on conditional terms. A common first condition is God's existence, as found in the ill-conceived preface to prayer, "Oh, God, if you are there …" Another popular condition is to ask to be guided to be a better … whatever faith a person happens to follow at the time: "O God, make me a better _____ (fill in the blank)."

But is that surrender? What if a person's chosen faith is wrong? What if *our* chosen religion is not *God's* chosen religion? Modesty forces us to acknowledge human capriciousness and the sensibility of entertaining all possibilities, including that of being wrong.

In this manner, surrender to God is only complete when selfless.

Surrender, in fact, is an easy word, an uneasy concept and a challenging act, for most of us associate surrender with submission to an adversary. However, whereas surrender to an adversary is a demoralizing defeat, surrender to the Creator is a victory of faith. An adversary threatens abuse, humiliation, imprisonment, torture, even death. The Creator promises mercy and benevolence, peace and salvation.

Similar to an adversarial surrender, religious surrender demands us to cast aside our tools of self-defense, abandon whatever social or family ties threaten to enslave us, reject the disapproval of friends and authorities who seek to obstruct us, and forsake those who threaten our faith. However, *unlike* an adversarial surrender, we do not disarm ourselves to a position of weakness, but to a position of strength. For what greater strength can we have than the love and support of Almighty God?

Those who submit to a wartime enemy seek to escape slaughter. Those who surrender to God flee from a world of lies and delusions, entangling hedonism, and magnetic seductions, to One whose mercy is guaranteed, whose love is assured, and whose security is absolute.

He is One we can trust to receive us with loving grace and incomparable hospitality.

He is The One Who made mankind,

The One Who sustains mankind,

The One Who awaits mankind.

And yet, He is the One who is denied by the majority of mankind.

And He deserves better from us.

The devout will humble themselves to the Creator, seeking salvation through recognizing and obeying Him. And to do this, they will sincerely seek His guidance.

Without compromise, without qualification, without resistance.

A total, unconditional surrender. Anything less is just bargaining.

Unlike an adversarial surrender, religious surrender demands work. We must examine the religions to which we are exposed and sift through the propaganda. Those who dismiss Judaism out of prejudice against the stereotypical avarice, or

Christianity out of revulsion for the pedophile priests, have judged according to human failings rather than tenets of faith. Similarly, those who reject Islam on the basis of popularized slanders judge the religion not by what God says but by what people say.

We also should not allow the customs and traditions of a people to obstruct our analysis. As Suzanne LaFollette so accurately stated, "There is nothing more innately human than the tendency to transmute what has become customary into what has been divinely ordained."[246] So although Christians may uniformly endorse Christmas trees and crucifixes, these practices are the product of traditions rather than scriptural teachings. In fact, many would argue that these traditions are condemned by biblical scripture as well as by the pious examples of the apostolic fathers.[247]

Similarly, many customs of Jewish and Muslim communities are religiously distracting. In the extreme, misguided fanatics commit atrocities that contradict the very tenets of their respective faiths.

For example, religious compulsion, terrorism, and oppression of women are not elements of the Islamic religion. These are anti-Islamic slanders built upon the deviant example of a few impious, headline-hugging Muslims, but they are not part of Islamic ideology. And if we judge religions by the poorer representatives of their faiths, of which there are many, we will throw out not just Islam, but all religions.

The problem is that current events, personal experience, and media spin can all create an unfair bias, which more often than not drives people to conceive marginal elements as normative. It is not the millions of fine Jews who make the news, but the Baruch Goldsteins. It is not the billions of kind and charitable Christians who hit the headlines, but the Jeffrey Dahmers and the abortion clinic bombers. And it is not the billion good Muslims, but the extremists and the militant fanatics. Not all Jews machine-gun Muslims while bowed down in prayer, not all Christians are psychopathic cannibals or abortion clinic bombers, and not all Muslims are terrorists or intolerant of other peoples' faiths. And if we allow ourselves to believe otherwise, then we end up judging institutions not by their true values but by the few deviants who give us reason to hate. And that destroys not only the broader reality, but our humanity.

So let us refrain from judging any religion based upon propaganda or the radical acts of its misguided followers, of whom there are far too many.

Once we look past these elements of religious distortion, we can complement our quest by praying for guidance. The Lord's Prayer might be a good starting point for Christians, or for anybody else for that matter. This prayer is non-denominational, and a reasonable person could hardly object to a request to be "delivered from evil." If any objection exists at all, it would have to either be that guidance is not specifically requested or that the two recorded forms of the prayer differ (compare Matthew 6:9–13 with Luke 11:2–4).

Which prayer, if either or both, was voiced by Jesus remains uncertain—all the more so considering that The Jesus Seminar, a body of prominent biblical scholars, announced that the only word of the Lord's Prayer that can be directly attributed to Jesus is "Father."[248] This conclusion is startling, for it not only shakes one of the most accepted trees in the forest of Christian faith, but it questions that very tree's legitimacy.

Some modern translations attempt to hide the disagreement between the two versions of the Lord's Prayer, but pretty much any Bible published prior to 1970 records the two-thousand-year-old discrepancy.

In view of this startling uncertainty, Muslims offer the following prayer as an acceptable alternative:

> In the name of Allah, Most Gracious, Most Merciful.
> Praise be to Allah, The Cherisher and Sustainer of the Worlds:
> Most Gracious, Most Merciful;
> Master of the Day of Judgment.
> You do we worship, and Your aide we seek.
> Show us the straight way,
> The way of those on whom You have bestowed Your grace,
> those whose portion is not wrath, and who go not astray.
>
> (TMQ 1:1–7)

Simple, non-denominational and to the point, Muslims recite this first *surah* of the Holy Qur'an a minimum of seventeen times a day the world over. Interestingly, this prayer glorifies God and requests His guidance, but nowhere mentions Islam by name. As is the case with the Lord's Prayer, it is difficult to object to a prayer so pure of sentiment and devoid of prejudice.

3
The Consequences of Logic

Logical consequences are the scarecrows of fools and the beacons of wise men.
　　　　　—Thomas Henry Huxley, *Animal Automatism*

Jews and Christians have pointed out that Ayah 2:136 of the Holy Qur'an teaches Muslims to acknowledge "what was given to Musa (Moses), 'Isa (Jesus) and the Prophets from their Lord. We make no distinction between one another among them ..."

The argument these Jews and Christians propose is this: If the Holy Qur'an tells the Muslims to acknowledge the revelations given to Moses and Jesus, and not to make distinctions between the prophets, then the Holy Qur'an validates the Old and New Testaments.

Not true.

"What was given to Musa (Moses), 'Isa (Jesus) and the Prophets from their Lord" was revelation. However, as all religious scholars know, the Torah of Moses and the Gospel of Jesus Christ are lost, and have been for millennia. What we have in the present day—and for that matter, what we have had for the last two thousand years—is significantly corrupted from the original texts.[249] Hence, although the Qur'an acknowledges the *original* revelation given to the prophets, in no way does it validate the Old and New Testaments in their present, impure forms.

Secondly, even taking the Jewish and Christian Bibles as they are, the Old Testament, New Testament, and Holy Qur'an establish continuity in the chain of prophethood, revelation, and monotheistic creed. What we *don't* find in the Old and New Testaments are the self-serving beliefs that so many have relied upon for salvation—such beliefs as the Jews still being the "chosen people," despite having broken their covenant with God, and Christians being "justified by faith," even though Jesus Christ never taught any such thing. For that matter, nowhere did Jesus teach any of the integrals of Trinitarian theology.[250]

Consequently, Muslims propose that those who follow the teachings of the prophets will discover the religion of Islam in their own books. In other words, all prophets taught the same monotheistic creed, the same continuity in the chain of prophethood and, with few amendments, the same divine law. However, just as we find consistency in the teachings of the prophets, we discover consistency among those who seek to distort revelation. The prophets lead us to truth, their antagonists (such as Paul) attempt to lead us astray; the tool of the prophets is revelation, and that of their antagonists: mysticism.

The Islamic view, then, is that each stage of revelation prepared true believers for the next. The creed was constant and the chain of prophethood unbroken. Those who follow this chain of prophethood and revelation will pass from one installment to the next, leading to the logical conclusion of accepting the final prophet, Muhammad, and the revelation of the Holy Qur'an.

Consequently, the entreaty is offered,

Say: "O People of the Book [i.e. Jews and Christians]! Come to common terms as between us and you: that we worship none but Allah; that we associate no partners with Him; that we erect not, from among ourselves, Lords and patrons other than Allah." If then they turn back, say you: "Bear witness that we (at least) are Muslims (bowing to Allah's Will)." (TMQ 3:64)

Will mankind come to these common terms? Will we all unite in the worship of Allah and Allah alone? Associating no partners or co-sharers in His divinity? Well, it hasn't happened yet.

But it is not all of mankind for whom each of us is responsible, but just ourselves:

O you who believe! Guard your own souls: if you follow (right) guidance, no hurt can come to you from those who stray. The goal of you all is to Allah: it is He that will show you the truth of all that you do."

(TMQ 5:105).

Islam can thus legitimate itself through Abraham as the oldest and most authentic religion, taught by all the prophets (the same thing was revealed to all of them) and finally proclaimed in a new and definitive way by Muhammad, the confirming "seal" of the prophets, after the Prophet had received it directly through an angel from the one true God, without the errors and distortions of the Jews and Christians. For the Qur'an, it is clear that Muslims stand closest to Abraham; in the descent from Abraham they are not the only worshippers of God but they are his only true worshippers.

—Hans Küng. 2007. *Islam, Past, Present and Future.* One World Publications. p. 51

APPENDIX 1
Idolatry

It is a strange irony that those who reverence stones live in glass ideologies.

—L. Brown

Idolatry—every monotheist abhors the thought, and yet many commit the crime themselves. Few today fully grasp the complexities of this issue, for the definition of *idolatry* has been buried beneath nearly 1,700 years of church tradition.

The second commandment states, "You shall not make for yourself a carved image—any likeness *of anything* that is in heaven above, or that is in the earth beneath, or that is in the water under the earth; you shall not bow down to them nor serve them" (Exodus 20:4–5). Alternate translations employ slightly different, though significant, wording, as for example: "You shall not bow down to them or *worship* them" (NRSV, NIV).

The commandment not to make carved images speaks for itself, as does the subsequent decree not to make any likeness whatsoever.

These directives could not be clearer.

It is man's nature, however, to seek loopholes in laws, taxes, and scripture. Consequently, there are those who consider the initial order not to make "carved images" or "any likeness of anything" conditional upon the following decree not to serve or worship the images—the argument being that if nobody actually worships the image itself, then it's permissible to make it. But that's *not* what the commandment says. And in any case, caution dictates avoiding what God has forbidden, for the one who trespasses can expect to be held accountable.

But let's take a step backward. What do the words *serve* and *worship* really mean?

The verb *to serve,* according to Merriam-Webster's Dictionary, means "to give the service and respect due to (a superior)."[251] Sooo, if placing images in exalted positions (statues of saints literally placed upon pedestals, religious icons framed, etc.), spending time, energy and money to dust, clean, beautify, and preserve them are not acts of service and respect, what are?

The typical Christian response? That these acts of *service* are not acts of *worship.*

Now, wait a minute. The word *worship* wasn't even around two thousand years ago. In fact, it wasn't around one thousand years ago. It didn't exist in the English language during the period of revelation, even if the New Testament had been written in English, which it wasn't. So what words were available in biblical times? What is the meaning from which the word *worship* was derived?

Not surprisingly, we trace the word *worship* back to a sense of having worth: a sense of worthiness:

> *Worship* began life as a compound noun meaning virtually "worthiness." It was formed from the adjective *worth* and the noun suffix *-ship* "state, condition," and at first was used for "distinction, credit, dignity." This soon passed into "respect, reverence," but it was not used in specifically religious contexts until the 13th century. The verb dates from the 12th century.[252]

And this from the *New Catholic Encyclopedia:*

> Worship: In Anglo-Saxon, "weorð-scipe" meant "worth-ship," in which "worth" is to be understood in the sense of value or honor. Worship, therefore, originally meant the state of worth, the quality of being valuable or worthy.[253]

So what does the second commandment really say? Not only should one not bow or pray to man-made images (in the manner of many Catholics), but one should not even value these images.

"But we don't value them!" the average Christian responds.

Oh, really? Well, in that case, you won't mind if we just toss them into the garbage or flush them down the toilet. I mean, they're worthless, right? Without value, right? And what do we do with worthless things? We throw them away, don't we?

The point is that, yes, Christians value their images, and in this manner they violate the second commandment.

Does idolatry manifest itself in other ways?

Sure. Ever wonder why people used to (and in some cases, still do) greet upper-tier clergy, royalty, and members of the social elite as "Your worship?" By this phrase, commoners venerate men and women of high worth, position, and social status. So is that worship? According to the definition of the word, yes. "Your worship" meant "Your worthiness," and conveyed the distinction of high value.

So does this mean the commoners who used this phrase worshipped those they addressed in such a manner? Uh, yes. Yup, that's about it. Not only did they worship them, they *idolized* them, and we see this dynamic applied as much to music, sports, and movie stars in the present day as we do to clergy, royalty, and the social elite.

"Oh, come on," you might say, "You're being ridiculous."
No, I'm being precise.

I'm not saying God has forbidden us to honor such individuals; I'm just saying that, yes, addressing individuals in such terms as "Your worship" is a form of worship. However, where this crosses the line into the forbidden zone is when people revere others *as gods*, or grant them the honor and respect reserved for our Creator. Should they prefer these individuals' guidance to the laws and guidance of revelation, they usurp God's authority. Likewise, should they revere such an individual by, oh let's say, claiming him to be infallible or by bowing down to him (even if just to kiss his ring), they grant him the rights and special honor reserved for Almighty God.

In this manner, idolatry does not require a statue, although statues certainly heighten the offense. After all, "idolatry refers to the worship of gods other than the one, true God, and the use of images is characteristic of the life of the heathen."[254]

It is interesting to have a Catholic encyclopedia provide such a definition, isn't it? Why, we don't even need to read between the lines to realize it is self-condemning!

Unfortunately, many modern Christian denominations justify their practices more on the basis of tradition than scripture. Rarely is scripture given priority over tradition. Examples do exist, however. As recently as the 1500s, the Nestorian Christians of the Malabar Coast in India were presented with an image of the Virgin Mary for the first time. Largely sheltered from European influence, these Malabar Coast Christians had remained ignorant of the changes instituted by the various councils and synods of the European churches. Only with the establishment of sea routes in the sixteenth century did the two begin to interact. As Edward Gibbon noted,

Their separation from the Western world had left them in ignorance of the improvements or corruptions of a thousand years; and their conformity with the faith and practice of the fifth century, would equally disappoint the prejudices of a Papist or a Protestant.[255]

So how did they respond when presented with an image of the Virgin Mary?

The title of Mother of God was offensive to their ear, and they measured with scrupulous avarice the honours of the Virgin Mary, whom the superstition of the Latins had almost exalted to the rank of a goddess. When her image was first presented to the disciples of St. Thomas, they indignantly exclaimed, "We are Christians, not idolaters!"[256]

It is worth nothing that these Malabar Coast Christians were neither incorrect nor alone in their views:

The primitive Christians were possessed with an unconquerable repugnance to the use and abuse of images, and this aversion may be ascribed to their descent from the Jews, and their enmity to the Greeks. The Mosaic law had severely proscribed all representations of the Deity; and that precept was firmly established in the principles and practice of the chosen people. The wit of the Christian apologists was pointed against the foolish idolaters, who bowed before the workmanship of their own hands, the images of brass and marble, which, had *they* been endowed with sense and motion, should have started rather from the pedestal to adore the creative powers of the artist.[257]

Or, to put it in simpler and more modern English,

> The primitive Christians had attacked image worship as the work of the devil and there had been wholesale destruction of every type of idol when Christianity had at last triumphed. But over the succeeding centuries, the images crept back, appearing under new names but, to the critical eye, with an identical role. It was the Christians of the East who first began to feel that much of the pagan religion that their forefathers had destroyed, at such cost in martyrs' blood, was insensibly being restored.[258]

Religious art nonetheless was approved at the Council of Nicaea in 325 CE, and idol worship invaded Catholic services from that time on. Gibbon comments:

> At first the experiment was made with caution and scruple; and the venerable pictures were discreetly allowed to instruct the ignorant, to awaken the cold, and to gratify the prejudices of the heathen proselytes. By a slow though inevitable progression, the honours of the original were transferred to the copy; the devout Christian prayed before the image of a saint; and the pagan rites of genuflexion, luminaries, and incense, again stole into the Catholic Church.[259]

Given time (Gibbon continues),

> The worship of images had stolen into the church by insensible degrees, and each petty step was pleasing to the superstitious mind, as productive of comfort and innocent of sin. But in the beginning of the eighth century, in the full magnitude of the abuse, the more timorous Greeks were awakened by an apprehension,

that, under the mask of Christianity, they had restored the religion of their fathers; they heard, with grief and impatience, the name of idolaters; the incessant charge of the Jews and Mahometans, who derived from the law and the Koran an immortal hatred to graven images and all relative worship.[260]

All whose Christianity was based upon scripture, apostolic example, and the teachings of the prophets opposed the introduction of idol worship. Hence, when Emperor Constantine's congruently named sister, Constantina, requested a representation of Jesus Christ in 326 CE, Eusebius of Nicomedia answered haughtily, "What, and what kind of likeness of Christ is there? Such images are forbidden by the second commandment."[261]

Over two centuries ago, Joseph Priestley penned a summary that not only explained the history, but also the reason for this corruption of Christian orthodoxy:

Temples being now built in honour of particular saints, and especially the martyrs, it was natural to ornament them with paintings and sculptures representing the great exploits of such saints and martyrs; and this was a circumstance that made the Christian churches still more like the heathen temples, which were also adorned with statues and pictures; and this also would tend to draw the ignorant multitude to the new worship, making the transition the easier.

Paulinus, a convert from paganism, a person of senatorial rank, celebrated for his parts and learning, and who died afterwards bishop of Nola in Italy, distinguished himself in this way. He rebuilt, in a splendid manner, his own episcopal church, dedicated to Felix the martyr, and in the porticoes of it, he had painted the miracles

of Moses and of Christ, together with the acts of Felix
and of other martyrs, whose relics were deposited in it.
This, he says, was done with a design to draw the rude
multitude, habituated to the profane rites of paganism, to
a knowledge and good opinion of the Christian doctrine,
by learning from those pictures what they were not
capable of learning from books, of the lives and acts of
Christian saints.

The custom of having pictures in churches being once
begun (which was about the end of the fourth or the
beginning of the fifth century, and generally by converts
from paganism) the more wealthy among the Christians
seem to have vied with each other, who should build and
ornament their churches in the most expensive manner,
and nothing perhaps contributed more to it than the
example of this Paulinus.

It appears from Chrysostom, that pictures and images
were to be seen in the principal churches of his time, but
this was in the East. In Italy, they were but rare in the
beginning of the fifth century, and the bishop of that
country, who had got his church painted, thought proper
to make an apology for it, by saying that the people being
amused with the pictures would have less time for regaling
themselves. The origin of this custom was probably in
Cappadocia, where Gregory Nyssenus was bishop, the
same who commended Gregory Thaumaturgus for
contriving to make the Christian festivals resemble the
pagan ones.

Though many churches in this age were adorned with
the images of saints and martyrs, there do not appear to
have been many of Christ. These are said to have been
introduced by the Cappodocians; and the first of these
were only symbolical ones, being made in the form of a
lamb. One of this kind Epiphanius found in the year 389,
and he was so provoked at it, that he tore it. It was not

till the Council of Constantinople, called *In Trullo*, held as late as the year 707 CE, that pictures of Christ were ordered to be drawn in the form of men.[262]

In 726 CE, a scant nineteen years following the Council of Constantinople, the Emperor of Constantinople, Leo III (also known as Leo the Isaurian, but best known as Leo the Iconoclast) began to destroy images within the expanding circle of his influence. Thomas Hodgkin noted,

It was the contact with Mohammedanism which opened the eyes of Leo and the men who stood around his throne, ecclesiastics as well as laymen, to the degrading and idolatrous superstitions that had crept into the Church and were overlaying the life of a religion which, at its proclamation the purest and most spiritual, was fast becoming one of the most superstitious and materialistic that the world had ever seen. Shrinking at first from any representation whatever of visible objects, then allowing herself the use of beautiful and pathetic emblems (such as the Good Shepherd), in the fourth century the Christian Church sought to instruct the converts whom her victory under Constantine was bringing to her in myriads, by representations on the walls of the churches of the chief event of Scripture history. From this the transition to specially reverenced pictures of Christ, the Virgin and the Saints, was natural and easy. The crowning absurdity and blasphemy, the representation of the Almighty Maker of the Universe as a bearded old man, floating in the sky, was not yet perpetrated, nor was to be dared till the human race had taken several steps downward into the darkness of the Middle Ages; but enough had been already done to show whither the Church was tending, and to give point to the sarcasm of the followers of the Prophet when they hurled the epithet "idolaters" at the craven and servile populations of Egypt and Syria.[263]

The irony of Emperor Leo's transition from victor over the Saracens in Eastern Europe to Leo the Iconoclast is inescapable. After he defeated the Muslims, he adopted their drive to abolish idolatry. In any case, Pope Gregory II attempted to dampen Leo's enthusiasm with the following counsel:

> Are you ignorant that the popes are the bond of union, the mediators of peace between the East and West? The eyes of the nations are fixed on our humility; and they revere, as a God upon earth, the apostle St. Peter, whose image you threaten to destroy …Abandon your rash and fatal enterprise; reflect, tremble, and repent. If you persist, we are innocent of the blood that will be spilt in the contest; may it fall on your own head.[264]

As George Bernard Shaw stated in the preface to his play, *Saint Joan*, "The Churches must learn humility as well as teach it."[265] No doubt the person who shouts, "Look at how humble I am! Can't you tell I'm the most humble person you ever saw?" is instantly disqualified. More to the point, the pope who sanctioned images while at the same time stating, "But for the statue of St. Peter himself, which all the kingdoms of the West esteem as a god on earth, the whole West would take a terrible revenge"[266] should perceive an asteroid-sized theological inconsistency. Exactly who should "reflect, tremble and repent" should be boldly obvious.

That Pope Gregory II and his followers were willing to wage war in defense of their images testifies to the extraordinarily high value (that is to say, the worth, the worthiness—i.e., the *worship*) they placed on these images. And spill blood they did, to such an extent that the defeat of Leo's army at Ravenna turned the waters of the river Po red. So badly was the river polluted that "during six years, the public prejudice abstained from the fish of the river …"[267]

When the Synod of Constantinople convened in 754 CE, the Roman Catholic Church staged a boycott due to non-conformity of the Greek Church with Catholic teaching. Or at least, that was the excuse they offered. A more likely scenario, perhaps, was that the Catholics recognized their inability to defend a practice that was scripturally condemned by the Almighty God they claimed to worship.

Nevertheless, the Synod of Constantinople convened without them and,

> After a serious deliberation of six months the three hundred and thirty-eight bishops pronounced and subscribed a unanimous decree that all visible symbols of Christ, except in the Eucharist, were either blasphemous or heretical; that image worship was a corruption of Christianity and a renewal of Paganism; that all such monuments of idolatry should be broken or erased; and that those who should refuse to deliver the objects of their private superstition, were guilty of disobedience to the authority of the church and of the emperor.[268]

The fact that the synod exempted the Eucharist from association with paganism is particularly curious to those knowledgeable of ancient Persian and Egyptian rites and rituals. The Persians employed consecrated water and bread in the ancient cult of Mithras.[269] As T. W. Doane notes in his 1971 study, *Bible Myths and Their Parallels in Other Religions,*

> It is in the ancient religion of Persia—the religion of Mithra, the Mediator, the Redeemer and Saviour—that we find the

nearest resemblance to the sacrament of the Christians, and
from which it was evidently borrowed. Those who were
initiated into the mysteries of Mithra, or became *members*,
took the sacrament of bread and wine ...

This food they called the Eucharist, of which no one was
allowed to partake but the persons who believed that the
things they taught were true, and who had been washed
with the washing that is for the remission of sin. Tertullian,
who flourished from 193 to 220 A.D., also speaks of the
Mithraic devotees celebrating the Eucharist.

The Eucharist of the Lord and Saviour, as the Magi
called Mithra, the second person in their Trinity, or their
Eucharistic sacrifice, was always made exactly and in every
respect the same as that of the orthodox Christians, for
both sometimes used water instead of wine, or a mixture
of the two.[270]

The cult of Osiris (the ancient Egyptian god of life, death,
and fertility) offered the same allure of an easy salvation as did
Paul's concept of salvation through the atoning sacrifice of Jesus.
"The secret of that popularity was, that he [Osiris] had lived
on earth as benefactor, died for man's good, and lived again
as friend and judge."[271] The ancient Egyptians commemorated
Osiris' birth with a cradle and lights and annually celebrated
his alleged resurrection. They also commemorated his death by
eating sacred bread that had been consecrated by their priests.
They believed this consecration transmuted the bread to the
veritable flesh of Osiris.[272] If it all sounds familiar, it should,
for as James Bonwick comments, "As it is recognized that
the bread after sacerdotal rites becomes mystically the body
of Christ, so the men of the Nile declared their bread after
sacerdotal rites became mystically the body of Isis or Osiris: in
such manner they ate their god."[273]

Furthermore, as Bonwick writes,

The cakes of Isis were, like the cakes of Osiris, of a round shape. They were placed upon the altar. Gliddon writes that they were "identical in shape with the consecrated cake of the Roman and Eastern Churches." Melville assures us, "The Egyptians marked this holy bread with St. Andrew's Cross." The *Presence* bread was broken before being distributed by the priests to the people, and was supposed to become the flesh and blood of the Diety. The miracle was wrought by the hand of the officiating priest, who blessed the food.[274]

In like fashion, ancient Buddhists offered a sacrament of bread and wine, Hindus a Eucharist of soma juice (an intoxicating plant extract), and the ancient Greeks a sacrament of bread and wine in tribute to Demeter (aka Ceres, their goddess of corn) and Dionysos (aka Bacchus, their god of wine). In this manner, they ate the flesh and drank the blood of their gods.[275]

The religious parallels are so obvious as to demand explanation. We can reasonably question how the cults of Isis and Osiris placed the mark of St. Andrew's cross on their consecrated bread two thousand years before St. Andrew was born. Clairvoyance on the part of the Egyptians, or religious plagiarism on the part of St. Andrew? In addition, there are striking similarities between the mysteries of Pauline Christianity and those of the cults of Isis and Osiris— mysteries to include the virgin birth (Isis the virgin mother, Horus the child) and the atoning sacrifice of Osiris, followed by his resurrection and assumption of the role of redeemer. Justin Martyr, the famous Christian apologist, dismissed these similarities by claiming that Satan copied the Christian ceremonies in order to mislead the remainder of mankind.[276] However, taking note of the time sequence, these earlier

Eucharistic practices and mysteries of faith preceded those of Catholicism by more than two thousand years.

Considering this fact, T. W. Doane reasonably concluded,

> These facts show that the *Eucharist* is another piece of Paganism adopted by the Christians. The story of Jesus and his disciples being at supper, where the Master did break bread, may be true, but the statement that he said, "Do this in remembrance of me,"—"this is my body," and "this is my blood," was undoubtedly invented to give authority to the *mystic* ceremony, which had been borrowed from Paganism.[277]

Invented statements, in the Bible? How can that be, when all of the gospels record Jesus' words at the paschal meal? Well, all but one, that is. According to John 13:1, Jesus was arrested *before* the Passover feast. So it's John against the Synoptics. Or, to make the contest even, it's John against Q (abbreviation of the German word *Quelle,* meaning "source")—the hypothesized common source document of the Synoptic gospels.

Lest anybody misunderstand, Catholics do not tolerate a symbolic interpretation of their sacramental rites. The Council of Trent (1545–63 CE) established laws concerning the alleged transubstantiation of the Eucharist, and these laws stand to this day. Not even the more liberal Second Vatican Council (1962–65) effected a change. In short, the Council of Trent's judgment reads:

> Canon 1: If anyone denies that in the sacrament of the most Holy Eucharist are contained truly, really and substantially the body and blood together with the soul and divinity of our Lord Jesus Christ, and consequently

the whole Christ, but says that He is in it only as in a sign, or figure or force, let him be anathema.[278]

In other words, anyone who considers the bread and wine of the Eucharist to be merely symbolic is to be anathema (i.e., cursed and excommunicated). This judgment is reinforced by the following:

Canon 6: If anyone says that in the holy sacrament of the Eucharist, Christ, the only begotten Son of God, is not to be adored with the worship of *latria,*[279(EN)] also outwardly manifested, and is consequently neither to be venerated with a special festive solemnity, nor to be solemnly borne about in procession according to the laudable and universal rite and custom of the holy Church, or is not to be set publicly before the people to be adored and that the adorers thereof are idolaters, let him be anathema.[280]

In other words, those who refuse to adore, venerate, or glorify are to suffer the same fate as those who consider the Eucharist symbolic. These Catholic laws remain on the books to the present day, which explains why so many Protestant denominations have sidestepped away from their Catholic cousins and either abolished or watered-down their veneration of the Eucharist. This reaction is particularly easy to understand, for many pagan cultures taught assimilation of the qualities of the ancestral totem through eating "bread transmuted into flesh." Which group has the real sacred saltine remains the subject of ongoing debate.

Returning to the main subject, the Catholic Church responded to the Synod of Constantinople of 754 CE by calling a second Council of Nicaea in 787 CE. This council reinstated image worship on the basis that "the worship of images is agreeable to Scripture and reason, to the fathers and councils of the church ..."[281]

Suddenly, the theory that certain eighth-century clergy partook of hallucinogenic mushrooms begins to look pretty good. We have to wonder what apostolic fathers and which scripture this council consulted. For that matter, exactly how is this decision "agreeable to scripture and reason"?

In any case, those religious communities that objected to Christian idol worship were "cleansed" by the Catholic armies. Beginning with the slaughter of Unitarian Christians in the mid-ninth century, Empress Theodora gained the dubious distinction of being the one "who restored the images to the Oriental [i.e., Eastern Orthodox] church."[282] All subsequent efforts to eradicate images in the church were quashed, resulting in the idolatrous practices witnessed to this day.

Of even greater concern is the adoption of *human* idols. Priest-worship surfaced in the early thirteenth century, in the form of priests acting as intermediaries for confession and absolution of sins. Pope-worship became manifest in the form of ritual kissing of the Pope's foot or ring. The creative doctrine of papal infallibility, as defined by Pope Pius IX at the First Vatican Council in 1869–1870, set the pope as rival with God. The worship of Mary and the title "Mother of God" were canonized considerably earlier, at the Council of Ephesus in 431 CE. Directing prayers to saints, angels and the Virgin Mary was officially sanctioned from the early seventh century. The famous prayer to the Virgin Mary, *Ave Maria* (Hail Mary), lagged a thousand years behind, and received official formulation in the reformed Breviary of Pope Pius V in 1568. However, among all the human subjects of worship, Jesus Christ is hands down the most worshipped mortal ever to have walked the earth.

A powerful challenge to Trinitarian thought, initially attributed to Theophilus Lindsey (1723–1804 CE) and subsequently argued by Unitarian Christians worldwide, asks how those who worship Jesus would respond, were he to return and pose the following questions:

a) Why did you address your devotions to me? Did I ever direct you to do this, or propose myself as an object of worship?

b) Did I not uniformly and to the last set an example of praying to the Father, to my Father and your Father, to my God and your God? (John 20:17)

c) When my disciples requested me to teach them to pray (Luke 11:1–2), did I ever teach them to pray to myself? Did I not teach them to pray to no one but to the Father?

d) Did I ever call myself God, or tell you that I was the maker of the world and to be worshipped?

e) Solomon, after building the temple said, "Will God indeed dwell on the earth? Behold the heaven and heaven of heavens cannot contain thee; how much less this house which I have built" (I Kings 8:27). So how could God ever have dwelt on earth?

These questions are all the more relevant, for Christians expect that when Jesus returns, he will denounce many "Christians" as disbelievers. As stated in Matthew 7:21–23,

> Not everyone who says to me, "Lord, Lord," shall enter the kingdom of heaven, but he who does the will of my Father in heaven. *Many* will say to me in that day, "Lord, Lord, have we not prophesied in your name, cast out demons in your name, and done many wonders in your

name?" And then I will declare to them, "I never knew you; depart from me, you who practice lawlessness!"

So if Jesus will disown some Christians who prophesied, cast out demons, and performed wonders in his name (i.e., those who say "Lord, Lord"), who are these disbelievers going to be?

Answer: those who "practice lawlessness" (Jesus' words, not mine). And that is the point, isn't it? For what law did Jesus teach? During the period of his mission, "the will of my Father in heaven" was Old Testament law. *That* is what Jesus taught, and that is what Jesus lived.

So where in his teachings or example did Jesus command servitude and worship of himself? Nowhere. Just the opposite, in fact, for the Bible records him having taught, "'You shall worship the Lord your God, and Him *only* you shall serve'" (Luke 4:8). Furthermore, Jesus reportedly taught, "Why do you call me good: No one is good but One, that is, God" (Matthew 9:17, Mark 10–18, and Luke 18:19), and, "My Father is greater than I" (John 14:28).

Perhaps for these reasons, Christians focused the first eighteen centuries of their worship on the Father, and the Father alone. As Joseph Priestly tells us, praying to Jesus is a modern innovation, distant from both Jesus' teachings and time:

Accordingly, the practice of praying to the Father only, was long universal in the Christian church: the short addresses to Christ, as those in the Litany, "*Lord have mercy upon us, Christ have mercy upon us,*" being comparatively of late date. In the Clementine liturgy, the oldest that is extant, contained in the *Apostolical Constitutions*, which were probably composed about the fourth century, there is no trace of any such thing. Origen, in a large treatise on the subject of prayer, urges very forcibly the propriety of praying to the Father only, and not to Christ; and as he gives no hint that the public forms of prayer had anything reprehensible in them in that respect, we are naturally led to conclude that, in his time, such petitions to Christ were unknown in the public assemblies of Christians. And such hold have early established customs on the minds of men, that, excepting the Moravians only, whose prayers are always addressed to Christ, the general practice of Trinitarians themselves is, to pray to the Father only.

Now on what principle could this early and universal practice have been founded? What is there in the doctrine of a Trinity consisting of three equal persons, to entitle the Father to that distinction, in preference to the Son or the Spirit?[283]

What is there, indeed? Priestley records a little-known aspect of Christian history: namely, that up to his time (late eighteenth century) the "general practice of Trinitarians themselves is, to pray to the Father only." Those who draw upon their modern Christian experience might mistakenly believe that the twenty-first century practice of praying to Jesus Christ dates from early Christianity.

Nothing is further from the truth.

For nearly eighteen hundred years following the birth of Christianity, prayers were directed only to God. It wasn't until 1787 when the Moravian Church, a Protestant sect founded in fifteenth-century Bohemia (in what is present-day Czechoslovakia), underwent a profound Pentecostal transformation and began directing prayers to Jesus Christ.

So why, if the three persons of the proposed Trinity are considered coequal, should such a preference for the Father have prevailed? And not just for a decade or two, but for the first eighteen hundred years of Christianity? Unless, that is, a greater lesson is to be learned from the uniformity of early Christian devotions than from the inconsistencies of Trinitarian theology.

Priestley was just one of many who attempted to prevent the derailing of Christian devotions from the Creator to His creation—Jesus, Mary, the Holy Spirit, and the multitude of saints. However, no historical analysis of this subject would be complete without noting that Islam has always maintained a strictly monotheistic, iconoclastic faith, as described by Gibbon:

> The Mahometans have uniformly withstood the temptation of reducing the object of their faith and devotion to a level with the senses and imagination of man. "I believe in One God and Mahomet the apostle of God," is the simple and invariable profession of Islam. The intellectual image of the Deity has never been degraded by any visible idol; the honours of the prophet have never transgressed the measure of human virtue; and his living precepts have restrained the gratitude of his disciples within the bounds of reason and religion."[284]

Recommended Reading

Translations of the Meaning of the Holy Qur'an:

1) The Holy Qur'an (King Fahd Holy Qur-an Printing Complex, Al-Madinah Al-Munawarah, Saudi Arabia) and The Qur'an (Tahrike Tarsile Qur'an Inc., Elmhurst, New York) both present the translation of Abdullah Yusuf Ali—an excellent translation, enhanced by the beauty of more classical English than that found in more modern translations. A major shortcoming, however, is that the translator's commentary contains multiple errors, and is best avoided in favor of more classic, and respected, *tafaseer* (explanations of the meanings of the Qur'an).

2) *The Noble Qur'an* (King Fahd Holy Qur-an Printing Complex, Al-Madinah Al-Munawarah, Saudi Arabia) translated by Dr. Muhammad al-Hilali and Dr. Muhammad Muhsin Khan. A more modern and literal translation than that of Abdullah Yusuf Ali, thoroughly researched and complemented by explanations from the *tafaseer* of Ibn Katheer, Al-Qurtubee, and At-Tabaree, as well as quotations of authentic *hadith*, primarily from the collection of Al-Bukhari. This is without a doubt the most error-free of the English translations, yet this translation nonetheless suffers from a certain lack of fluency in the

English language. Although an exceptional reference book, dedicated reading can become tiresome due to the format and limitations of the language.

3) *The Qur'an* (revised and edited by Saheeh International, Abul-Qasim Publishing House, Jeddah, Saudi Arabia). An excellent, easily readable, and highly respected modern translation, thought by many to be the overall best available in the English language. Highly recommended as the first book for those seeking an easy, accurate, and pleasing translation of the meaning of the Qur'an.4)

Sciences of the Qur'an:

1) *An Introduction to the Sciences of the Qur'aan* (Al-Hidaayah Publishing, Birmingham, England), by Abu Ammaar Yasir Qadhi.

2) *Approaching the Qur'an* (White Cloud Press), by Michael Sells.

History of Islam:

1) *Muhammad, His Life Based on the Earliest Sources* (The Islamic Texts Society, Cambridge, England) by Martin Lings. An excellent and comprehensive history of the life of Muhammad, only slightly marred by the few aforementioned errors.

2) *When the Moon Split* by Safi-ur-Rahman al-Mubarakpuri. Published by Maktaba Dar-us-Salam, Saudi Arabia. An excellent, award-winning history of the Prophet, this English translation is slightly disappointing, but still readable and highly informative.

History of the Arabs:
1) *A History of the Arab Peoples* (Warner Books) by Albert Hourani. Scholarly and comprehensive.

Comparative Religion:
1) *MisGod'ed*, by Laurence B. Brown—the first book in this series.
2) *Misquoting Jesus* (Harper San Francisco), by Bart D. Ehrman. Perhaps the most readable book of biblical textual criticism ever written, backed up by the highest scholarship.
3) *Lost Christianities* (Oxford University Press), by Bart D. Ehrman. Another "must read."
4) *A Muslim Study of the Origins of the Christian Church* (Oxford University Press), by Ruqaiyyah Waris Maqsood. A sadly neglected treasure of theology written by a noted Muslim scholar.
5) *The Mysteries of Jesus* (Sakina Books, Oxford), by Ruqaiyyah Waris Maqsood. Same book, but published under a different title.

Basic Information on Islam:
1) *What Everyone Should Know About Islam and Muslims* (Kazi Publications, Chicago, IL), by Suzanne Haneef. A comprehensive, beautifully written primer.
2) *What Every Christian Should Know About Islam* (The Islamic Foundation, Markfield, England), by Ruqaiyyah Waris Maqsood. Shorter than Suzanne Haneef's book, but every bit as enjoyable and informative, with greater emphasis on theology, balanced by personal narrative.

Guidance to New Muslims:

1) *Bearing True Witness* (or, *Now That I've Found Islam, What Do I Do With It?*)—see author's website, www.leveltruth.com.

And Just for Pleasure:

1) *The Eighth Scroll,* by Laurence B. Brown. A historical thriller.
2) *The Road to Mecca* (Islamic Book Trust, Kuala Lumpur), by Muhammad Asad. A remarkable and heartwarming story of one man's journey, first to Islam, and then through the world of the Arabs.
3) *Desert Encounter*, by Knud Holmboe. Memoirs of a Danish Muslim's travels through "Italian" Africa.

BIBLIOGRAPHY

Abu Nu'aem. *Dala'el An-Noobowah.*

Al-Bukhari—the famous ninth century *hadith* scholar, Muhammed ibn Ismaiel ibn Ibrahim; translated by Dr. Muhammad Muhsin Khan. 1997. *Sahih Al-Bukhari.* Riyadh: Darussalam.

Al-Haakim.

Al-Hilali, Muhammad, Ph.D. and Dr. Muhammad Muhsin Khan, M.D. *Interpretation of the Meanings of The Noble Qur'an in the English Language; A Summarized Version of At-Tabari, Al-Qurtubi and Ibn Kathir with comments from Sahih Al-Bukhari.*

Al-Mubarakpuri, Safi-ur-Rahman. 1995. *Ar-Raheeq Al-Makhtum (The Sealed Nectar).* Riyadh: Maktaba Dar-us-Salam.

An-Nasa'ee.

Anthes, Richard A., John J. Cahir, Alistair B. Fraser, and Hans A. Panofsky. 1981. *The Atmosphere.* 3rd edition. Columbus: Charles E. Merrill Publishing Co.

Arberry, A. J. 1953. *The Holy Koran: An Introduction with Selections.* London: George Allen & Unwin Ltd.

Arberry, A. J. 1964. *The Koran Interpreted.* London: Oxford University Press.

Arberry, A. J. 1996. *The Koran Interpreted.* A Touchstone Book: Simon & Schuster.

Arbuthnot, F. F. 1885. *The Construction of the Bible and the Korân.* London: Watts & Co.

Ash-Shifa.

At-Tabarani, *Al-Mu'jam Al-Kabeer.*

Ayto, John. 1991. *Bloomsbury Dictionary of Word Origins.* London: Bloomsbury Publishing Limited.

Azzirikly, Al-Aa'lam.

Baigent, Michael and Richard Leigh. 1991. *The Dead Sea Scrolls Deception.* New York: Summit Books/Simon & Schuster Inc.

Bermant, Chaim and Michael Weitzman. 1979. *Ebla: A Revelation in Archaeology.* Times Books.

The Bible, Revised Standard Version. 1977. New York: American Bible Society.

Bonwick, James, F.R.G.S. 1956. *Egyptian Belief and Modern Thought.* Colorado: Falcon's Wing Press.

Bucaille, Maurice, M.D. 1977. *The Bible, the Qur'an and Science.* Lahore: Kazi Publications.

Bultmann, Rudolf. 1971. *The Gospel of John, a Commentary.* Translated by G. R. Beasley-Murray. Oxford: Basil Blackwell.

Butler, Trent C. (General Editor). *Holman Bible Dictionary.* Nashville: Holman Bible Publishers.

Cailleux, Andre. 1968. *Anatomy of the Earth.* New York: McGraw-Hill Book Company. Translated by J. Moody Stuart.

Carlyle, Thomas. 1841. *On Heros, Hero-Worship and the Heroic in History.* London: James Fraser, Regent Street.

Chamberlin, E. R. 1993. *The Bad Popes.* Barnes & Noble, Inc.

Cohen, M.J. and J.M. 1996. The Penguin Dictionary of Twentieth-Century Quotations. Penguin Books.

Davis, Richard A., Jr. 1972. *Principles of Oceanography.* Reading, Massachusetts: Addison-Wesley Publishing Co.

De Lamartine, A. 1854. *Histoire de la Turquie.* Paris.

Denzinger, Henricus & Schonmetzer, Adolfus. 1973. *Enchiridion Symbolorum, Definitionum et Declarationum de Rebus Fidei et Morum.* Barcinone: Herder.

Diamond, Jared. 1999. *Guns, Germs, and Steel.* W. W. Norton and Company, Inc.

Doane, Thomas W. 1971. *Bible Myths and Their Parallels in Other Religions.* New York: University Books.

Ehrman, Bart D. 2005. *Misquoting Jesus.* HarperCollins.

Ehrman, Bart D. 2005. *Lost Christianities.* Oxford University Press.

Elder, Danny; and John Pernetta. 1991. *Oceans.* London: Mitchell Beazley Publishers.

The Encyclopedia Americana International Edition. 1998. Grolier Inc.

Encyclopaedia Britannica. 1994–1998. CD-ROM.

Encyclopaedia Judaica. 1971. Jerusalem: Keter Publishing House Ltd.

Encyclopaedia Judaica, CD-ROM Edition. 1997. Judaica Multimedia (Israel) Limited.

Fath Al Bari Sharh Sahih Al Bukhari. Ibn Hajar Al Asqalani, Bab Alqadar. Cairo: Al Maktaba Assalafiyah.

Fossier, Robert (editor). 1986. *The Cambridge Illustrated History of The Middle Ages.* Cambridge: Cambridge University Press.

Fox, Robin Lane. 1991. *The Unauthorized Version: Truth and Fiction in the Bible.* Viking Press.

Gibbon, Edward, Esq. 1854. *The History of the Decline and Fall of the Roman Empire.* London: Henry G. Bohn.

Gilman, Arthur, M.A. 1908. *The Saracens.* New York: G. P. Putnam's Sons.

Gross, M. Grant. 1993. *Oceanography, a View of Earth.* 4th edition. Englewood Cliffs: Prentice-Hall, Inc.

Guillaume, Alfred. 1990. *Islam.* Penguin Books.

Hammad, Ahmad Zaki. 1997. *Father of Flame, Commentary & Vocabulary Reference of Surat al-Masad.* Bridgeview, Illinois: Quranic Literacy Institute.

Hastings, James (Editor). 1913. *The Encyclopedia of Religion and Ethics.* Charles Scribner's Sons.

Hastings, James (editor); Revised edition by Frederick C. Grant and H. H. Rowley. 1963. *Dictionary of The Bible.* 2nd edition. Charles Scribner's Sons.

Hirschfeld, Hartwig, Ph.D. 1902. *New Researches into the Composition and Exegesis of the Qoran.* London: Royal Asiatic Society.

Hodgkin, Thomas. 1967. *Italy and Her Invaders.* New York: Russell & Russell.

Hogarth, D.G. 1922. *Arabia.* Oxford: Clarendon Press.

The Holy Bible, New King James Version. 1982. Thomas Nelson Publishers.

The Holy Bible, New Revised Standard Version. Grand Rapids, MI: Zondervan Publishing House.

Hyndman, H. M. 1919. *The Awakening of Asia.* New York: Boni and Liveright.

Ibn Hisham. *As-Seerah An-Nabawiyyah.*

Imam At-Tirmithi. *Mukhtasar Ash-Shama'el Al Muhammadiyyah.*

Irving, Washington. 1973. *Mahomet and His Successors.* New York: G. P. Putnam's Sons.

Kähler, Martin. 1953. *Der sogennante historische Jesus und der geschichtliche, biblische Christus.* Munich: New edition by Ernst Wolf.

Kipling, Rudyard. *Life's Handicap.* 1891. "Bertran and Bimi."

Kraeling, Emil G. Ph. D. 1952. *Rand McNally Bible Atlas.* Rand McNally & Co.

Kuenen, Philip H. 1960. *Marine Geology.* New York: John Wiley & Sons, Inc.

Küng, Hans. 2007. Islam, Past, Present and Future. One World Publications.

Labbe, P. Venice, 1728–1733. *Sacrosancta Concilia.*

LaFollette, Suzanne. 1926. *Concerning Women.* "The Beginnings of Emancipation."

Lane, Edward William. 1980. *An Arabic-English Lexicon Derived From the Best and the Most Copious Eastern Sources.* Beirut, Lebanon: Librairie Du Liban.

Lane-Poole, Stanley. 1882. *The Speeches and Table-Talk of the Prophet Mohammad.* London: MacMillan and Co.

Lings, Martin. 1995. *Muhammad, His Life Based on the Earliest Sources.* The Islamic Texts Society.

Manaahil Al-Irfaan fi Uluum Al-Qur'an (Wells of Knowledge of the Sciences of the Qur'an). 1988. Muhammad Abdul-At-Theem Az-Ziqaani. Dar Al-Kutub Al-Ilmee'a.

McBrien, Richard P. (General Editor). 1995. *HarperCollins Encyclopedia of Catholicism.* New York: HarperCollins Publishers.

Meagher, Paul Kevin OP, S.T.M., Thomas C. O'Brien, Sister Consuelo Maria Aherne, SSJ (editors). 1979. *Encyclopedic Dictionary of Religion.* Philadelphia: Corpus Publications.

Merriam-Webster's Collegiate Dictionary. 1997. 10th edition. Merriam-Webster, Inc.

Michener, James A. May, 1955. "Islam: The Misunderstood Religion," in *Reader's Digest* (American Edition).

Miller, Albert and Jack C. Thompson. 1975. *Elements of Meteorology.* 2nd edition. Columbus: Charles E. Merrill Publishing Co.

Montet, Edward. 1929. *Traduction Francaise du Couran*. Paris.

Moore, Keith L. 1983. *The Developing Human, Clinically Oriented Embryology, With Islamic Additions*. 3rd edition. Jeddah: Dar Al-Qiblah with permission of W.B. Saunders Co.

Muata'h Imam Malik.

Muhammad ibn Ishaq ibn Yasar. 1963. *Seerat An-Nabi*. Maydan Al Azhar (Cairo): Muhammad Ali Sabi'eh & Children.

Muir, Sir William. 1923. *The Life of Mohammad*. Edinburgh: John Grant.

Muslim—the famous ninth century *hadith* scholar, Muslim ibn Al-Hajjaj.

Musnad Abu Ya'ala.

Musnad Ahmad.

Naish, John, M.A. 1937. *The Wisdom of the Qur'an*. Oxford.

National Geographic Society. "The Universe, Nature's Grandest Design." Cartographic division. 1995.

National Geographic. December, 1978.

New Catholic Encyclopedia. 1967. Washington, D.C.: The Catholic University of America.

The New International Encyclopaedia. 1917. 2nd edition. New York: Dodd, Mead and Company.

Newsweek. October 31, 1988.

Nydell, Margaret K. 2006. *Understanding Arabs*. Intercultural Press.

Ostrogorsky, George. 1969. *History of the Byzantine State*. (Translated from the German by Joan Hussey). New Brunswick: Rutgers University Press.

Press, Frank and Raymond Siever. 1982. *Earth*. 3rd edition. San Francisco: W. H. Freeman and Co.

Priestley, Joseph, LL.D. F.R.S. 1782. *An History of the Corruptions of Christianity*. Birmingham: Piercy and Jones.

Priestley, Joseph. 1786. *The Theological and Miscellaneous Works of Joseph Priestley*. Edited by John Towill Rutt. Hackney: George Smallfield.

Qadhi, Abu Ammaar Yasir. 1999. *An Introduction to the Sciences of the Qur'an*. Birmingham: Al-Hidaayah Publishing.

Ranke, Hermann. *Die Ägyptischen Personennamen (Dictionary of Personal Names of the New Kingdom)*. Verzeichnis der Namen, Verlag Von J J Augustin in Glückstadt, Band I (1935); Band II (1952).

Rippin, Andrew (editor). 1988. *Approaches to the History of the Interpretation of the Qur'an*. Chapter: "Value of Hafs and Warsh Transmissions," by Adrian Brockett. Oxford: Clarendon Press.

Robinson, Victor, M.D. 1943. *The Story of Medicine*. New York: The New Home Library.

Ross, Alexander. 1718. *The Life of Mahomet: Together with The Alcoran at Large*. London.

Sa'eid Hawwa. 1990. *Ar-Rasool, Salallahu Alayhi Wa Salam*. 2nd edition. Cairo: Dar As-Salaam Publishing.

Sahih Al-Bukhari.

Saheeh International Version of The Holy Qur'an. 1997. Abul-Qasim Publishing House. Jeddah, Saudi Arabia.

Said Qutub, *Fi Thilal Al-Qur'an*.

Sale, George. 1734. *The Koran*. London: C. Ackers.

Schroeder, Rev. Henry J., O.P. 1941. *Canons and Decrees of the Council of Trent* (Original Text with English Translation). London: B. Herder Book Co.

Seeley, Rod R., Trent D. Stephens and Philip Tate. 1996. *Essentials of Anatomy and Physiology*. 2nd edition. St. Louis: Mosby-Year Book, Inc.

Shaw, George Bernard. 1944. *Everybody's Political What's What?*

Shaw, George Bernard. 1924. *Saint Joan.*

Smith, R. Bosworth, M.A. 1986. *Mohammad and Mohammadanism.* London: Darf Publishers Ltd.

Stubbe, Dr. Henry, M.A. 1975. *An Account of the Rise and Progress of Mohomedanism, with the Life of Mahomet.* Lahore: Oxford and Cambridge Press.

Sunan Tirmithee.

Sykes, Sir Percy Molesworth. 1951. *A History of Persia.* 3rd edition. London: Macmillan & Co., Ltd.

Tafheem-ul-Qur'an.

Tafseer ibn Kathir.

Tarbuck, Edward J. and Frederick K. Lutgens. 1982. *Earth Science.* 3rd edition. Columbus: Charles E. Merrill Publishing Company.

Thompson, Della (editor). *The Oxford Dictionary of Current English.* 1993. 2nd edition. Oxford University Press.

Vaglieri, Dr. Laura Veccia. Translated from Italian by Dr. Aldo Caselli, Haverford College, Pennsylvania. Originally published in Italian under the title: *Apologia dell' Islamismo* (Rome, A. F. Formiggini, 1925). 1980. *An Interpretation of Islam.* Zurich: Islamic Foundation.

Watt, W. Montgomery. 1953. *Muhammad at Mecca.* Oxford: Clarendon Press.

Wegner, Paul D. *The Journey from Texts to Translations.* 1999. Grand Rapids: Baker Books.

Wehr, Hans. *A Dictionary of Modern Written Arabic.* 3rd printing. Beirut: Librairie Du Liban; London: MacDonald & Evans Ltd. 1980.

Weinberg, Steven. 1988. *The First Three Minutes, A Modern View of the Origin of the Universe.* Basic Books; Harper Collins Publishers.

Wells, H. G. 1922. *The Outline of History*. 4th edition. Volume 2. Section XXXI —"Muhammad and Islam". New York: The Review of Reviews Company.

Whiston, William, A.M. 1998. *Josephus, The Complete Works*. Nashville: Thomas Nelson Publishers.

Zad Al-Ma'ad.

Zahrnt, Heinz. 1817. *The Historical Jesus*. (Translated from the German by J. S. Bowden). New York: Harper and Row.

GLOSSARY OF TERMS

AH: "After Hijra." The zero point of the Islamic calendar corresponds to the Muslim Hijra (migration) from Makkah to Medina in July of the year 622 CE. Subsequent dates were calculated according to the lunar calendar, which differs from the Julian calendar by roughly ten days each year.

Ayah: Plural of *ayat*: Verse of the Holy Qur'an.

BH: "Before Hijra." See *AH* for explanation.

Bint: "Daughter of."

CE: "Common Era" or "Christian Era."

Fitrah: The innate nature instilled by Allah as human birthright. *Fitrah* includes the recognition and understanding of Allah as Lord and Creator, and the inborn ability to discriminate between good and evil.

Hadith: A tradition recording the words, actions, appearance, or implied consents of Muhammad ibn Abdullah.

Hafith: A memorizer of the Holy Qur'an.

Haj: The annual Muslim pilgrimage to Makkah.

Hijra: The Muslim migration from Makkah to Medina in July of the year 622 CE.

Ibn: "Son of."

Imam: Leader of the prayer, the one who goes out in front of the congregation.

Makkah: aka Mecca, Bakka, Becca, Baca. The holy city to

which Muslims make pilgrimage. The Kaba, to which Muslims direct prayers, and the well of Zam-Zam is contained in the central, sacred mosque.

Mecca: See Makkah.

Mushaf: "Book."

Muslim: A famous ninth-century hadith scholar, Muslim ibn Al-Hajjaj. Not to be confused with *muslim*, a follower of Islam.

Sahaba: The companions of the prophet Muhammad.

Sunni: Orthodox sect of Islam, accounting for ninety-five percent of all Muslims.

Surah: Chapter of the Holy Qur'an.

Tawheed: Islamic monotheism.

Zakat: The poor-due incumbent upon Muslims, akin to tithing or alms.

ENDNOTES

[1] Guillaume, Alfred. 1990. *Islam.* Penguin Books. pp. 73–74.

[2] Cohen, M.J. and J.M. 1996. *The Penguin Dictionary of Twentieth-Century Quotations.* Penguin Books.

[3] Nydell, Margaret K. 2006. *Understanding Arabs.* Intercultural Press. p. 34.

[4] As per the *Encyclopaedia Britannica,* "The history of the term's [*apocrypha*] usage indicates that it referred to a body of esoteric writings that were at first prized, later tolerated, and finally excluded." It is interesting to note that the apocrypha, though initially "prized," eventually fell to the station of simply being tolerated, and subsequently to being rejected. The assertion that the same sequence of religious evolution ultimately resulted in the modification and/or rejection of Jesus Christ's teachings does not exactly remain distant. And how can it, when the very history of early "Christianity" is shaded in doubt? To quote from the Encyclopaedia Britannica once again,

> The writers of the four Gospels included in the New Testament were bearing witness to assured truths that the faithful ought to know, and *no convincing reconstruction of historical facts is possible* from these books of the New Testament. The only avowedly historical book in it (i.e., the New Testament) is the Acts of the Apostles. The New Testament as a whole represents merely a selection from the early Christian writings. It includes *only* what conformed to the doctrine of the church when, later on,

that doctrine became fixed in one form. Between the Acts of the Apostles, dating probably from the late 1st century, and the writings of Eusebius of Caesarea (died *c.* 340) and his contemporaries in the first quarter of the 4th century, there is an almost complete gap in Christian historiography. (Above italics mine.)

And so, we have to wonder, "What did the early first-, second-, and third-century "Christians" know that we don't?"

[5] Ehrman, Bart D. 2005. *Misquoting Jesus*. HarperCollins. p. 89.

[6] Ibid., p. 90.

[7] Watt, W. Montgomery. 1953. *Muhammad at Mecca*. Oxford: Clarendon Press. p. 57.

[8] Hirschfeld, Hartwig, Ph.D. 1902. *New Researches into the Composition and Exegesis of the Qoran*. London: Royal Asiatic Society. Preface, ii.

[9] Ibid., p. 32.

[10] *New Catholic Encyclopedia*. 1967. Washington, D.C.: The Catholic University of America. Vol 9, p. 1001.

[11] Carlyle, Thomas. 1841. *On Heros, Hero-Worship and the Heroic in History*. London: James Fraser, Regent Street. pp. 86–87, 89.

[12] Islam lacks clergy or a papal equivalent, but it does have officers (i.e., judges, governors, etc.) who serve to govern the Islamic nation. The caliph is the highest of these officials, but this does not give him power over the religion. On the contrary, his decrees are subject to approval by religious scholars.

[13] Vaglieri, Dr. Laura Veccia. Translated from Italian by Dr. Aldo Caselli, Haverford College, Pennsylvania. Originally published in Italian under the title *Apologia dell' Islamismo* (Rome, A. F. Formiggini, 1925). 1980. *An Interpretation of Islam*. Zurich: Islamic Foundation. pp. 41–42.

[14] Arberry, Arthur J. 1964. *The Koran Interpreted*. London: Oxford University Press. Introduction, p. ix.

[15] Muir, Sir William. 1923. *The Life of Mohammad*. Edinburgh: John Grant. Introduction, pp. xxii–xxiii.

[16] Rippin, Andrew (editor). 1988. *Approaches to the History of the Interpretation of the Qur'an*. Chapter: "Value of Hafs and Warsh Transmissions," by Adrian Brockett. Oxford: Clarendon Press. pp. 44–45.

[17] See Part 1, Chapter 4 for more on this issue.

[18] Ehrman, Bart D. 2003. *Lost Christianities*. Oxford University Press. p. 102.

[19] Fossier, Robert (editor). 1986. *The Cambridge Illustrated History of The Middle Ages*. Cambridge: Cambridge University Press. Vol. 3, p. 495.

[20] Denzinger, Henricus & Schonmetzer, Adolfus. 1973. *Enchiridion Symbolorum, Definitionum et Declarationum de Rebus Fidei et Morum*. Barcinone: Herder. p. 246.

[21] Arbuthnot, F. F. 1885. *The Construction of the Bible and the Korân*. London: Watts & Co. pp. 5–6.

[22] The Bible, Revised Standard Version. 1977. New York: American Bible Society. Preface, p. v.

[23] Ibid., Preface, p. iii.

[24] This last book is available through Al-Hidaayah Publishing, P.O. Box 3332, Birmingham, U.K. B10 9AW.

[25] Bucaille, Maurice, M.D. 1977. *The Bible, the Qur'an and Science*. Lahore: Kazi Publications. pp. 110–111.

[26] Wells, H. G. 1922. *The Outline of History*. Fourth Edition. Volume 2, pp. 686–688.

[27] The seventh to eleventh-century Jewish scribes who devised the diacritical marks which standardized pronunciation, verse division, and vowel notation in the Old Testament.

[28] *Encyclopaedia Britannica*. CD-ROM.

[29] The Bible, Revised Standard Version. Preface, p. iv.

[30] Arbuthnot, F. F. p. 10.

[31] The Bible, Revised Standard Version. Preface, pp. iv-v.

[32] Ibid., Preface, p. iv.

[33] Gibbon, Edward, Esq. 1854. *The History of the Decline and Fall of the Roman Empire*. London: Henry G. Bohn. Vol. 5, Chapter L, p. 452.

[34] Ibid., Chapter L, p. 453.

[35] Smith, R. Bosworth, M.A. 1986. *Mohammad and Mohammadanism*. London: Darf Publishers Ltd. pp. 64–65.

[36] Michener, James A. May, 1955. "Islam: The Misunderstood Religion," in *Reader's Digest* (American Edition). p. 70.

[37] Muhammad Ibn Ishaq ibn Yasar. 1963. *Seerat An-Nabi*. Maydan Al Azhar (Cairo): Muhammad Ali Sabi'eh & Children. Vol. 1. p. 207

[38] Narrated by *Muslim* (the famous ninth century *hadith* scholar, Muslim ibn Al-Hajjaj).

[39] *Manaahil Al-Irfaan fi Uluum Al-Qur'an (Wells of Knowledge of the Sciences of the Qur'an)*. 1988. Muhammad Abdul-At-Theem Az-Zarqaani. Dar Al-Kutub Al-Ilmee'a. Vol 1. p. 216.

[40] Arberry, A. J. 1953. *The Holy Koran: An Introduction with Selections*. London: George Allen & Unwin Ltd. p. 28.

[41] Vaglieri, Dr. Laura Veccia. pp. 40–41.

[42] Guillaume, Alfred. pp. 73–74.

[43] Narrated by *Muslim*.

[44] Vaglieri, Dr. Laura Veccia. pp. 40–41.

[45] Arberry, A. J. *The Holy Koran: An Introduction with Selections*. pp. 31–32.

[46] On the same page as the preceding quote (i.e., p. 31), Professor Arberry wrote, "As for the faithful, I will not conceal from them, what they will not in any case imagine, that I am no Muslim, nor could ever be."

[47] Said Qutub, *Fi Thilal Al-Qur'an.*

[48] The Arabs considered poetry so potent that wars were sometimes initiated, fought and concluded on its basis. In these cases, literary wars escalated from sharp tongues to sharp swords. Such feuds of verse and violence typically ended as they had begun, with a wise poet reminding both tribes in heart-rending verse of their losses and the bleak future of continued hostility, as compared to the benefits of reconciling differences.

[49] Arberry, A. J. 1996. *The Koran Interpreted.* A Touchstone Book: Simon & Schuster. Preface, p. 25.

[50] Hastings, James. 1913. *The Encyclopedia of Religion and Ethics.* Charles Scribner's Sons. Vol X, p. 540.

[51] Hastings, James (editor); Revised edition by Frederick C. Grant and H. H. Rowley. 1963. *Dictionary of The Bible.* 2nd edition. Charles Scribner's Sons. p. 105.

[52] *Encyclopaedia Judaica.* 1971. Jerusalem: Keter Publishing House Ltd. Vol 4, p. 863.

[53] *New Catholic Encyclopedia.* Vol 9, p. 1001.

[54] Wegner, Paul D. *The Journey from Texts to Translations.* 1999. Grand Rapids: Baker Books. p. 250.

[55] Fox, Robin Lane. 1991. *The Unauthorized Version: Truth and Fiction in the Bible.* Viking Press. pp. 28–34.

[56] Whiston, William, A.M. 1998. *Josephus, The Complete Works.* Nashville: Thomas Nelson Publishers. 18.4.6., p. 580.

[57] Wehr, Hans. *A Dictionary of Modern Written Arabic.* 3rd printing. Beirut: Librairie Du Liban; London: MacDonald & Evans Ltd. 1980.

[58] *Encyclopaedia Britannica.* CD-ROM.

[59] *The Encyclopedia Americana International Edition.* 1998. Grolier Inc. Vol 21. p. 848.

[60] Ibid., Vol 26. p. 714.

[61] Thompson, Della (editor). *The Oxford Dictionary of Current English*. 1993. Second Edition. Oxford University Press. p. 26.

[62] Ranke, Hermann. *Die Ägyptischen Personennamen* (*Dictionary of Personal Names of the New Kingdom*). Verzeichnis der Namen, Verlag Von J J Augustin in Glückstadt, Band I (1935); Band II (1952).

[63] Meagher, Paul Kevin OP, S.T.M., Thomas C. O'Brien, Sister Consuelo Maria Aherne, SSJ (editors). 1979. *Encyclopedic Dictionary of Religion*. Philadelphia: Corpus Publications. Vol 1, p. 741.

[64] Those with deeper interest may wish to research *Atlantis of the Sands*, by Ranulph Frennes, *Ebla: A Revelation in Archeology,* by Chaim Bermant and Michael Weitzman, and *Lost Civilizations*, by Bill Harris.

[65] *National Geographic*. December, 1978. pp. 731–5.

[66] Ibid. p. 735.

[67] Ibid.

[68] Ibid., p. 731.

[69] Ibid., p. 748.

[70] Ibid., p. 736.

[71] Bermant, Chaim and Michael Weitzman. 1979. *Ebla: A Revelation in Archaeology*. Times Books. p. 191.

[72] Kraeling, Emil G. Ph.D. 1952. *Rand McNally Bible Atlas*. Rand McNally & Co. p. 358.

[73] *Encyclopaedia Judaica*, CD-ROM Edition. 1997. Judaica Multimedia (Israel) Limited. "Nazareth" entry.

[74] Baigent, Michael and Richard Leigh. 1991. *The Dead Sea Scrolls Deception*. New York: Summit Books/Simon & Schuster Inc. p. 174.

[75] Ibid.

[76] *Musnad Ahmad*.

[77] Narrated by *Al-Bukhari*.

[78] When Muhammad's beloved uncle Hamzah was slain in battle and horribly mutilated, he promised to do the same to seventy of the enemy. In *surah* Nahl, 16:126–128, Muhammad was corrected and commanded to no greater than equal punishment, and patience and restraint. Years later, the Muslims conquered Makkah and the woman who commissioned Hamzah's murder presented herself to Muhammad. She had not only ordered Hamzah killed, but had cut out and chewed the liver of his corpse. Yet Muhammad forgave her.

[79] On the occasion of Muhammad having ransomed a group of captives—men who were aggressive enemies of God, and who were captured while fighting the Muslims for their faith. (TMQ 8:67)

[80] A point needs to be made in this regard. Orthodox (Sunni) Muslims are sensitive to the fact that because Muhammad is recognized as having suffered the rare error of human judgment, certain "Muslims" have misinterpreted this fact, and have sought to discredit whichever of his statements and actions are to their personal distaste. Such people take what they want from the *sunnah* of the prophet, and selectively disavow all that which goes against their preference, manufacturing the excuse that perhaps Muhammad's judgment with regard to specific matters was faulty. The essential element of Islamic faith compromised by such suggestions is that the Islamic religion teaches that any error of the prophet was corrected within his lifetime, for Allah would not allow the words or actions of His messenger to convey an error. Hence, whereas the rare fault of judgment was consistent with the humanity of the messenger, the prompt correction of those errors is consistent with the perfection of the Creator, and with the perfection of the message He chose to transmit, both in revelation and in the living example of the prophet.

[81] A traditional Arab desert composed of layers of shredded wheat, chopped nuts, and either cream or melted cheese, seasoned with cardamom and drenched with sugar-syrup spiced with cinnamon and cloves.

[82] Sa'eid Hawwa. 1990. *Ar-Rasool, Salallahu Alayhi Wa Salam.* Second Edition. Cairo: Dar As-Salaam Publishing. pp. 282–3.

[83] Lings, Martin. 1995. *Muhammad, His Life Based on the Earliest Sources.* The Islamic Texts Society. p. 148.

[84] Al-Mubarakpuri, Safi-ur-Rahman. 1995. *Ar-Raheeq Al-Makhtum (The Sealed Nectar).* Riyadh: Maktaba Dar-us-Salam. pp. 210–226.

[85] A.H.—"After Hijra"—the Islamic calendar's zero point being the Prophet's migration from Makkah to Medina in July of 622 CE.

[86] Muhammad Al-Hilali and Muhammad Khan translation.

[87] Ibid.

[88] Hammad, Ahmad Zaki. 1997. *Father of Flame, Commentary & Vocabulary Reference of Surat al-Masad.* Bridgeview, Illinois: Quranic Literacy Institute. p. 42.

[89] Ibid.

[90] Al-Hilali, Muhammad, Ph.D. and Dr. Muhammad Muhsin Khan, M.D. *Interpretation of the Meanings of The Noble Qur'an in the English Language; A Summarized Version of At-Tabari, Al-Qurtubi and Ibn Kathir with comments from Sahih Al-Bukhari.* Surah 74, Ayah 11.

[91] *Tafseer ibn Kathir.*

[92] Ibn Hisham, *As-Seerah An-Nabawiyyah,* and Azzirikly, *Al-Aa'lam.*

[93] Ostrogorsky, George. 1969. *History of the Byzantine State.* (Translated from the German by Joan Hussey). New Brunswick: Rutgers University Press. p. 95.

[94] Sykes, Sir Percy Molesworth. 1951. *A History of Persia.* 3rd edition. Vol 1. London: Macmillan & Co., Ltd. p. 483.

[95] Ostrogorsky, George. p. 95.

[96] Ibid., pp. 100–101.

[97] Sykes, Sir Percy Molesworth. Vol 1. pp. 483–484.

[98] Muhammad Al-Hilali and Muhammad Khan translation.

[99] *Tafseer Ibn Kathir, Musnad Ahmad, Sunan Tirmithee and An-Nasa'ee.*

[100] Narrated by *At-Tirmithi* and *Al-Haakim.*

[101] Bucaille, Maurice. p. 239.

[102] Diamond, Jared. 1999. *Guns, Germs, and Steel.* W. W. Norton and Company, Inc. p. 253.

[103] Authored by Shabir Ahmed, Anas Abdul Muntaqim, and Abdul-Sattar Siddiq, and published by the Islamic Cultural Workshop, P.O. Box 1932, Walnut, CA 91789; (909) 399–4708.

[104] Robinson, Victor, M.D. 1943. *The Story of Medicine.* New York: The New Home Library. p. 164.

[105] Wells, H. G. Volume 2, pp. 708–710.

[106] Michener, James A. p. 74.

[107] Hirschfeld, Hartwig. p. 9.

[108] The authors (Thatcher and Schwill, as quoted by H. G. Wells) must be excused from any charge of inaccuracy on this point. The fact of the matter is that from the time of revelation to the present, there have always been Muslims who willfully persisted upon the forbidden. Most acted as individuals, but deviant practices grew to engulf entire societies far more often than most Muslims would like to admit. The common example of Muslim owners/operators of liquor-based businesses such as convenience stores, restaurants, and off-licenses illustrates that the hypocritical practice persists to the present day—openly in non-Muslim lands, and underground in those few countries where Islamic law is enforced.

[109] Wells, H. G. Volume 2, pp. 710–712.

[110] Related by Ibn Abbas.

[111] Available on the Internet at http://www.islam-brief-guide. org, and through The Islamic Foundation of America, P.O. Box 3415, Merrifield, VA 22116, USA, Tel.: (703) 914–4982, e-mail: ifam@erols.com.

[112] Tarbuck, Edward J. and Frederick K. Lutgens. 1982. *Earth Science.* 3rd ed. Columbus: Charles E. Merrill Publishing Company. p. 157.

[113] Press, Frank and Raymond Siever. 1982. *Earth.* 3rd ed. San Francisco: W. H. Freeman and Co. p. 435; Cailleux, Andre. 1968. *Anatomy of the Earth.* New York: McGraw-Hill Book Company. Translated by J. Moody Stuart. pp. 218–222; Tarbuck, Edward J. and Frederick K. Lutgens. 1982. p. 158.

[114] Cailleux, Andre. p. 222.

[115] Weinberg, Steven. 1988. *The First Three Minutes, A Modern View of the Origin of the Universe.* Basic Books; Harper-Collins Publishers. pp. 101–121.

[116] In addition to the evidence cited above, the paleontologic record shows the earliest marine deposits on the Atlantic coast of Africa and South America to date from the Jurassic period of 208–144 million years ago, suggesting the lack of an ocean separating these continents before that time.

[117] Remnant magnetism: ferromagnetic materials crystallize with orientation along the Earth's magnetic field. Subsequent liberation of crystals, reorientation, and re-deposition in sedimentary deposits provides a layered record of each continent's changing orientation through time.

[118] Lane, Edward William. 1980. *An Arabic-English Lexicon Derived From the Best and the Most Copious Eastern Sources.* Beirut, Lebanon: Librairie Du Liban. Book I, Part 8, p. 2865, column 3.

[119] Seeley, Rod R., Trent D. Stephens and Philip Tate. 1996.

Essentials of Anatomy and Physiology. 2nd edition. St. Louis: Mosby-Year Book, Inc. p. 211.

[120] Wehr, Hans.

[121] Davis, Richard A., Jr. 1972. *Principles of Oceanography.* Reading, Massachusetts: Addison-Wesley Publishing Co. pp. 92–93.

[122] Kuenen, Philip H. 1960. *Marine Geology.* New York: John Wiley & Sons, Inc. p. 43.

[123] Gross, M. Grant. 1993. *Oceanography, a View of Earth.* 4th ed. Englewood Cliffs: Prentice-Hall, Inc. p. 223.

[124] Ibid., p. 224.

[125] Muhammad Al-Hilali and Muhammad Khan translation.

[126] Elder, Danny; and John Pernetta. 1991. *Oceans.* London: Mitchell Beazley Publishers. p. 27.

[127] *Encyclopaedia Britannica.* CD-ROM. "Altitude Sickness" entry.

[128] Anthes, Richard A., John J. Cahir, Alistair B. Fraser, and Hans A. Panofsky. 1981. *The Atmosphere.* 3rd ed. Columbus: Charles E. Merrill Publishing Co. pp. 268–269.

[129] Miller, Albert and Jack C. Thompson. 1975. *Elements of Meteorology.* 2nd ed. Columbus: Charles E. Merrill Publishing Co. p. 141.

[130] Ibid., p. 141.

[131] *Encyclopaedia Britannica.* CD-ROM.

[132] *Fath Al Bari Sharh Sahih Al Bukhari.* Ibn Hajar Al Asqalani, Bab Alqadar. Cairo: Al Maktaba Assalafiyah. Vol II, p. 480.

[133] *Musnad Ahmad.*

[134] Narrated by *Muslim.*

[135] Lane, Edward William. Book I, Part 5, p. 2134, column 3.

[136] Moore, Keith L. 1983. *The Developing Human, Clinically Oriented Embryology, With Islamic Additions.* 3rd ed. Jeddah: Dar Al-Qiblah with permission of W.B. Saunders Co. Foreword.

[137] Dr. Keith L. Moore is a man many would like to discredit for his work in the field of human development. However, the following list of his credentials and awards show that discrediting one of the world's foremost anatomists and embryologists is not particularly easy: Professor Emeritus of Anatomy and Cell Biology at the University of Toronto; past Associate Dean of Basic Sciences at the Faculty of Medicine and Chairman of the Department of Anatomy for eight years; 1984 recipient of the J.C.B. Grant Award from the Canadian Association of Anatomists (the most distinguished award in the field of anatomy in Canada); and past director of the international associations known as the Canadian and American Association of Anatomists and the Council of the Union of Biological Sciences. *The Developing Human* has been translated into eight languages, the third edition (1983) complete with Islamic additions.

[138] Another excellent reference is Dr. Mohammed Ali Albar's *Human Development, As Revealed in the Holy Quran and Hadith*, available through many Islamic bookstores.

[139] *Al-Bukhari*, Muhammed ibn Ismaiel; translated by Dr. Muhammad Muhsin Khan. 1997. *Sahih Al-Bukhari*. Riyadh: Darussalam. Volume 7, *hadith* #5678, p. 326.

[140] Bucaille, Maurice. p. 162.

[141] Ibid., p. 148.

[142] Montet, Edward. 1929. *Traduction Francaise du Couran*. Paris. Introduction, p. 53.

[143] Stubbe, Dr. Henry, M.A. 1975. *An Account of the Rise and Progress of Mohomedanism, with the Life of Mahomet*. Lahore: Oxford and Cambridge Press. p. 158.

[144] Naish, John, M.A. 1937. *The Wisdom of the Qur'an*. Oxford. Preface, p. viii.

[145] Let us remember that it was not Jesus, but Paul who

abolished Old Testament law. Jesus taught "Do not think that I came to destroy the Law or the Prophets. I did not come to destroy but to fulfill" (Matthew 5:17). For full discussion, see *MisGod'ed*.

[146] The Isaac/Ishmael question, as well as other relevant OT errors, are discussed in more detail in *MisGoded*, Part IV, Chapter 1.

[147] Zahrnt, Heinz. 1817. *The Historical Jesus*. (Translated from the German by J. S. Bowden). New York: Harper and Row. p. 43.

[148] Ibid., pp. 47–48.

[149] Kähler, Martin. 1953. *Der sogemnante historische Jesus und der geschichtliche, biblische Christus*. Munich: New edition by Ernst Wolf. p. 16, as quoted by H. Zahrnt.

[150] Zahrnt, Heinz. p. 61.

[151] Gibbon, Edward. Vol. 5, Chapter XLVII, p. 206.

[152] Bultmann, Rudolf. 1971. *The Gospel of John, a Commentary*. Translated by G. R. Beasley-Murray. Oxford: Basil Blackwell. p. 567.

[153] To this day, Christian theologians acknowledge this remarkable facet of Muhammad's character: "The Prophet's subjective honesty may not be doubted. In principle, one can agree or disagree with the content of his revelations but one shouldn't cheapen the disagreement by disparaging Muhammad as a person."— Küng, Hans. 2007. *Islam, Past, Present and Future*. One World Publications. p. 118.

[154] Few works, including those of excellence, are without error, and the biography by Martin Lings proves this point. The two errors significant enough to warrant mention are the assertion that Muhammad preserved icons of Jesus and Mary, as well as a picture of Abraham, when he destroyed the idols of the Kaaba, and that Muhammad sought Zainab in marriage due to

physical attraction. Neither of these assertions is supported by the textual evidences (i.e., the *hadith*), and both are condemned by the scholars of the Sunni orthodoxy. The biography is otherwise comprehensive, well-researched, beautifully written, inspirational, and highly regarded among Muslims and Orientalists alike. Consequently, the common opinion among the members of the educated Islamic community is that despite the few errors encountered therein, there is probably no better biography of Muhammad in the English language at the present time than Martin Lings'.

[155] *Ibn* translates as "son of." The full name of Muhammad's father is Abdullah ibn 'Abdul-Muttalib ibn Hashim.

[156] Ross, Alexander. 1718. *The Life of Mahomet: Together with The Alcoran at Large.* London. p. 7.

[157] Lane-Poole, Stanley. 1882. *The Speeches and Table-Talk of the Prophet Mohammad.* London: MacMillan and Co. Introduction, pp. xxvii-xxix.

[158] Sale, George. 1734. *The Koran.* London: C. Ackers. "To the Reader." Page v.

[159] Narrated by At-Tabarani in *Al-Mu'jam Al-Kabeer.*

[160] *Mukhtasar Ash-Shama'el Al Muhammadiyyah* by Imam At-Tirmithi, pg 18, *hadith* No. 6. Second paragraph also narrated by *At-Tabarani* in *Al-Mu'jam Al-Kabeer.*

[161] Narrated by *Al-Bukhari* and *Muslim.*

[162] Hogarth, D.G. 1922. *Arabia.* Oxford: Clarendon Press. p. 52.

[163] Irving, Washington. 1973. *Mahomet and His Successors.* Vol 1. New York: G. P. Putnam's Sons. pp. 342–4.

[164] See Part I, Chapter 4 and Part III, Chapter 11.

[165] *New Catholic Encyclopedia.* Vol 7, p. 677.

[166] Ibn Hisham. *As-Seerah An-Nabawiyyah.*

[167] Abu Nu'aem. *Dala'el An-Noobowah.*

[168] *Al-Bukhari* and *Muslim.*

[169] Ibn Hisham. *As-Seerah An-Nabawiyyah.*

[170] Ibid.

[171] *Musnad Ahmad* and *As-Seerah An-Nabawiyyah*, by Ibn Hisham.

[172] *Musnad Ahmad.*

[173] Ibn Hisham. *As-Seerah An-Nabawiyyah.*

[174] *Sahih Al-Bukhari.*

[175] Al-Mubarakpuri, Safi-ur-Rahman. pp. 210–226.

[176] Lings, Martin. p. 148.

[177] Al-Mubarakpuri, Safi-ur-Rahman. pp. 117–119.

[178] Ibn Hisham. *As-Seerah An-Nabawiyyah.*

[179] *Musnad Ahmad.*

[180] The second century in the Muslim calendar (After Hijra, or AH) corresponds to 719–816 CE in the Gregorian calendar.

[181] Ibn Hisham. *As-Seerah An-Nabawiyyah.*

[182] See al-Waada'ee, Muqbil ibn Haadee, *Saheeh al-Musnad min Dalaa'il an-Nubuwwah*, Kuwait: Dar al-Arqam, 1987 for one of the best references in this category.

[183] Sa'eid Hawwa. p. 322.

[184] *Fath Al-Bari.*

[185] *Zad Al-Ma'ad.*

[186] *Sahih Al-Bukhari.*

[187] Al-Mubarakpuri, Safi-ur-Rahman. p. 454.

[188] Ibid., p. 454.

[189] *Sahih Muslim* and *Sahih Al-Bukhari.*

[190] *Sahih Al-Bukhari*, narrated by Jabir ibn Samurah.

[191] *The New International Encyclopaedia.* 1917. 2nd Ed. Vol XVI. New York: Dodd, Mead and Company. p. 72.

[192] Watt, W. Montgomery. p. 52.

[193] *Ash-Shifa.*

[194] The annual *zakat*, or poor-due, is one of the five pillars of

Islam, alongside the declaration of Islamic faith, prayer, the fast of the month of Ramadan, and pilgrimage to Makkah—each in accordance with the rules of the religion. Muslims believe that just as practicing the other pillars of Islam purifies their person and lives, paying *zakat* (typically 2.5% of what a person owns for a full year above and beyond his or her needs) purifies a person's wealth.

[195] Smith, R. Bosworth. pp. 288–289.

[196] *Sahih Al-Bukhari.*

[197] Narrated by *Muslim* and *Al-Bukhari.*

[198] Narrated by *At-Tirmithi.*

[199] Saheeh International version. 1997. Abul-Qasim Publishing House. Jeddah, Saudi Arabia.

[200] Ibn Hisham. *As-Seerah An-Nabawiyyah.*

[201] Lions are no longer found, but both lions and tigers used to exist in the Arabian Peninsula.

[202] *Tafheem-ul-Qur'an.*

[203] The other being *Muslim*, meaning the body of *hadith* collected by the famous scholar of Islam, Muslim ibn Al-Hajjaj.

[204] Banu Abdul-Manaf (meaning the children of Abdul-Manaf) was the tribe of Muhammad.

[205] *Sahih Al-Bukhari.*

[206] Ibn Hisham. *As-Seerah An-Nabawiyyah.*

[207] *New Catholic Encyclopedia.* Vol 7, p. 677.

[208] Narrated by *Al Bukhari.*

[209] Narrated by *Muslim.*

[210] Narrated by *Al-Bukhari* and *Muslim.*

[211] Ibid.

[212] *Sahih Al-Bukhari* and *Muata'h Imam Malik.*

[213] Narrated by *Al-Bukhari* and *Muslim.*

[214] Lane-Poole, Stanley. Introduction, pp. xlvi-xlvii.

[215] Gilman, Arthur, M.A. 1908. *The Saracens.* New York: G. P. Putnam's Sons. pp. 184-5.

[216] Ibn Hisham. *As-Seerah An-Nabawiyyah.*

[217] *As-Seerah An-Nabawiyyah* by Ibn Hisham, and *Musnad Abu Ya'ala.*

[218] Qadhi, Abu Ammaar Yasir. 1999. *An Introduction to the Sciences of the Qur'an.* Birmingham: Al-Hidaayah Publishing. p. 94.

[219] Hyndman, H. M. 1919. *The Awakening of Asia.* New York: Boni and Liveright. p. 9.

[220] Irving, Washington. Vol 1, p. 345.

[221] Carlyle, Thomas. pp. 115–116.

[222] Some historians believe it was as few as six hundred; others as many as nine hundred.

[223] Ibn Hisham. *As-Seerah An-Nabawiyyah.*

[224] See *MisGod'ed*, Part I, Chapter 1.

[225] Al-Mubarakpuri, Safi-ur-Rahman. pp. 483–485.

[226] Ibid., p. 485.

[227] See Part III, Chapter 6 of *MisGod'ed.*

[228] Carlyle, Thomas. pp. 114–115.

[229] Since the mid-nineteenth century, some have regarded Unitarianism as synonymous with Universalism, despite separate and distinct theologies. The union of the Universalist Church of America with the American Unitarian Association in 1961, to form the Unitarian Universalist Association, has done little to alleviate this misunderstanding. However, while most Universalists may be Unitarians, the opposite is certainly not the case, for the Universalist concept of salvation of all souls is contrary to the creed of Unitarian Christianity, which teaches salvation conditional upon correct belief and practice, according to the teachings of Jesus. Perhaps for this reason, in combination with the diversity of Universalist beliefs, the Universalist church has failed to formulate a statement of creed accepted by all affiliates. Furthermore, Universalist

theology is more heavily based upon philosophy than scripture, which explains the disunity. For the purposes of this work, "Unitarian Christianity" refers to the classic Unitarian theology founded upon scripture and united in affirming divine unity. Universalism is by no means to be inferred in the mention of Unitarianism herein, and will not be discussed any further in this work.

[230] See *MisGod'ed,* Part III, Chapter 8.

[231] *Musnad Ahmad.*

[232] De Lamartine, A. 1854. *Histoire de la Turquie.* Paris. Vol. II, pp. 276–277.

[233] *National Geographic Society.* "The Universe, Nature's Grandest Design." Cartographic division. 1995.

[234] Kipling, Rudyard. *Life's Handicap.* 1891. "Bertran and Bimi."

[235] Butler, Trent C. (General Editor). *Holman Bible Dictionary.* Nashville: Holman Bible Publishers. Under "John, the Gospel of," (subsection: "Election").

[236] *Encyclopaedia Judaica.* Vol 5, p. 499 (under "Chosen People").

[237] *New Catholic Encyclopedia.* Vol 11, p. 713.

[238] Ibid., Vol 11, p. 719.

[239] Ibid., Vol 11, p. 714.

[240] See Luther's *De servo arbitrio – The Will Enslaved.*

[241] See Calvin's *Institutes of the Christian Religion.*

[242] Narrated by *Al-Bukhari.*

[243] Narrated by *Muslim.*

[244] Narrated by *At-Tirmithi.*

[245] Ibid.

[246] LaFollette, Suzanne. 1926. *Concerning Women.* "The Beginnings of Emancipation."

[247] See Jeremiah 10:2–4 regarding Christmas trees, Appendix 1 of this book regarding statues.

[248] *Newsweek*. October 31, 1988. p. 80.

[249] For evidence and discussion, see *MisGod'ed*, Part IV.

[250] See *MisGod'ed*, Part III: Doctrinal Differences.

[251] *Merriam-Webster's Collegiate Dictionary*. 1997. Tenth edition. Merriam-Webster, Inc.

[252] Ayto, John. 1991. *Bloomsbury Dictionary of Word Origins*. London: Bloomsbury Publishing Limited.

[253] *New Catholic Encyclopedia*. Vol 14, p. 1030.

[254] Ibid., Vol 7, p. 348.

[255] Gibbon, Edward, Esq. Vol. 5, Chapter XLVII, p. 263.

[256] Ibid.

[257] Ibid., Chapter XLIX, p. 359.

[258] Chamberlin, E. R. 1993. *The Bad Popes*. Barnes & Noble, Inc. p. 11.

[259] Gibbon, Edward, Esq. Vol. 5, Chapter XLIX, p. 361.

[260] Ibid., p. 365.

[261] Hodgkin, Thomas. 1967. *Italy and Her Invaders*. Vol. VI, Book VII. New York: Russell & Russell. p. 431.

[262] Priestley, Joseph, LL.D. F.R.S. 1782. *An History of the Corruptions of Christianity*. Birmingham: Piercy and Jones. Vol. 1; "The History of Opinions relating to Saints and Angels," Section 1, Part 2— "Of Pictures and Images in Churches." pp. 337–339.

[263] Hodgkin, Thomas. Vol. VI, Book VII, p. 431.

[264] Gibbon, Edward, Esq. Vol. 5, Chapter XLIX, pp. 376–7.

[265] Shaw, George Bernard. 1924. *Saint Joan*. Preface.

[266] Labbe, P. Venice, 1728–1733. *Sacrosancta Concilia*. Vol. VII, p. 7.

[267] Gibbon, Edward, Esq. Vol. 5, Chapter XLIX, p. 379.

[268] Ibid., p. 369.

[269] Bonwick, James, F.R.G.S. 1956. *Egyptian Belief and Modern Thought*. Colorado: Falcon's Wing Press. p. 417.

[270] Doane, Thomas W. 1971. *Bible Myths and Their Parallels in Other Religions.* New York: University Books. pp. 307–308.

[271] Bonwick, James. p. 162.

[272] Ibid., p. 163.

[273] Ibid., p. 417.

[274] Ibid., pp. 417–418.

[275] Doane, Thomas W. pp. 305–309.

[276] Ibid., p. 307.

[277] Ibid., p. 312.

[278] Schroeder, Rev. Henry J., O.P. 1941. *Canons and Decrees of the Council of Trent* (Original Text with English Translation). London: B. Herder Book Co. p. 79.

[279] *latria*, the worship or adoration owed to God alone, as opposed to *dulia* (the honor given to the saints) and *hyperdulia* (the honor given the Virgin Mary) – McBrien, Richard P. (General Editor). 1995. *HarperCollins Encyclopedia of Catholicism.* New York: HarperCollins Publishers.

[280] Schroeder, Rev. Henry J. p. 80.

[281] Gibbon, Edward, Esq. Vol. 5, Chapter XLIX, p. 397.

[282] Ibid., Vol. 6, Chapter LIV, p. 242.

[283] Priestley, Joseph. 1786. *The Theological and Miscellaneous Works of Joseph Priestley.* Edited by John Towill Rutt. Hackney: George Smallfield. Vol VI, p. 29.

[284] Gibbon, Edward, Esq. Vol. 5, Chapter L, p. 533.